IDENTITIES IN
NORTH AMERICA

IDENTITIES IN

NORTH AMERICA

The Search for Community

EDITED BY ROBERT L. EARLE

AND JOHN D. WIRTH

STANFORD UNIVERSITY PRESS

Stanford, California   1995

COMPARATIVE STUDIES IN HISTORY, INSTITUTIONS, AND PUBLIC POLICY

Edited by John D. Wirth

Sponsored by the North American Institute using grants from the Hewlett Foundation and the Government of Canada.

Stanford University Press
Stanford, California
© 1995 by the Board of Trustees of the
Leland Stanford Junior University
Printed in the United States of America

CIP data are at the end of the book

Stanford University Press publications are
distributed exclusively by Stanford University Press
within the United States, Canada, and Mexico; they
are distributed exclusively by Cambridge University Press
throughout the rest of the world

Preface

The editors wish to thank the co-conveners of the North American Institute's November 1992 Santa Fe Forum on Identities—Sen. Jack Austin of Canada, Dr. George Cowan of the United States, and Lic. Emilio Carrillo Gamboa of Mexico—for making the meeting such a success. The Forum was essential to launching this book project. Returning to Santa Fe in early 1993, the authors engaged in an intense discussion at the Sol y Sombra Center for the Study of Community, and this is a better book because of it.

Funding for the NAMI Forum was provided by the John D. and Catherine T. MacArthur Foundation, which, with a Canadian Studies Conference grant from the Department of Foreign Affairs and International Trade, underwrote the costs of bringing the authors back to Santa Fe. The book itself was subsidized from NAMI's Hewlett grant, and from the Government of Canada's conference grant. We received additional support from the Sol y Sombra Foundation in Santa Fe. Finally, we wish to thank Norris Pope, Director of the Stanford University Press, and President Miguel de la Madrid, Chairman of the Fondo de Cultura Economica, for their commitment to bringing this book to Spanish readers.

R. L. E.
J. D. W.

Contents

Contributors

JORGE A. BUSTAMANTE is Professor of Sociology and President of the Colegio de la Frontera Norte in Tijuana. He is on the Joint Public Advisory Committee (JPAC) to the North American Commission for Environmental Cooperation, and is also a member of the Border Environmental Cooperation Commission.

DAVID CROMBIE, P.C., is Commissioner of the Waterfront Regeneration Trust in Toronto; he was the minister responsible for multiculturalism in the Mulroney cabinet, and was mayor of Toronto between 1972 and 1978.

ROBERT L. EARLE is a member of the senior Foreign Service with the U.S. Information Agency; he served as Minister Counselor for Public Affairs, U.S. Embassy, Mexico City, 1989–92, and currently holds that post in Bonn.

RICHARD ESTRADA is Associate Editor of the editorial page of *The Dallas Morning News* and a member of the U.S. Commission on Immigration Reform.

JOHN HAMER is a Senior Fellow of the Discovery Institute and a freelance writer in Seattle.

RICHARD KIY is a specialist on United States–Mexico border affairs with the U.S. Environmental Protection Agency and served most recently as Acting Environmental Attache in the Mexico City Embassy.

ALEJANDRA LAJOUS VARGAS is Director of the television station Canal Once in Mexico City.

DANIEL LATOUCHE is Research Professor of Political Science at the National Institute of Scientific Research, an affiliate of the Université du Québec.

MARC PACHTER is Deputy Assistant Secretary for External Affairs at the Smithsonian Institution in Washington, D.C.

ALBERTO RUY-SÁNCHEZ, a novelist and critic, is founding Editor of *Artes de México*.

PAUL SCHELL is Co-Chairman of the Board of the Discovery Institute, and a Seattle Port Commissioner.

KEITH SPICER chaired the Citizens' Forum on Canada's Future (Spicer Commission) and is currently Chairman of the Canadian Radio-Television and Telecommunications Commission.

JOHN D. WIRTH is Gildred Professor of Latin American Studies at Stanford University and President of the North American Institute in Santa Fe, New Mexico. He also serves on the Joint Public Advisory Committee (JPAC) to the North American Commission for Environmental Cooperation.

IDENTITIES IN
NORTH AMERICA

Introduction

ROBERT L. EARLE AND JOHN D. WIRTH

Santa Fe, Jamestown, and Quebec City, the outposts and gateways for North America's three founding European cultures, were established almost simultaneously—but only to spearhead a clash of empires and nation-states that, over the next two hundred years, would redraw the political map of North America, creating the nineteenth-century boundaries of Canada, the United States, and Mexico, with their separate national histories and distinct national interests.

Yet even as that political map endures, the signing of the North American Free Trade Agreement (NAFTA) in 1993 has brought the legacy of continental intersection back into focus. As market integration and regionalization accelerate, we are drawn to the deepest-running aspects of identity, or all that is most authentic to North American peoples. Knowing who we are and what we want, we can speculate on how our interdependence might yield forms of association that go beyond trade toward a broader sense of common interests and the forging of community.

Facing North, Santa Fe (1610) was a frontier outpost of New Spain, one of the most socially enduring colonial regimes in modern times. Blocked from further expansion by hard-riding Comanches and Apaches, the agro-pastoral society of New Mexico survived at the end of a long supply line over the Camino Real to Chihuahua and the South while living in close proximity with native peoples. Later, in the 1820's, New Mexicans were hosts to an early example of North American social convergence in Taos, an Indian trade zone and southern terminus of the continental fur trade linked to Canada. The centuries-long exchange of Spanish/Mexican culture with Amerindians was already well established when French fur trappers, American mountain men, and traders from all three founding cultures established the fleeting basis for a true multicultural exchange in Taos and Santa Fe.[1]

Jamestown (1607) quickly foundered, but the westward-moving frontier of English America became a founding metaphor for the United States, a continental nation of immigrants. An abundance of cheap land attracted the population tide from Europe out of which the United States was largely formed: two and a half million people by 1760, on the eve of independence, 40 million by the time California joined the Union in 1850.[2]

Yet the founding of Jamestown also links us to the troubled legacy of plantation America. The Founding Fathers who created a new, liberal polity also presided over a society with taproots into the Atlantic slave trade. Meanwhile, the displaced native peoples struggled for survival, creating what has been called "the persistence of natives" as another enduring facet of the American experience.[3]

An alternative future was opened for Canada by Great Britain's successful efforts to reform and regroup after the American Revolution. Bestowed initially by the colonial power, Canada's political identity was based on order, responsible government (the cabinet-driven parliamentary system), and a society more collectivist in outlook than the United States.[4] In this sense, counterrevolutionary Canada was more fully formed by its colonial experience than the United States, or at least went further down the colonial road.

Yet during the nineteenth and early twentieth centuries, Canada, too, became a nation of immigrants, albeit geographically confined within the habitable fringes of a vast northern hinterland that constantly raised the question of physical and social survival in the Canadian mind.

For its part, sparsely populated New France, though defeated by Great Britain in 1758, left a legacy of French speakers across the continent whose *cultural* survival is the touchstone of Québécois identity today. Quebec (1608), the homeland of seven million people, claims recognition as a founding nation of North America and looks to continental economic integration to provide the economic bolstering for that claim.

To touch upon identity, then, is to locate those aspects of our history that matter most. Mexico has the longest colonial past of the three, being deeply rooted in the syncretic society of its foundation through its conquest in the sixteenth century. The pragmatic flexibility and inventiveness of its multiethnic society are arguably more fundamental to Mexican identity and nationality than the form of government itself.

Not so with the United States, which finds its locus of identity in political values. Here, the nation of immigrants centers its identity on the political compact, accommodating a myriad of cultures but holding citizenship as the test of universal allegiance while expecting, and finding throughout its history, enough cultural assimilation to sustain it.

By contrast, Canadian identity is weaker in both the sociohistorical sense of Mexico, which follows the path of syncretism, and the compactual or covenantal sense of the United States, which historically has required a unified political credo for its immigrant society. More regionalistic than the other two, Canada is still working out the consequences of having had two founding European cultures and of having followed the evolutionary path to state formation in 1867 and subsequent independence. Thus, in the case of Canada, there was no war of independence and there is no independence day, unlike in Mexico and the United States, where the modern state was formed in the crucible of great revolutions—1910 and 1776, respectively—and mid-nineteenth-century civil wars.

Historically, the United States has had intimate relations with both Mexico and Canada. But it is only now, with the passage of NAFTA and the regionalization of world trade, that Canada and Mexico are being drawn together into a close relationship, and that Canada has joined the Organization of American States. A new historiography will probe the remoter origins of this Canada-Mexico intersection: some will stress the continental filling-in that shook them both in the age of Sir John Macdonald, Ulysses S. Grant, and Benito Juárez, and the intense development of regional resource economies; others will emphasize the lack of close contacts between Mexico and Canada, with exceptions such as the Spanish exploration from Mexico of what is now British Columbia or the cowboy accouterments Alberta received via the United States. Meanwhile, realists will say that Mexicans and Canadians shared little on the same continent except asymmetrical linkages with the Americans.

Complicating the question of identities are the indicators of wealth and poverty that roughly group Canada and the United States on one side of the global North/South divide and Mexico on the other. Can nations so different in history and conditions find common ground?

I

This book is an inquiry, an attempt by thirteen North American authors to assess the dynamics of North American identities and our collective future on this continent. The book's underlying premise is not the inevitability of community in North America, but its possibility. Where and how might Canadians, Americans, and Mexicans interact more fruitfully? Looking beyond free trade, are there fresh opportunities for cooperation to be found in North America's value structures, social groupings, institutions, and regions? If so, what costs and what benefits might accompany interactions that touch on each nation's civic culture, basically its profound sense of self?

We recognize that these are broad questions—questions this volume may do more to frame than answer. This is appropriate in these early days of a new continental self-awareness. What follows are some suggestions on how to read this book, highlighting the themes and topics that each author, based on his or her own experience and point of view, was asked to address.

The first part, on core values, recognizes the necessary statements that have to be made about each country. The premise is that historically our countries share a strong Atlantic link, but also what we, in our concluding essay, call a New World amplitude of vision that sets us apart from Europe. We North Americans share a history of geographic proximity, which produced intense contacts. Also, we share an engagement with indigenous cultures. Nevertheless, we are different, and our differences are manifest in the way we create and re-create ourselves. Core values are not givens; rather, they are constantly subject to redefinition and change. Understanding this is all the more important in an age of globalism, in which North America has emerged as both a trading bloc and a multifaceted community in formation. As Daniel Latouche has pointed out, "How we define our localism is the key to it, because we are all global."[5]

In his spirited lead chapter, Keith Spicer takes what might be called a "building block" approach to national identity and distinctiveness. In contrast to the United States, Canada's national self-image is presented as that of an ironic, self-deprecating society, but also a nation more caring, tolerant, and inclusive than its giant southern other. Emerging in this essay is a Canadian model of identity building, the way Canadians imagine themselves, affirmed in certain core practices and beliefs, such as social programs and international cooperation. The addition of Mexico to Canada's continental perspective is welcomed for the way it broadens North American horizons and diminishes relentless concerns and comparisons with the United States.

Marc Pachter limns out the values of a U.S. nationality that is also defined politically, but that unlike Canada's, is defined almost wholly in terms of itself. Here, identity is contextualized by explicit reference to public values, among which he singles out freedom of choice. Americans are universalists, in the sense that all citizens are asked to subscribe to these public values, and identity is created through participation in a profoundly civic process. Americans have reveled in their sense of exceptionalism. Unlike Canadians or Mexicans, they define these values not so much in reference to either the European or the indigenous "other" as in reference to ideational factors. Traditionally, the fault line in the American value structure has been race, seen as an internal dilemma. Now, however, the need to focus on the validity of values other than their own may catch Americans unprepared to grasp the new realities of interdependence. The United States is now inescapably located in relation to others, and this may be harder for us than for Canadians and Mexicans to deal with.[6]

It follows that Pachter's final sentence could be taken as a warning that the NAFTA partnership may not work. It is not clear that either the U.S. Congress or the U.S. public will accept "that being North American is not the same as being American"; that is, they may lack the flexibility to join in a cooperative relationship. If Canada and Mexico do not wish to play by U.S. rules, the giant nation in the middle may not wish to stay in the game.

Alberto Ruy-Sánchez's Mexico is always in the process of creation, and he explicitly rejects earlier attempts (by Samuel Ramos, especially) to locate an essential Mexican identity based on *mestizaje* (the intermarriage of Spaniards and Mexican-born Creoles with indigenous peoples) or a shared sense of collective lessons from the past. Rather, following Octavio Paz's analysis, Ruy-Sánchez says that Mexicans are adept at putting on masks, revealing only those parts of themselves that are adequate to the situation. In a sense, all cultures do this, and he argues that what is needed now in North America is a "dance of the masks" based on listening, understanding, and complex signaling among the three.

The upshot of this part is that a conversation has begun. The differences are real, and these are different voices, each producing a sort of snapshot of where we are now at this point in the process of being North American. Canadians, more than Mexicans, are concerned about a "loss" of identity. Americans in their universalism also question whether their civic culture is under strain from too much cultural particularism from the outside, meaning the consequences of another wave of massive immigration. Responses will be found in the next part, on group identities and interactions.

II

Canadian cities as focal points for multiculturalism, as well as nodes of coherence in a nation of strong regionalism, are the focus of David Crombie's paper. Under the Crown, there never was a presumption of universalism, and all groups were recognized. Crombie draws on his experience as mayor of Toronto to show that the idea of neighborhoods based on ethnicity and distinctness has deep historical sanction. History has a great deal to do with the way cities developed on both sides of the border. Toronto is also seen by Crombie as a testing ground for what Canadians want with respect to civic order and urban ecology.

The example of multicultural Toronto is given as a sort of assurance by proxy that Canadian pluralism will endure. But that is to ignore the counterexample of Montreal, once home to many so-called English Canadians who, having lost or been displaced from *their* neighborhoods, have left Quebec altogether because of its restrictive language laws. In Mordecai Richler's words, "Just about everything has been done to make the Anglophone youth, even those who are fluently bilingual, feel unwelcome in Quebec."[7]

Officially, there never was a melting-pot ideology in Canada, and assimilation is disavowed. Yet it can be argued that in fact English-speaking Canada has been indistinguishable from the United States in this respect. Official multiculturalism lending legitimacy to immigrant groups may actually facilitate the melting-pot process, since if one is accepted by the general community, one has less reason to resist incorporation within it. Hence the rejectionism of Quebec, in sharp contrast to Toronto and still more to Vancouver, with its widening window on Asia.

The highly charged topic of assimilation in the United States is the subject of Richard Estrada's chapter. Every wave of immigration has produced worries about the fate of national cohesion. The current movement of peoples into the United States, the largest since the big immigration of 1890–1914, is no exception. The important question Estrada addresses is whether assimilation will be able to function effectively this time around, or whether the process has already broken down. As Estrada points out, free trade is not likely to slow undocumented immigration from Mexico in the short run.

Given the proximity of Mexico and other sending nations in the hemisphere, a complex situation of assimilation *and* cultural maintenance has emerged in this generation of Latino immigrants. Thus Estrada sees traditional assimilation as under stress, creating an important public policy issue. Polls do show that among Hispanics, in particular, there is little desire for cultural or language maintenance, whatever their leaders say or the roadblocks the majority society places in their way. On the contrary, Latino immigrants want their share of the American dream and see assimilation as the fastest way to get there.[8] An interesting parallel may be the Quebeckers, hundreds of thousands of whom went to New England and assimilated after 1850.

The Mexican communications industry exemplifies Mexico's ability to adapt tools and processes to its own national purposes. This is the thesis of Alejandra Lajous Vargas, who sees Mexican television programming, with its national thrust, as an example of Mexican skill in adapting to changing technologies and circumstances. When asked whether in our global information age this characteristic was up to the task of culturally incorporating such a young population—half of all Mexicans are under twenty—her response was yes and strongly so, based on the capacity of this syncretic culture to re-create itself. Still, given the youthful profile of the general population, it is difficult for Mexican TV advertisers to know what the market is.

This part adds up to a vote of confidence in ourselves. In the words of Ruy-Sánchez, "True living culture everywhere changes a bit every day." Some of us worry about cultural coherence, but the social process moves along. The New World is no Europe, with its fears of homogenization and loss of identity as the institutions of the Economic Community grow stronger. Nor could it be. Products of what is now called "the encounter phenomenon," we are each of us a blend of races and cultures. As Pachter has pointed out, this is something really new. "It defines us as New World peoples; we are comfortable with culture clashes which define us."[9]

If, as Ruy-Sánchez says in his paper, "our new challenge is to share our differences, our national identities," then the emerging transborder regions of North America are one place to observe whether this is in fact already occurring. Are we building community first by parts? Having located identities at the center, the book now attempts to find communities at, on, and over the borders. This is the logical working out of what it means to "think globally, act locally" in today's interconnected world.

III

Quebec is an important actor in this process, although Daniel Latouche in his stimulating discussion of Québécois nationality would deny that Quebec is a region at all. Today, its way of operating is defined fundamentally by insertion into the larger market of North America, and for this reason, Quebec is enthusiastic about NAFTA. Whether the logic is for separation or for some sort of accommodation with the rest of Canada, Quebec has cast its lot with North America.

The challenge of Quebec—which is demanding recognition at the very least as a distinct, founding nation and at the most as a separate state—is crowding Canadian federalism. As Latouche sees it, the emerging nationalism of English Canada is a reaction to Quebec exceptionalism and to market-driven social change, a reaction that explains in part English Canada's bridling at the idea and consequences of NAFTA, while affirming Canadian social programs.

"Cascadia," the concern of Paul Shell and John Hamer, is a socio-economic region in rapid formation. Whether the states and provinces of the Pacific Northwest will develop regional political institutions as part of their common identity is open to question. But the fact stands that national governments are leaving certain functions to the states and provinces. Will these be formalized in transborder councils of some sort, based on need and a twenty-first-century flexibility toward sovereignty? In any event, integration North to South, and out to Asian markets, is happening rapidly as a sense of shared regional identity is developing.

The Gulf region, according to Richard Kiy, is a shared maritime frontier between Mexico and the United States defined by the arc of eight major port cities from Veracruz to Miami. The Gulf itself is a commons, ripe for coordinated environmental management. This underappreciated region of agriculture, manufacturing, tourism, and energy resources is geographically coherent and economically complementary. Historically, the French, Spanish, and British empires intersected here. Whether a shared Gulf mentality is developing remains to be seen. There are signs that political vision and leadership are lacking, but prospects for rapid economic growth are strong nonetheless. One result of NAFTA will be to foster the incorporation of Caribbean island economies into the Gulf region. (Their labor markets are already heavily integrated with the mainland.) Next, the Gulf region's likely role will be to tie North and South America more tightly together, drawing on its strategic location, as well as its transportation, financial, natural, and human resources.

Finally, the land border defines a well-developed identity on the Mexican side, the result of policy, ethnicity, and the cultural preferences of the *fronterizos* themselves. The sociologist Jorge Bustamante is concerned with the people who live and work on the Mexican side, not with the millions who pass through. He rejects the notion of "MexAmerica," a concept advanced a decade ago by Joel Garreau that aroused little interest in Mexico but achieved wide currency in the United States.[10]

In Bustamante's view, the border is defined by the intensity and extension of interactions, primarily between paired cities with their commercial interdependence and the large in-bond manufacturing industry (*maquiladoras*) on the Mexican side. Bustamante sees continued prosperity and development along the border as not being threatening to Mexican cultural identity. Rather, his concern is that unless free trade is extended to all of Mexico, the nation risks internal divisions as the poorer south and the macrocephalic center fall farther behind, deepening a north/south divide within Mexico. The January 1994 rising in Chiapas underscores his point.

To sum up: these transborder areas are the testing grounds of socio-economic integration in North America. This is because North America is a space-oriented community, where the givens of geography matter a great deal. Integration at the very least requires good transportation, shared problem solving, and the ability to deal with other perspectives in all aspects of daily life. These regions are developing rapidly, and they are proving grounds for a complex layering of communities, the subject of the final paper.

IV

Exploring further the points of intersection and potential overlap between the different identities of North America, we devote our concluding essay explicitly to the question of community. Looking beyond market integration for the deeper rhythms of interdependency, we seek the elements that form a continental context and favor community building in an era of partnership and increased flow.

By no means is this a NAFTA-driven thesis. While we give due weight to the forces of economic convergence that favor regionalization, our thesis is that the three North American nations share a *perceptual* heritage, or context, as well as economic regionalism and geography. This context draws on a shared and recuperable liberal tradition, and what we call the "amplitude of vision" of New World peoples. For in fact, Mexico has a strain of liberalism in its past, one that was unable to survive the nineteenth century but appears ready to reassert itself in the late twentieth century. Furthermore, a history of incorporating many voices underlies the amplitude of vision we speak of. This provides a viable intellectual framework for each of the three countries to play its full role.

We begin by presenting examples of the thinking needed to build community drawn from the literature and philosophy of each country. These examples are not offered as prefigurations or latent imperatives, but as a mixture of historical and contemporary resources available for use as inspiration or vehicles of cooperation.

Two concepts order our assessment of the new ways of thinking.

The first is the need for a "fusion of horizons," a willingness to think about issues from different national perspectives without abandoning one's own. Our national civic cultures are deepened thereby: one's own, what is most near and dear, is broadened and enhanced by convergence, proximity, and understanding, to the point of taking pleasure in the civic culture of the others. The end result is to develop multiple allegiances, without inevitably or even necessarily giving up one's own.

Our second assumption is that the greatest single difference among the three countries (greater than the wealth factor) is the relative importance assigned to individual and collective rights. This may be the central question pertaining to North American identities and community. Influenced by John Dewey, the American exponent of *pragmatic* liberalism and community, and by Charles Taylor, the Canadian champion of *relativistic* liberalism in the debate on multiculturalism and national identity, we attempt to reconcile individualism, a value that lies at the heart of American-style process liberalism, with the values of collectivism and group rights, which are stronger in both Canada and Mexico.

We then show how the dynamics of identity are being worked out in certain exemplary institutions and in the emerging transborder regions and subnational units of North America. Yet this search for community occurs within the existing framework of the nation-states of North America. Far from joining in what Sen. Daniel Patrick Moynihan calls "the liberal expectancy," according to which bigger markets will supposedly create bigger and somehow better states, we see the persistence of different identities, values, and ways of thinking as essential for the process of creating community.[11] We conclude by suggesting ways to cross the threshold of institution building in North America, noting that it is in functional institutions that nations, localities, and individuals often find their finest self-expression.

PART ONE

Core Values

Canada: Values in Search of a Vision

KEITH SPICER

Canada's identity is its identity crisis. Remember the old British Airways slogan, "Getting there is half the fun"? For Canadians, forever seeking their collective identity (and failing to find it) seems perversely almost *all* the fun: angst is our ecstasy. Cynics, or fatalists, believe that Canada's perpetual, chattering trip to nationhood long ago became our national destination, or at least our destiny. Anguished introspection about what Canada is, why it exists, and where its elusive spirit should take it has bedeviled political discourse for generations and made constitutional reform both a permanent feature and a permanent frustration of Canadian statecraft. Arguing over how or even whether to weave our various peoples (beginning but not ending with our French- and English-speaking ones) into some kind of single people obsesses armies of otherwise imaginative intellectuals and commentators. It exasperates our citizens and makes them despise elites they see as fiddling while our economy and society burn for reform. Strange? Debilitating? Yes. But for now it's the only way we know how to be who we are. And it's why—until we can fuse our many common values into a unifying vision broader than the stunting, and embarrassing, claim that we're "not Americans"—Canadians appear to condemn themselves to endless, inconclusive attempts at self-definition.

Canada may win the world championship of insecurity among satellites of much larger nations, at least in the industrial world. It's a country mired in ceaseless self-psychoanalysis. It is, as I said long before Mia Farrow muddled my metaphor, the Woody Allen of nations.

The jokes Canadians tell about themselves to illustrate this national neurosis are devastating. Some classics: Canadians, in Olympic terms, strive ferociously to seize the bronze medal; or, why does a Canadian cross the road? Not, like the heroic chicken, to get to the other side, but to get to the middle. Our kissin' cousins, the Yanks, are unapologetic Americans. We Canadians (since we are trafficking in stereotypes) tend to apologize for existing.

For existing. Deep down, do we feel guilty for messing up the Americans' Manifest Destiny? Canadians and Mexicans thought the North American Free Trade Agreement was meant to swap a few products and services. But when President Bush lyricized in December 1992 that NAFTA was really the prelude to a Bolivar-style union from Yukon to Yucatan, the only restraint to Canadians' usual outrage at such ideas was pity that Bush may have been suffering from post-electoral *tristesse*. At Bush's prediction, our resolutely nationalist prime minister John Diefenbaker twitched in his tomb, and a couple of Toronto editorial writers coughed almost audibly. Canadians, like Mexicans, do not dream of wrapping themselves in the Stars and Stripes. We Canadians are reluctant enough to wrap ourselves in our own flag. We prefer to imagine (perhaps with a touch of malice?) that our stubborn persistence as an independent country perplexes, even vaguely annoys, some American patriots.

(Whatever else you may think of Canadians, they do have a sense of humor. Or, rather, they export a lot of it, usually as a wacky sense of irony: from the King of Comedy Mack Sennett in the 1920's down to the contemporary stars Rich Little and Dan Ackroyd, Hollywood and the U.S. media have been massively infiltrated by Canadian comic writers, producers and actors.[1] To the extent that news is sometimes funnier than fact, you might tack onto that list other well-disguised Canadian passport-holders, such as ABC's Peter Jennings, CBS's Morley Safer, and PBS's Robert MacNeil, as well as dozens of lesser Canadian media professionals all over the United States. President Reagan's top gag writer was a Canadian. And on the loftier plane of scholarly wit, you might recall those "two greatest Canadians that America ever produced," John Kenneth Galbraith and Marshall McLuhan, both born and educated in Canada but made famous in the United States. I lack space here to catalog the entire Canadian *maquis* in U.S. academe, government, science, literature, and the arts; suffice it to observe that for countless talented English-speaking Canadians the United States naturally offers a grander stage than the much smaller—and usually less welcoming—one they find at home.)

Since all stereotypes, though unfair, carry some grain of truth, let's just say that while the secret dream of every Mexican may be to become a *caudillo*, and that of every American to become an entrepreneur, there may lurk in every Canadian the reckless fantasy of becoming a civil servant.

My French-speaking Quebec compatriots will tell you that only the three-quarters of Canadians who normally speak English suffer from Woody Allenism; that the quarter of our population called Québécois is a complex-free, self-confident *nation* within a political and economic country. Well, *oui et non*. In cultural, social, legal, and some economic terms, our Québécois countrymen clearly and happily form a very "distinct society," as our politicians have fumbled to label them. But the Québécois nationalist elites (whose orthodoxies permeate media, culture, and schools) tend to live out vis-à-vis English-speaking Canada something very like the traumas and complexes that our Anglo nationalist elites display toward Americans. The ultranationalists among Québécois elites are haunted by nightmares of assimilation and constant "humiliation" by an Anglo majority they perceive to be—at best—domineering, insensitive, and indifferent. That's a fair copy of Anglo-Canadians' resentment of Americans, although Anglo-Canadians feel very close to Americans on cultural and personal levels, and, when overseas, find themselves defending Americans quite zealously (if only on the naive grounds that Canadians think they know the *real* reasons to be paranoid about Americans).

If, as Albert Einstein argued, nationalism (unlike patriotism, which he considered the positive love of country) always tries to unite a people *against* outsiders, English Canadians have decisively, though inadvertently, helped fashion the Québécois's sense of themselves by playing the historic role of their "threatening foreigners"; while the Americans, with equally unaware generosity, have glued the rest of us together. "Everybody needs somebody," as the love song goes. If you're unsure of yourself as a nation, you probably need somebody to fear and/or distrust, ideally somebody portrayable as a hereditary enemy. Any bigger neighbor will do just fine. And if you're as lucky as Canadians are, you can find one whose economic and cultural influence over your country is so pervasive that its potential military ambitions lose all raison d'être.

Moreover, Québécois are archetypally Canadian in their political culture: like all Canadian communities and regional interest groups, they pursue high principles through fiery brinksmanship politics choreographed to end in a boringly peaceful, usually less-than-lofty deal. In some other countries, revolutionaries toss bombs, or at least pamphlets; in Canada, sworn political enemies put in joint applications to the Canada Council (our national arts body) for a grant to hold a colloquium.

Over two centuries of living with, and quarreling with, us English Canadians may have made Québécois the only Latins in the world who don't automatically interpret compromise as defeat—who, recalling two usefully distinct French words, don't take *compromis* for *compromission*. In language and folklore, in the arts high and low, Canada has many "cultures" or, as Québécois and dozens of native groups like to say, many "nations." But in political style, mores, and expectations, Québécois and all of us share a fascinating, if often infuriating, political nationality.

That political culture, which I'll spell out a bit later, is a key characteristic defining Canada's "soul" or identity. To explore that identity, let's recall first the *sources* of our values, then the *core values* Canadians share, and finally Canadians' evolving—some might say dissolving—sense of *citizenship*.

The Sources of Canadian Values

Where do Canada's distinctive values come from? Three factors shape the worldviews of Canadians of almost all backgrounds.

Climate. The poet Gilles Vigneault's song "*Mon pays, ce n'est pas un pays, c'est l'hiver*" and the pianist Glenn Gould's essay on the "Idea of North" both illustrate Canadians' deep collective memory of the cold and the snow and the long pioneer darknesses until the spring came. Although our West Coast almost never sees snow, and even our Siberian capital, Ottawa, knows temperatures ranging from 30 degrees below zero (Celsius) to 30 degrees above (about $-25°$ F to $95°$ F), part of the psyche of all Canadians lies somewhere in cold storage on a blizzard-swept Arctic plain. The unspoken awareness of a brutal climate chills our souls even more piercingly than the Great White North on U.S. weather maps threatens Americans with all manner of frigid horrors from Canada. As Montesquieu could have argued from climatological determinism, such a bitter challenge to life itself inclines human beings to hardiness, doggedness, and resourcefulness, but also to caution, conservatism, and an obligatory caring for each other.

Geography. Three other features of our land mark all Canadians: its immensity, its natural riches, and its immediate proximity to the most powerful nation on earth. Never study a political map of Canada. To understand the miracle of making any kind of Canada, look at a population map of North America. Canada then looks not like the top half of a continent, whose almost 10 million square kilometers make it the world's second largest landmass after Russia; it looks like a fragile, scattered archipelago of isolated human settlements crammed into a narrow corridor between the empty, forbidding north and the massive magnet of the United States. Even with one of the world's most advanced communications, media, and travel networks, Canadians must grapple with, in Prime Minister William Lyon Mackenzie King's words, "too much geography" (as well as "too little history"). This mammoth territory, like Russia, contains a treasure vault of natural resources: every kind of energy and minerals, as well as seemingly limitless forests, agricultural land, and, until recently, fish. Such abundance tempts foreigners to invest in Canada; it leads Canadians to be more smug (some say lazier) than less favored peoples; and it provides our ever-turf-conscious federal and provincial politicians still another chance to quarrel over jurisdiction, once again proving our national genius of making opportunities into problems.

Our third geographical reality—sharing the world's longest undefended (and indefensible?) border with the United States—overwhelms us in ways that no American can understand, but in ways that every Mexican can begin to—culturally, economically, socially, politically, diplomatically. Except for Quebec, Canada (unlike Mexico) cannot even build a sense of nationhood behind the rampart of a distinct language. American ideas, fads, products, media, and mores sweep and swirl about us at every turn, from our factories to our magazine stands to our TV screens. English-speaking Canadians, at least, are not just seduced by American influences; they are totally vulnerable to them. At a very superficial level, we English-speaking Canadians look and sound so much like our southern neighbors that most Americans innocently, but enragingly for us, love to tell us we're "just like" them, then sublimely ignore us. No wonder wags have suggested we should plot to get Americans' attention by growing beards, speaking Spanish, and invading North Dakota.

History. Making a country on such a land is hard enough. Add a history that structured our society into two major European language and cultural communities, a multitude of more recent immigrant cultures (arriving at widely staggered intervals), and a series of renascent native cultures—none of them sharing common memories of when and how and with whom Canada began, and none sharing a common vision of Canada—and you have a human puzzle of epic proportions. Tack on a highly decentralized federal system covering ten provinces and two, soon three, territories, seven distinctive and often competing economic regions, and a parliamentary democracy crowned by a nonresident monarchy a majority of Canadians no longer identify with, and you have, believe me, a devil of a time developing shared dreams, symbols, and leadership. (We couldn't manage to adopt a distinctive national flag until 1965 or a national anthem until 1980.) As in most federations, but with a sometimes corrosive mean-spiritedness, our constitutional pendulum swings constantly between centralization and decentralization. But in Canada it swings farther: between versions of the Liberal Pierre Elliott Trudeau's "One Canada" emphasizing strong individual rights and the Conservative Joe Clark's "community of communities" emphasizing strong collective (especially regional) rights.

Astoundingly, and destructively, Canadian schools outside Quebec teach almost no Canadian history at all before late high school, and provincial education authorities resist attempts at even writing a shared history for English-speaking Canada. In Quebec, where local history is omnipresent in schools, the history and current realities of Canada outside the province rarely infiltrate books or classrooms. History is definitely a source of Canadians' values; sadly, it shapes us mainly by its absence as a unifying force.

Canadians' Core Values

The broadest view of a nation's core values includes shared beliefs and ideas that underpin a sense of national community. Such values—dreams or "myths" in André Malraux's terms—eclipse the ideas peculiar to countless subtribes of language, culture, and region, not to mention the new Politically Correct subtribes of gender, sexual orientation, and physical ability.

Following the failure of the Meech Lake constitutional accord in June 1990 (which sought to recognize Quebec's status as a "distinct society" within confederation), Prime Minister Brian Mulroney asked me to set up and chair a group—the Citizens' Forum on Canada's Future—to solicit the views of grass-roots Canadians on the broad directions they wished their country to take. After an eight-month consultation by "kitchen meetings," 1-800 telephone calls, and electronic town halls of over 700,000 Canadians (including 300,000 elementary and secondary school students), the Citizens' Forum confirmed seven universal beliefs as intrinsic to "Canadianness."

From native Canadians to Québécois to British-background Canadians to "traditional ethnic" Canadians to recent "nontraditional" immigrants, citizens claimed that the following made them feel distinctly Canadian (that is, for most, non-American):

- A belief in equality and fairness in a democratic society—meaning respect for all minorities
- A belief in consultation and dialogue, both between government and citizens and among various groups of citizens

- A belief in accommodation and tolerance—the legendary Canadian belief in compromise
- A commitment to diversity—our belief that the more we emphasize our differences, the more we will feel united
- An abiding compassion and generosity—our deep attachment to Canada's social safety nets of universal health care and pensions
- A respect for Canada's natural beauty—embracing both environmentalism and awe for the grandeur of our great empty land
- Canada's world image of being committed to freedom, peace, and nonviolent change.[2]

This last point came through as probably the strongest and most promising of all our core values. Why? Because it takes us outside our internal obsessions and quarrels, and forces us to see the great value of Canada in the world as an almost ideal peaceful and peace-making society.

To dig a little deeper into the Canadian psyche, I would suggest a slight reshuffling of these core values as stated by our citizens. I think that a more succinct list of what makes Canadians tick would pare the elements to five:

Survival. This theme is the primordial Canadian fear and hope. As Margaret Atwood showed in her classic work of that title, and Laure Rièse anthologized in *L'Ame de la poésie canadienne-française*, both English- and French-speaking literatures in Canada echo the early pioneer's fear of not surviving climate, famine, illness, and the hostility of the aboriginal peoples, who, for their part, were worried about surviving the white settlers. The survival theme also plays off the perennial political, economic, and cultural threat of domination by the United States. For French-speaking Canadians, the theme plainly includes cultural and linguistic survival against assimilation by English-speaking Canada. In the late 1860's and 1870's, Canadians' haunting wish to survive drove them to build the transcontinental railway; without it, Canada literally could not have existed above that interminable, invisible border with the United States. At least until the mid-1980's, that drive to survive led us to try to hold back the rising tidal waves of U.S. investment, which some nationalists suspected only developed Canada to make it attractive enough to take over. This view now lodges mainly in the New Democratic Party and Mel Hurtig's freshly minted National Party.

Tolerance. Canadians pride themselves on their respect for differences and on their alleged genius for compromise to make differences livable. Some examples: our officially sanctioned welcome for immigrant cultures and languages, our very generous and color-blind refugee policies, and our strong federal and provincial human rights laws and commissions. Not a few homegrown skeptics would now argue that our tolerance is really fatalism before the difficulty of weaving our countless human strands into a country. They would also argue that our true genius is the self-indulgent one of turning opportunities into problems: inheriting two world languages becomes a "burden," and finding a cornucopia of natural resources turns into a federal-provincial holy war (as almost everything in Canada does, sooner or later). At any rate, diversity for Canadians is almost synonymous with unity.

Equality. Canadians' cult of tolerance may encourage our cult of mediocrity. Treating everybody the same, and granting everybody the same rights, can come close to saying everybody enjoys the same talents and deserves the same attainments. But deeper reasons explain our ease with the ordinary. Arguably three times colonized (by France, Britain, and now the United States), Canadians tend to fear excellence as success deserved by, and proclaimable by, only our betters. A typical Canadian self-deprecation: "We Canadians landed on the moon a year before the Americans, but we were too shy to tell anybody." In 1992, when the United Nations declared that Canada had displaced Japan as the best place in the world to live, a cartoon in the *Ottawa Citizen* showed one Canadian whining to another that those perfidious Japanese had robbed us of our rightful place . . . as number two.

(Speaking of Japan, the Japanese adage "The nail that stands out will get hammered down" fits us Anglos all too well, though much less so the more self-assured Québécois. In Quebec, the only nails that risk hammering down are mavericks who defy nationalist orthodoxies or people who bring up the unmentionable in international publications. The explosion of fury in Quebec nationalist circles against Mordecai Richler's 1992 *New Yorker* polemic on Quebec's anti-Semitic past and its law banning English signs was a painfully telling episode. In English-speaking Canada, we do not excommunicate dissenters; we ridicule and marginalize them. The result is the same.)

Order. Compared with Americans, Canadians show astounding respect for authority. Given a choice between order and freedom, Canadians tend not so much to mind putting the public interest (as incarnated by established authority) over the interest of individuals. Like the good Prussians in the 1929 German cult movie *Der Hauptmann von Koepenick*, Canadians—at least until recently—have historically enjoyed revering anybody with a title. This had its beginnings with our foundation, on both

French and English sides, as an eighteenth-century counterrevolutionary state, as a country faithful to Crown and Altar. It became entrenched in the eastern half of Canada under churchly and conservative political elites who ruled well into the twentieth century. And it spread throughout the nineteenth-century West, where a single red-coated Mountie would lay down Her Majesty's law in frontier towns without benefit of cavalry, vigilantes, posses, or Colt .44s. This ingrained respect for authority is weakening: our 1982 Charter of Rights and Freedoms empowers individuals and groups in their contest with the state, and a worldwide phenomenon of discredit saps our political elites. But Canadians still keep "peace, order, and good government" as desiderata in their Constitution—a somewhat stodgier motto, as many have pointed out, than the Americans' "life, liberty, and the pursuit of happiness."

A Beacon of Peace. Cynics aside, and there are a few, the most powerful positive force uniting Canadians is their universal belief that if Canada stands for anything, it stands for peace in the world. This is "Pearsonian idealism"—symbolized and inspired by Lester Pearson's Nobel Prize–winning success in creating a U.N. Peace Force at Suez in 1956. Pierre Trudeau and his fellow Québécois Jacques Parizeau tried to ridicule the idea of Canada as a "boy scout." But Canadians, drawing on a century-old missionary tradition, a significant role in both world wars and Korea, and an image of themselves as an unthreatening friend to all, have insisted that Pearson's idealism is their lucid realism: helping out abroad unites us at home. Canada, the only nation to win the U.N. High Commissioner for Refugees' Nansen Medal for generous treatment of refugees, is also the only country to have contributed troops and money to *all 34* U.N. peacekeeping missions since 1947. Canadians may forever squabble over trivia at home; but they will probably forever want to be good guys—helpful fixers—in the world. It's who we are at our best; it's who we want to believe we are deep down. Personally, I believe that Canadians can never build a nation together unless they help build a happier, more peaceful world together. Isolation for us would amount to disintegration.

Can helping fashion a new North America, and perhaps later a new Western Hemisphere, replace our European, Asian, and African engagements as a unifying focus? To a degree, yes, as I'll suggest later in sketching out some possible new solidarities and dynamics offered by the rise of Mexico in the 1990's and beyond. But I think we will always seek attachments far from home to keep us from drowning in the attractions of our overwhelming neighbor.

These are the main ideas that make Canadians Canadians. If you're a typically well-intentioned American not richly informed about Canada, you may still say: "Hey, we're still just about the same." Then ponder two issues, which I urge upon U.S. diplomats newly appointed to that minefield of misunderstanding called Canada: gun control and universal health care. Canadians hate guns and love tax-supported health care for everybody. So far, although Mr. and Mrs. Clinton may change things a bit, America's reality seems to us to say that Americans like guns a lot and think free health care for all is some kind of "socialist" boondoggle.

To anchor the above values or beliefs, Canadians have devised homegrown institutions and mechanisms. These are worth study by Americans and Mexicans because they may prove instructive for either emulation or rejection.

Our system of social safety nets—under financial strain, as everywhere else—lies deep in our untouchable unconscious. Our foremost social program is a universal health care system that, though not perfect, is probably the most apt example the United States could possibly learn good things from. Other programs: a plethora of pensions, payments, grants, and loans to less-favored individuals and groups of every kind, from the aged to the disabled to social activists outside the economic mainstream. "Social" solidarity even includes state support for many interest or protest groups defending cultural, ethnic, or gender causes.

On the economic side, we have built up an almost sacred system of grants and loans to overcome "regional economic disparities." And in many ways, we allow our provinces more economic autonomy than sovereign states in the European Common Market. To cite a few examples: only now are the final barriers being lowered to allow beer sales among provinces; construction workers (and sometimes materials) from outside Quebec cannot be used with total freedom on projects in Quebec; and marketing boards galore protect provincial markets from domestic competition. The roughly 500 interprovincial trade barriers we tolerate cost us an estimated $5.2 billion (U.S.) a year. Recent reforms to the contrary, we accept many of them as underpinnings of regional distinctiveness and equal opportunity. For better or worse, we try to abolish geography.

Politically, we have tried to broker regional, cultural, and linguistic differences in three major or "traditional" parties: the Progressive Conservative Party (only foreigners untutored in our wondrous ways find this name an oxymoron), the Liberal Party, and the New Democratic Party. Some free-enterprise Americans (for us a tautology, not an oxymoron), having studied the programs of these parties, would probably argue that we have three socialist parties. To assert that is to ignore the whole value structure of our country. Canadians share many core beliefs and myths different from Americans', including our belief that governments, on balance, do more good than harm. The comparatively greater willingness of all our mainstream parties to intervene in society and the economy only confirms these cultural differences.

The fall 1993 federal election almost wiped out two of these traditional brokerage parties, the Conservatives and the NDP, and brought into Parliament two strong regional parties, the west's right-wing Reform Party and Quebec's separatist Bloc Québécois. The latter is now—entertainingly for foreigners—Her Majesty's Loyal Official Opposition. Pessimists argue that such parties herald the end of Canada, the homeland of compromise; optimists see them as symptoms of tensions rising to provoke a classic Canadian compromise.

Given our climate, our scattered peopling of a vast land, and our history of struggling to carve out a way of life distinct from the American Way, it's not surprising that Canadians have emphasized sharing burdens and putting the community's welfare over the individual's. We are not a nation of Wyatt Earps or Lone Rangers, much as we might like to be after watching a bracing western movie. Our historical memory sees the rugged individualist who goes it alone as quite likely just a selfish egomaniac who hogs all the food and blankets, then endangers the village by getting drunk and needlessly provoking the Indians. Boringly but reliably, we like to talk things out as a group, then *authorize* our representatives to do things of benefit to us all. In the Canadian grain, our heroes are mainly anti-heroes.

On a symbolic level, this willingness to let the State intervene is well summed up by two nation-knitting creations of Conservative governments that did not even call themselves "progressive." In the late nineteenth century, Tories built the national railway (for English-speaking Canada, a genuine myth of song and story) that literally created this country coast to coast. And, in the 1930's, to prevent U.S. domination of our airwaves, Conservatives set up the Canadian Broadcasting Corporation, a BBC-style arm's-length network that Canadians often rail against but cling to, in times of national insecurity, as an electronic security blanket.

In 1974 in Alberta, and 1981 in Ontario, Progressive Conservative governments bought, respectively, an airline and a big chunk of an oil company. In 1990 a Conservative government in Ottawa legislated Canada's long-term participation in a huge undersea oilfield off Newfoundland.

Of the three new parties active in 1993—the regionalist Reform Party, the Bloc Québécois, and the National Party—only the western-rooted Reform Party treats government as a barely necessary evil, and that is so partly because it believes the old parties used government to exclude the West. The other two new parties, to put it kindly, are not inclined to equate state intervention with meddling.

A word about political style. Contradictions of region, culture, language, social beliefs, and economic interest have imposed on Canadian politics two characteristics. The first is a tendency, brilliantly analyzed by Herschel Hardin in his book *A Nation Unaware*, to mix public and private enterprise in that classic Canadian hybrid, the Crown Corporation.[3] A second contradiction, perhaps common to all politics at some level, might be called creative ambiguity. The main three fault-lines we have to paper over pit West against East ("East" actually means the central provinces of Ontario and Quebec, not so much the Atlantic region); provinces against Ottawa (i.e., decentralization vs. centralization); and, most notoriously, Quebec against the rest of Canada. Canadians cannot define their country too clearly or too symmetrically without blowing it up, or provoking federalist gridlock: the repeated failure of our constitutional talks for decades is frustrating evidence. Our politicians seem condemned to hedge and tack and weave even more than most. It's too cynical to say that the great advantage of having two official languages is that politicians can state opposite truths, when necessary, in English and French; but in a country that defines unity as diversity, plain truth often needs various shades of varnish. Orwell would have understood.

Canadians' Evolving (Dissolving?) Citizenship

Canadians' sense of themselves and their country is now under assault from powerful external and internal forces. Worldwide, tribal insecurities are attacking efforts good and bad to build larger loyalties. Even forgetting the former Soviet Union and Yugoslavia, where armed ideology could no longer keep the lid on ethnic nationalism, the European Community, Belgium, Britain, and the former Czechoslovakia have faced, or are facing, challenges to long-admired collective dreams. Even the Italy of Mazzini and Garibaldi is looking shaky as North talks of cutting loose South. Closer to home, Mexico's "Norte" has long felt constrained by a distant "Centro" dominated by Mexico City. The doubtfully analogous but seductive examples of the Baltic states, Scotland, and Slovakia tempt always temptable Quebec secessionists (as did, before the horror in Bosnia-

Herzegovina, the Balkan states). At the same time, the Canada–U.S. Free Trade Agreement (FTA) has strengthened North-South economic links while weakening Canada's own East-West links. NAFTA, too, is likely to make our old internal bargains less relevant.

Within Canada itself, two factors have sapped our solidarities with each other. On the one hand, government, especially our federal one, has drastically weakened programs allowing Canadians to learn about one another. In the past nine years, Ottawa has killed, or cut, the kind of youth exchanges that 30 years ago de Gaulle and Adenauer found vital to building Franco-German friendship. And turf-protecting provincial educational bureaucracies still fight off all suggestions of teaching a common national history—and in many cases, any Canadian history to speak of before the mid-teen years. On the other hand, as in so many democracies, our people feel divorced from their leaders. The result: simmering animosities among groups and regions, and a sense of rudderlessness as a nation.

In sum, Canada is living through a period of spiritual destabilization. Is this destabilization the antechamber of disintegration? Or is it a transition to a more exciting remaking of our country?

Argument and evidence abound to back either view. The decisive factor, in spite of all the obvious economic, cultural, social, and political determinisms, will be the ability of Canadians to articulate and share a unique, compelling vision. For that we need unique, compelling leaders not yet on the horizon.

I am thinking here of leaders able to reflect upon the nature of a nation. Leaders who can reach the hearts, and capture the dreams, of the many peoples called Canadian and, without suffocating their originalities, weld them into a single people.

What is a nation? Ernest Renan, responding to his own question in the classic lecture of that title given at the Sorbonne in 1882, rejected all theories rooted in race, language, religion, geography, or mere history.[4] Renan defined the nation in terms admirably suited to Canada's deep dilemma: how to translate a mosaic into a melting pot; how to give nationality to a nation whose existence rests all too much on a name; how to focus values into a vision.

Do you doubt that the key to a unifying vision—a "spiritual principle" or "moral conscience," as Renan put it—lies in defining Canada's special place in the world? In 1992 Canadians thrilled to only two events: the demonstrated leadership of our general Lewis Mackenzie as head of the U.N. forces in Sarajevo and . . . the Toronto Blue Jays' winning of the

World Series. If you believed our editorialists and elected leaders as they reflected on this second, highly spiritual experience, about 25 American, Dominican, and Puerto Rican baseball players saved Canada from disintegration. The point in both cases is that we yearned for the world (or at least the Americans) to legitimize our triumph, and maybe to tell us who we are. That should tell you all you need to know about both our country's aching to achieve its potential and our politicians' often hard-to-glimpse potential.

I've spoken about how the United States and Canada interact, so often causing Canada to seek a different vision. In the broadening context of North American interdependence, how might Canada's groping for identity mesh, and perhaps evolve, with Mexico's personality as we both deal with our powerful neighbor?

Canada's growing relations with Mexico can bring a hopeful new dimension to Canadians' thinking and destiny. The closeness Mexicans and Canadians feel to Europe, our partly shared Latinity, our relatively harmonious (current) racial experiences, our instinct to use the State for common projects (including cultural ones), our wish to be seen as independent of the United States, even a certain interpersonal reticence—such factors ought to facilitate dialogue.

In a passive sense, it may be consoling for both Mexicans and Canadians to feel they are no longer alone against their generally benign, but huge and self-centered, common neighbor. And in a more positive sense, Canada and Mexico, by finding strong new avenues for pulling together, may be able to underpin and highlight their own identities in ways less touchily hostile to Americans.

Some possible avenues for Mexican-Canadian cooperation? The Pacific Rim, for example, in offering joint projects for Japanese investment; some niche manufacturing, such as telecommunications and small aircraft; agricultural research and market development; joint peace-keeping initiatives; inter-American diplomacy, notably in helping build the huge new trading community linking North, Central, and South America that many dream of; and of course large-scale exchanges of students and professionals to knit the human fabric vital to a good international relationship. The Organization of American States can prove an admirable forum for joint efforts: both Mexico and Canada are trusted activists in their own right and valued as useful bridges to U.S. policy.

Such efforts, because they would be positive and not directed against the Yankees/gringos, might over decades soften the paranoia of both Canadians and Mexicans about their American neighbor. Subtly, and along with the evolution of Quebec and the Canadian West toward greater self-affirmation, Canadians might find in their new Mexican partners true allies of the spirit. In the now-less-threatening environs of a trilateral North America, Mexico and Canada might even stop seeing America as the elephant in their beds, and more as the ham in their sandwich—not as a problem, but as an extraordinary and nourishing opportunity. In short, they might help each other discover more mature identities rooted in their ability to offer widely respected values and original models of civilization.

All of these bilateral affinities and potentials stir plausible hopes. But weaving Mexico into Canada's political imagination might pay another dividend to Canadians: a fresh and broader perspective on their elusive national purpose. As the twenty-first century dawns, Canadians just may be able to transcend some internal quarrels by integrating Mexico into a continental, Renan-style national purpose—into a vision of a destiny where all three North American nations begin to rise above old purposes, old missions, and old illusions, and to share certain common hopes. Until now (though much less in Quebec, securely insecure behind its linguistic rampart), "North America" to Canadians has meant standing alone against an assimilationist tidal wave from the United States. As a serious interlocutor and ally, Mexico was invisible to Canadians, as Canada was to Mexicans. A three-nation North America, where new Mexican-Canadian solidarities could grow and link America's two suspicious neighbors, might well move Canadians to translate their strivings for a transcendent national purpose onto a wider stage, one grand enough to suck the melodrama from many internal Canadian tensions. No longer would Canada's "identity" consist mainly in clinging to an obsessive, sulky anti-Americanism and playing world boy scout through the United Nations and other multilateral groups. It might rest on the idea of Canada—all parts and peoples of it—participating enthusiastically in a three-nation North America, a North America no longer resembling a U.S. hegemony but, for the first time, something like a partnership.

In such an outlook, Canada could continue to find itself by acting in the world. But the faraway adventures in peace-making and aid-giving that have defined Canada since the Second World War could now find a spiritual center of gravity closer to home. They could draw on a vision of North America anchored in new interests and new intimacies shared with Mexicans as well as Americans.

Both Mexicans and Americans, notwithstanding strong and enduring national egos, appear to find power enough in the North American idea to rethink many national assumptions and to tackle historic structural reforms. Can Canadians find similar national purpose, and perhaps greater national cohesion, by stretching their imagination to embrace all of North America? Can they assume a strongly felt identity as North Americans that might, like Rilke's two love-solitudes, "protect and limit and greet" their identity as Canadians?

In a word: can Canada's distinctive values as a country refocus themselves into the more sweeping vision of a continent? At this early stage in developing a new North American family, much of the above flirts with wishful thinking. But is not such dreaming precisely how futures are born? Three centuries ago, Mexico's brilliant feminist poet-philosopher Sor Juana de la Cruz would certainly have agreed; so, two centuries ago, would have America's Thomas Jefferson; and so today, no doubt, could even Woody Allen and his spiritual compatriots in Canada.

American Identity: A Political Compact

MARC PACHTER

> The political activity that pervades the United States must be
> seen in order to be understood. No sooner do you set foot
> upon American ground than you are stunned by a kind of
> tumult. . . . It is impossible to spend more effort in the pursuit
> of happiness.
> —Alexis de Tocqueville, *Democracy in America*

Attempts to define the nature of American society often begin with a quo-
tation from Alexis de Tocqueville's nineteenth-century masterpiece, *Democracy in America*. It is remarkable that a book written about a country
thought to be perpetually changing, relentlessly modern, and completely
without a sense of tradition could be produced over 150 years ago and still
seem so *right* as a current description. It is even more surprising that Tocqueville's study of a people principally rural, Protestant, and Anglo-Saxon
(and enslaved African-American) could have anything to say to or about
the urban, industrial, multicultural nation that hundreds of millions rest-
lessly inhabit today.

If observations rendered in the first half of the nineteenth century are
still applicable to the United States of the late twentieth century, it is reasonable to assume that there exists an enduring "core" nature of American
society. But to understand it, one has to distinguish America's sense of
nationhood from that of traditional societies, which draw their identity
from bonds of faith, ethnicity, and memory. To speak of an American
identity requires that we reexamine what it is that holds a national community together and what it is that constitutes a national culture.

Being fully American, as the United States defines its citizens, does
not presuppose an ancestral linkage to the nation or to its predominant
ethnic cultures or religious traditions. Americans, as individuals, participate in a multitude of historic cultures, but what they share with one
another is something quite different. At the heart of their nationhood is
an enduring social contract and the energetic process it sets in motion. It

is the task of this essay to capture the sense of that contract and the evolution of that process.

Membership in the national community demands only the decision to become American, a political decision that contains within it a moral dimension as well. *All* Americans, including the native-born, are assumed to be Americans by choice, not merely by historical legacy. They have agreed to participate in a political and social construct. (This welcoming notion of community has a darker side. If one is judged American through allegiance to a process and principle, then one can be labeled "un-American" as well. It is hard to imagine a Committee on Un-French or Un-Mexican Activities.)

A passion for "choice" may, in fact, be the central thrust and value of the society. It is the active mode of freedom, and assumes not only an absence of political or economic restraint, but an opportunity to select from a rich menu of possibilities. At its most trivial, the culture indulges this value in the proliferation of an endless and often meaningless variety of consumer options. There is a breezy assumption of the virtue of choice for its own sake, which crops up in comments like the following from the social critic Richard Reeves: "Radio in America is like Baskin-Robbins without the calories. Thirty-one choices can make you anxious, but you are proud to know they are all there. . . . In most parts of the world the dead hand of government controls the dial, limiting radio listeners to good music, bad music and predictable news from the provinces."[1]

At a deeper level there is, in the love of choice, a memory of the chance to escape the dead end of lives in ancestral cultures and to create in a New World the life one chooses to live. Many Americans repeat this pattern of migration, literally, by moving to the western states, or symbolically, in their professional or social lives, looking for new starts, for second chances. And while the tragic experience of Native Americans and African-Americans has long mocked the national ethos of choice, they too have come to demand a right to shape their own destinies and to share in the possibilities assumed to be an American birthright.

America believes in self-creation and celebrates the "self-made man," and now "the self-made woman." At the heart of this faith is the conviction that inherited circumstances and forebears are far less important than the direction one chooses for oneself and the effort one invests in that choice. America's heroes "come from nowhere" and "make it on their own." Its singers insist, "I Did It My Way." Except for the stubborn and heretical barriers of race, to be discussed later, Americans assume of themselves and of others that their origins may enrich their lives but do not shape their destinies.

Though liberating as an assumption and an ideal, this concept of social and economic free will also places on the individual the burden of responsibility for his or her own fate. In a society that is in a perpetual state of becoming, there are no social or economic absolutes, and no allowance for the inability to improve one's life, for whatever reason. When ambition is frustrated and prosperity denied, Americans see a perversion of the natural order of things. American rage, when it erupts, is fueled by the encounter with limits.

Although a passion for choice is the engine of American individualism (the term was first coined by Tocqueville to describe American democratic behavior), it also provides a corrective to selfish behavior. From the vantage point of more traditional societies, Americans may seem to be a nation of atomized individuals in social free-fall; but in fact they have not eliminated a sense of social obligation. They have merely replaced its hereditary base.

Americans are joiners and volunteers and philanthropists. They embrace a series of obligations and responsibilities freely chosen, and thereby harness their individualism to social purpose. If Europeans, Asians, Africans, and Latin Americans marvel at the lack of a sense of extended family, ancestral ties, and class allegiance in the United States, so do Americans marvel at what they see as the ungenerous reluctance of members of traditional cultures to embrace nonreligious or nonfamilial opportunities for volunteerism and to provide financial support for good causes.

American society has married an ethic of choice to an endless variety of traditions, ideas, and opportunities. The mix of peoples and customs encountered in American daily life and the dramatic interruption most communities have experienced in their emigration from their homelands has led to a practice of sampling and borrowing and intermingling of styles, rituals, and above all foods. This eclecticism, which may seem messy to more historically unified cultures, becomes in America a value and a signpost of vitality. It is what gives national shape, ultimately, to much of the country's art and literature. America's artists, writers, and architects have taken as their prerogative picking and choosing among elements in foreign and domestic cultures and combining them into a new American whole.

The dynamic at the heart of America's system of values, beliefs, and identity found its most lyrical early expression in the "inalienable rights" of all human beings, which the Declaration of Independence listed as "life, liberty, and the pursuit of happiness." It was not happiness that the author of the Declaration, Thomas Jefferson, claimed for his countrymen and all humanity, but its "pursuit." From the start, there has been very little utopianism in the American political mainstream, little sense of an ideal State or an ideal human condition to be constructed through social planning. It is, instead, the very condition of striving, of becoming, the experience of unfettered living, that excites the national imagination. The words that move Americans are revealing: "freedom," "mobility," "individualism," "opportunity," "energy," "pragmatism," "progress," "renewal," "competition." These are not dry, descriptive words; they speak to the American spirit.

Bill Clinton, in his successful 1992 presidential campaign, chose as his rallying cry one of the most evocative words in the American vocabulary: "Change." Although one word alone does not win an election, the slogan was inspired in its appeal to national yearnings. The constant American hunger for change may be one of the most bewildering aspects of the national system to those outside it, a deliberate and seemingly perverse invitation to disorder or at least to endless beginnings. Over a century and a half ago, one writer caught the mood of perplexity in a speech he recorded by a not yet Americanized Louisiana Creole:

"Ah, *messieurs*," he shouted. "Do you remember Mister Jefferson. . . . How glad we were to have such a glorious statesman. Bah! In less than a year nothing was right. After four years he had to make room for Mister Madison, and Mr. Madison remained *la creme de perfection* for a time. Then they played the same game, off he went and Mister Monroe appeared, and Mister Monroe was given his marching orders and Mister Adams arrived. And now they want Mr. Jackson. Always something new, something better. *Morbleau*, why don't they keep Jefferson or Madison or Adams if they are good? Why always this restlessness, disorder, and confusion in the whole country? Why always start afresh? And that they call self-government."[2]

Part of the attraction of change in American culture is rooted in the hope that every change will bring improvement. But the optimistic expectation that change represents progress ipso facto is far less important than a strong tendency to dislike and even to fear permanence in authority or policy. During the debate over the approval of the proposed Constitution, Thomas Jefferson warned that even permitting a president more than one four-year term, without guaranteed rotation, might lead to his becoming a virtual "officer for life."[3] Jefferson's concern was based on the fundamental American assumption that sovereignty rests in the people and is only temporarily and conditionally bestowed on the officeholder.

The churning, antagonistic nature of the American process is meant to provide a guarantee against entrenchment. No party or individual can be trusted with authority for too long a period. People are corruptible; policies grow stale. When one party occupies the White House too long, a restlessness rises in the electorate. No one set of ideas or leaders will hold their allegiance over time. It is the dynamic of the system itself that brings Americans what they need and trust: a balancing of forces, a monitoring of truth through challenge and exposure, a reminder of the conceits and danger of power, of the benefits of change and growth and experimentation, and, not least, of the charm of starting afresh.

Paradoxically, then, America achieves its continuity through an insistence on change, and its stability through the incorporation of conflict. This is not simply the habit of a raucous electoral tradition, but a strategy built into the very framework of government. The historian Michael Kammen has described the system set in motion in 1789 by the framers of the Constitution as one of "conflict within consensus."[4] As another historian, Marcus Cunliffe, puts it: "They built friction into the document, intentionally, as a safeguard against corruption and dictatorship."[5]

This is certainly not a formula for efficiency. While American technology and management celebrate the ideal of efficiency, the nation as a political culture nurtures a profound distrust of long-term planning, of the concentration of power, of too-smooth national decision making. The constitutional government deliberately frustrates unified action through the separation of powers and a system of checks and balances. It has as its base a philosophy that assumes, in the formulation of James Madison, the Father of the Constitution, that men are not angels. "If men were angels," he wrote in a classic *Federalist* essay, "no government would be necessary. If angels were to govern men, neither external nor internal controls on government would be necessary." The public interest could therefore best be served by pitting "opposite and rival interests" against one another to create the effect of "better motives."[6] This political system can and does lead to conflict, frustration, and occasional gridlock in the absence of statesmanlike compromise or of the compatibility of political philosophy across the executive, legislative, and judicial branches. But it also achieves a virtual guarantee against the usurpation of authority.

The political system promotes as well the balancing act of federal, state, and municipal authority, which leads to a strong reluctance at the national level to mandate policy in many areas. The United States has no one educational system, no Ministry of Culture, and, so far, no health system directly administered from Washington. Policy on these and other issues emerges principally through persuasion, coordination, coalition building, and negotiation across parties, constituencies, interest groups, and regions. A very strong role is played by the large private sector, which reflects the released energy of an open marketplace of ideas, programs, and resources; and another significant actor is the suspicious press.

Despite the tradition of restrained government, many Americans over the last century have proposed a new view of the State's role. If a society needs only to be released from the yoke of government to enjoy the benefits of freedom, then the task of political reform is complete when the worst tendencies of government are offset and social energies are released. But this assumes that the underlying political, social, and economic realities allow for equal participation in the full benefits of freedom, or, conversely, that only certain members of society qualify as active participants. Generations of American reformers have demanded that their society acknowledge those it has excluded and then use government as a guarantor of their freedom to share in the American promise. They have consistently been challenged by others, who fear the empowerment of government as an assault on freedom. In the end, the question for American democracy has been easy to pose but very difficult to answer: what is the relationship between equality and freedom?

By the standards of the eighteenth century, the new nation had radicalized the idea of political consent by vesting final authority in the people, all of whom, in the words of the Declaration of Independence, were "created equal." But actual participation in the new political community of the United States was constrained in ways modern Americans would find intolerable and even inconceivable.

The Constitution left the question of voting rights to the decision of the separate states, which varied considerably in their commitment to universal suffrage even among white men. Property qualifications at the time the government was formed made over four-fifths of adult white males ineligible to vote or hold office.[7] Added to this community of the excluded were the entire population of women and the large population of slaves, referred to by the Constitution as "other Persons" (valued as three-fifths of "free Persons" for purposes of taxation and representation[8]), as well as all members of the Native American tribes. The enfranchised political population was therefore a mere fraction of the larger community.

But the appeal to universal rights had an irresistible momentum that carried the nation far beyond the limited applications of its first decades. American history is in large part the tumultuous unfolding of the logic of its origins. By the time Tocqueville visited the United States in the early 1830's, at that point caught up in the revolutionary mood of Jacksonian democracy, universal suffrage was in sight for most white males. The term "universal" had been stretched as a boundary of political community, but only so far. The Civil War of the 1860's corrected the obscenity of the tolerance of slavery in a free society and was followed by the 14th and 15th Amendments to the Constitution which extended political rights to half the African-American population. The female half had to await the passage of the 19th Amendment in 1920, which finally swept into the political community the largest group of disenfranchised Americans.

Even after several years of deliberate, targeted enforcement of basic political rights and the insistent demands of the civil rights movement, the most basic question of the nature of equality as a precondition of freedom remained unresolved in American culture. Fair and equal access to political rights, whenever finally resolved, would not itself guarantee for everyone full participation in the promise of American life. Any argument that this inequality of circumstance was due to "innate" limitations among the excluded communities and categories of Americans threatened the very idea of American individualism. The very idea that an individual could be boxed in by his or her fate, playing out narrow dramas of class and caste and race and gender, was abhorrent. If it was a matter, instead, of artificial barriers set up by society—particularly racism, but also sexism and social and economic factors—then the responsibility of the nation became to guarantee, not simply assume, equality among all Americans at the starting gate in their pursuit of happiness. But by what means? The answer for the growing reformist tradition was the active use of the nation's authority in a program of social justice. The central government was no longer the problem; it was the solution.

Reformers have generally argued their case for intervention within the framework of the American dynamic. Government was introduced as an active player in the economic life of the nation during the Progressive Era of the early twentieth century and then, in Franklin Delano Roosevelt's New Deal Administration, as itself a counterbalance to social and economic forces that threatened the fairness of the society. More recently, social policy setting has become even more activist in seeking to affect the terms on which Americans prepare, compete, and interact. The issue at the heart of American reform is simply this: what does it take for an individual American, and especially one encumbered by the experience of prejudice, by economic condition, and, more recently, by disability, to have an equal shot at success? What does it take, truly, for all Americans to be free?

When most Americans speak of equality, they mean equality of opportunity, not of outcome. From the first, Americans have rarely argued for or demonstrated a commitment to a society with equality of property or condition. Part of the American Dream is the belief, the "value," that individuals, differing as they do in initiative, energy, and talent, should enjoy the disparate fruits of their effort. There are meant to be no guarantees of equal results. Most Americans do not want a level society; they do, however, want a level playing field.

Or do they? It is a perpetual dilemma in American life that generalizations about the goals, values, and circumstances of the society break down when confronted by the stubborn heritage of a racial divide. It was possible for the new nation to see itself as an embodiment of the Enlightenment and yet count a slave as three-fifths of a human being. It was possible for the infant nation to celebrate its democratic momentum during the Jacksonian Era of the early nineteenth century and yet increase its population of slaves and the number of slave states. It was possible for the reunited nation to pass a constitutional amendment enfranchising all African-Americans and yet take a full century to enforce its most basic provisions. And, despite the progress of the civil rights movement, it continues to be possible to predict different destinies and experiences for an American child solely on the basis of his or her race. This is more than an American dilemma: it is an American heresy calling into question the very viability of the society as a community of shared values and expectations.

The renewed awareness of the intractability of race as a factor mocking American ideals has led to assertiveness and hostility among many groups and a mood of crisis in the American sense of self. The danger of fragmentation, of the fraying of the fabric of national identity, is real. But it is also true that Americans have long *used* acrimonious self-criticism, passionate rhetoric, and the clash of social forces to propel themselves forward. The jeremiads warning of the decline of individual communities or of the nation as a whole date back to the era of the Puritans, serving then, as in every succeeding era, as an incentive to change and action and as a measure of American impatience and stubborn expectations.

What is demanded by the mainstream activism of the late twentieth century (there are more radical separatist arguments as well) is a fulfillment of the logic of American democracy. The question is not only political and economic, but cultural as well. Even if the expressed values of the society defined being American as participating in a social contract rather than a particular heritage, the assumption persisted that the true, the *essential*, American came of a certain racial and cultural background (Anglo-Saxon, later broadened to European), faith (Protestant, broadened, after years of hostility, to include Catholic and, even more reluctantly, Jewish) and, for purposes of political and economic status, gender (male). The early-twentieth-century idea of the melting pot asserted, at least for certain communities, that they did not have to be born to a particular heritage but were expected to become American culturally no less than politically—to lose, in effect, their marks of difference from the majority of Americans. Even this did not forestall a dramatic restriction in immigration policies in the 1920's that assumed the "suitability" of only certain groups for American citizenship.

The argument for the recognition of the diversity of cultures and backgrounds as being fundamental, not only to American reality, but to American ideals has forced the society to debate anew the implications of its unusual notion of national community as process and interaction. From the 1960's, advocates of diversity have vied to create an apt metaphor for American society that would include rather than exclude or melt down. In Jesse Jackson's words: "There is talk about [America] being a melting pot. But it is really more like a vegetable soup. There are separate pieces of corn, meat, and so on, each with its own identity." Another advocate, Manuel Guerra, an educator of Mexican-American background, does not see the need to "substitute mashed potatoes for *frijoles*" as the price of being considered truly American. "Rather than the melting pot, we believe in the heterogeneity of American society, including the give and take with other peoples and other cultures."[9]

Guerra's appeal to the "give and take" of American society is a classic tenet of the national faith applied to a new era. Each generation of Americans has pushed the notion of the American blend of opinions, peoples, faiths, cultures, and, most recently, languages to the point where many have feared that the center would no longer hold. So far the record of national cohesion gives hope for the future, but that future is far from being guaranteed in the face of concerns among some members of the majority communities that the national fabric is unraveling and among disenchanted members of minority communities that they will never be genuinely welcomed into the American mix.

In other respects, as well, the current "crisis" in American values represents not their repudiation, but a testing of their application to widened circumstances. The growth of the American feminist movement is a reminder that biology was assumed to exempt half of all Americans from political and then professional and economic inclusion in the dynamic of national life. The barrier of gender has not yet fallen, but it is under continuous attack. Also caught up in the continuing revolution in American expectations are fundamental social constructs like that of the family, which are continually susceptible to the ethic of choice and self-realization. As early as the nineteenth century, Americans transformed marriage traditions to allow the free choice of partners. This notion expanded over time to include the right to choose to live together "without benefit of clergy" or to marry and then divorce; and increasingly, even to the redefining of what constitutes a family within or outside of legal frameworks. Increasingly, relations between children and parents and between younger and older generations test the boundaries of authority and consent to an extent unimaginable in earlier eras.

These are current American tendencies, but they are also, to a somewhat lesser extent, tendencies of all industrial democratic cultures. (The American writer Gertrude Stein once defined the United States as "the oldest country in the twentieth century.") Americans must begin to wonder how much the culture that once defined them as unique has become, in at least some of its aspects, the culture of global modernism. Some of this has not been easy to take. It has been a shock to see Japan hailed in its technological and industrial advancement as the nation of the twenty-first century; to see West Europeans identified with the notion of a grand union of states and a dynamic commonwealth; and to see the emerging, if tortured, democracies of Central and Eastern Europe become identified with the aspirations of an excited electorate.

But for all that, Americans can see the advantage they have in their long history of political openness and change, tolerance of conflict, entrepreneurial energy, and cultural mix. Their flexible history can serve as a formula for stability during the ongoing shocks of global modernism, confirming rather than undermining national traditions. What remains uncertain is how they will react to the toughest challenge to their assumptions: an emerging universe of shrinking resources and global and regional interdependence.

If a belief in limitless possibilities lies at the heart of American culture and community, then a sense of shared destiny with our neighbors to the North and South, requiring compromise and adjustment, will take time to develop. The dynamic of American belief and action has so far happened primarily within the confines of the country's own borders and "destiny." As a laboratory of democracy, the United States has felt protected by two oceans, unaffected by the border to the North and defensive of the border to the South.

In the immediate future, America will remain preoccupied by the working out of its own democratic logic at home. In the long run, its growing association with Mexico and Canada will require of it a tolerance of diversity in political style and national culture functioning *outside* the moral dynamic and purpose of its own national life. It will find, in the end, that being North American is not the same as being American.

Approaches to the Problem of Mexican Identity

ALBERTO RUY-SÁNCHEZ

Every nation has its own "tradition of ideas" about its existence, its history, and its essence. Mexico is no exception in that perennial search for a national self. As with any other culture or nation, however, to write about a Mexican national self means also, somehow, to reinvent it.

Some ancient Mexicans, the Aztecs for example, made an effort to present themselves as the personification of Mexicanness. They believed, and made believe, that their empire was the natural extension of their essential nature and calling. Historians among the Aztecs even went so far as to burn earlier versions of Mesoamerican history in order to establish theirs as the only one.

Many people, in many countries, have harbored in their hearts that very same desire and have performed the same kinds of immolation of the past in the name of some glory for the present—and in the name of a future for their glory.

Perhaps humankind's construction of an epic image of itself cannot exist without some sort of symbolic immolation. The heroic image of the self is always built over an ancient garden: it is a marble statue embedded in ground that was once fertile, a petrified flower that wants to live forever.

Any definition of a national self, even as the conclusion of a vivid chronicle, then, is a work of fiction; and more precisely, a symbolic work of fiction. But it is certainly a kind of fiction that humans need, or at least believe they need—which, in symbolic terms, is precisely the same thing. If we consider the symbolic dimension of our everyday lives, we are forced to treat all attempts at defining our national character as a work of symbols, as an elaboration of symbols.

Yet even to speak about the personal image of each one of us is already a complex problem. If I see myself in a mirror and try to describe my face, that description—even if expressed in the most detached and precise terms—is necessarily full of psychological dynamics, tensions, and pretensions. A great deal of Lacanian psychoanalytic theory is based on the primal scene of the infant child looking at himself in a mirror for the first time. It is a problem that has been christened "the construction of the self."

Obviously, the problem is all the more complex when someone looks at himself in a mirror and—based solely on that reflection—tries to construct the image of a national self. If an *I* speaking of an *I* is a complicated phenomenon (fraught with side effects and profound implications), consider how much more complicated it is for an *I* to speak of an *Us*.

The Search for the Ideal Mexican

There is a long tradition of inquiry in Mexico into the notion of an ideal Mexican. In this century alone, the tradition has given us—among the many books dedicated to Mexicanness, or *Mexicanidad*—two classics that are still studied, consulted, read, and quoted: *El perfil del hombre y la cultura en México*, by Samuel Ramos, and *El laberinto de la soledad*, by Octavio Paz.[1] Together, they constitute two of the archetypical studies of the Mexican self, two approaches that are still obligatory references. I will comment on both.

Their dates of publication are significant. The essay by the philosopher Samuel Ramos appeared in 1934, in the midst of the nationalist euphoria Mexico experienced after the Revolution and at the onset of the populist government spearheaded by General Lázaro Cárdenas.

It is no coincidence that this sort of intellectual probing should have occurred at that time. Ramos's reflection was plainly a nationalistic attempt to gain insight into who "*the* Mexican" might be. But even if he accepted a nationalistic and highly mythological notion of the existence of a quintessential Mexican, he was certainly not the blindest of nationalists. In his book, Ramos reacted against the radical nationalism that wanted to spare the country from all foreign contact, which it considered damaging. Nevertheless, Ramos did argue in favor of keeping the country free of any foreign system or idea that could stop "the high impulses of the Mexican soul." Though he failed to mention it, Ramos was referring to Marxism. He did not fit the stereotype of the leftist nationalist, as did Diego Rivera, for example, about whom Ramos was to write a book the following year, admiring the painter precisely on account of his Mexicanness.[2]

The national euphoria soon diminished as the Mexican Revolution began to be seen as an increasingly petrified myth, an institution. Hence the time came to criticize the official versions of the national self as presented by Mexicans from the various artistic horizons, from mural painting and dance to literature and film.

Octavio Paz's essay appeared in 1950, at the end of this general nationalistic enthusiasm and at the dawn of a new period in Mexican culture: the decades marked by disillusion with the Mexican Revolution, and the resulting desire to situate Mexico alongside other nations and to propel the country into the international modernity of the times.

Time, however, is a strange thing. Its acids consume books and ideas to varying degrees. Hence the effects of time on cultural products recall Spinoza's aphorism on the relativity of life: "The same sun that melts wax solidifies clay." If Ramos's search seems somewhat dated, Paz's work is still alive, eternally criticized but nonetheless provocative. While a lapse of only 16 years separates their dates of publication, a century now seems to separate their respective aims and forms.

Like other philosophers—including Emilio Uranga and his *Análisis del ser del mexicano*[3]—Ramos addressed the problem of "being Mexican" for his readers and in so doing, constructed a new psychological portrait of *the* Mexican based on the national mentality during the first half of this century. Paz, by contrast, proposed a moral critique of "being Mexican," a mythological and paradoxical portrait of *the* Mexican to be directed toward the intellectual climate of the second half of this century. Thus, while Ramos was looking backwards, Paz was staring straight ahead. Indeed, Ramos was closing an intellectual period, whereas Paz was opening up a new one.

It seems natural that a moral critique should feel closer to us than the psychological portrait. We are at the far edge of an era in which "being critical" has been a dominant intellectual value.

We can readily admit that *the* Mexican, whether Ramos's or Paz's, no longer exists, so rapidly has Mexico been changing. But maybe neither of the ideal Mexicans they portrayed ever existed. Maybe we will discover that, however eloquently, they were only discussing the perspectives and preoccupations of their times, along with an awareness of being different from their foreign neighbors, as they constructed their own personal images of Mexicanness. So perhaps the time has come to create a new, different portrait of the ideal Mexican, to view ourselves from the perspective of the close of the century—in short, to look into a different mirror in the hope of finding our plural image, an *Us* within the deepest vision of an individual *I*.

As a writer and editor involved in various fields of Mexican culture, observing the contemporary changes in the intellectual and psychological landscape, I am firmly under the impression that a new sensibility is beginning to emerge in Mexico. My points of reference are the early symptoms that are manifesting themselves in the visual arts, where—as we enter the final decade of this century—a new aesthetic has come to modify the artistic panorama of Mexico. For it has been in the visual arts that important cultural movements in Mexico have always first been given expression. It is there that they manifest their character.

The most diverse group of painters now share common concerns, pursuing a spiritual quest that in various ways makes painting, sculpture, and photography rituals of transcendence. Echoes and references to prehispanic rites abound, some of which are ahistorical fictions, pure inventions of the artists themselves. More intensely than ever before in this century, artists conceive of themselves as wounded souls. In this they follow Frida Kahlo, the visual historian of the "I-in-pain," the "I" equally repressed in the social epic of the 1930's and the neo-avant-garde abstractionist movement of the 1960's. There is a new concern for the populist feeling of traditional Mexico. But above all, for a large portion of the art world, there is a fresh interest in what it means to be Mexican and what, after all, is "Mexico." The search for Mexico's essential images has become a reinvention of those images by the artists who would pursue them. In sum, we are witnessing a search for what is most fundamental to art and to Mexico at one and the same time. This search is a deep expression of fantasy; it bursts forth in daily reality with the creative force of pure invention.

This new sensibility (which I have elsewhere called "the fantastic fundamentalism of new Mexican art") may well be the third great cultural movement in Mexico during this century.[4] The two previous movements (the nationalism of the 1930's; the neo-avant-garde of the late 1950's and early 1960's) perfectly coincide with the books published by Samuel Ramos and Octavio Paz. Seemingly, then, if this new sensibility eventually touches the field of philosophical inquiry, we should sooner or later expect to encounter a new portrait of *the* Mexican, a new examination of the problem of "being Mexican."

If there is one step that can be taken now in this direction, it is certainly not to make a simple list of Mexican "core values." That is a fiction that has outlived whatever usefulness it may have had. Even following in the footsteps of Paz and Ramos, we have consistently moved ahead on blazing saddles. The world has changed—not just nations. And our consciousness of the nature of the world has also changed. We cannot pretend that the portrait of the Mexican, or that of any other nationality in our *fin de siècle*, is as solidly grounded in reality as any thinker may have believed it was, many years ago, when those two books were written.

As an indication of that change of consciousness, we now tend to feel that all the attributes that Paz and Ramos claimed for the "ideal Mexican" cannot be accepted without qualification. Where Paz has written, "Mexicans consider life a battle," we need to say, "*Some* Mexicans consider life a battle" (and the same holds true for each ascription he makes). It is significant that all these ascriptions can and must be understood in another, more complex and relative way. Interesting and appealing though they may be, these "core values" are not the heart of the book. If *The Labyrinth of Solitude* is still valid, it is precisely thanks to its complex understanding of Mexican life at its most symbolic—and not on account of a list of adjectives pretending to describe Mexican nature.

It is not a question of whether Paz's analysis is true or false. It is true insofar as it is taken in good faith and with a reasonable dose of relativity. The Mexico he describes clearly has become much more complex, both in real life and in our minds. It cannot be described now without taking note of a certain degree of heterogeneity, to the extent of growing beyond or even diminishing the notion of something called *the* Mexican.

One interesting aspect of cultural relations today is how developed countries like the United States continue making specific demands on countries like Mexico. This demand implies conforming to their idea of what constitutes the Other country. As the United States becomes increasingly diverse, multiethnic, and multicultural—and increasingly less definable as one specific and linear culture—more and more Americans want to believe in a Mexico of one rigidly defined culture, instead of a complex plurality. For their own purposes they would rather see a primitive list of core values, what they want the other to be, and in this case, the ideal other is *le bon sauvage*. Increasingly, more and more Americans interested in Mexico want it to have the very unity of being and the solid identity they feel they themselves are permanently losing. Is this a mechanism of compensation? Is it a way of finding in the Other something that one can no longer possess oneself?

The mythic purity of cultures or races is less convincing now than it was in Ramos's day. We are all a mixture of races, and no purity is believable. As Henri Focillon wrote even then:

Nowhere in the universe are there greenhouses in which pure races may be found in flower. The most careful practices of endogamy do not prevent crossbreeding; the best-protected insular environments are open both to infiltration and to invasion. Even the constancy of anthropological indices by no means implies that values are changeless. Man works on himself. But he does not, it is true, rid himself of the age-old deposits laid down by time, and they are something that must be accounted for. What they constitute is a tonality, rather than an armature or a foundation. They introduce into the complex equilibrium of a culture inflections and accents similar to those that characterize a spoken language.[5]

Something to be especially noted in this observation by Focillon is the relativity he underlines in respect to that dimension of identity he calls "a tonality, rather than an armature or a foundation." National identity, then, cannot be a founding whole of core values, or a moral armature. It is a gesture full of meanings, a vision that is different at the very outset from that of Ramos and Paz.

Let's briefly examine these two archetypal images of the Mexican looking for himself in the forest of images of the world.

Samuel Ramos's analysis is based on a psychological theory, namely, the notion proposed by Adler that the neurotic harbors equivocal ideas of himself—undervalues himself—and hence directs all his acts to demonstrate to others and to himself his greatness, his power. For Ramos, to be Mexican, to parade the commonplaces of "the Mexican being," is an act of compensation. And that is the key concept in his portrait of the ideal Mexican. The development of this idea is rooted in Mexican history. And throughout this history, he seeks several basic "Mexican attitudes," such as self-deprecation and mechanical imitation.

Even in the establishment of Mexico's independence from Spain, Ramos sees the workings of an essentially Spanish value: individualism. "In America," he writes, "each one of the different colonies tended to be another Spain. When the revolutionaries raised a flag against Spain with the cry of '*mueran los gachupines*,' Spanish psychology was expressing itself in that attitude of refusal. We did nothing but emancipate ourselves from Spain in a Spanish style."[6]

To achieve legitimacy, this kind of psychological analysis applied to a country needed to accept the notion of a parallel between individual and race, in the sense that races are also assumed to experience childhood, maturity, and senility. What we now call underdevelopment would accordingly be considered the extreme youth, or immaturity, of a society, of a culture, or of a race. Ramos argues that the Mexican belongs to a young race that needs to grow into maturity, and—he writes—"to learn how to live instead of how to die." What he calls with great respect "the modern psychological doctrines" revealed that "the individual character needs to explore his childhood so as to seek an experience that gave a definitive orientation to his life."[7] Thus, he explores the history of Mexico looking for a traumatic experience, which he finds in the Conquest: for the Indians, the humiliation of being conquered; for the descendants of the conqueror, the humiliation of not being true Europeans. The Mexican finds himself in the middle, and to be there is his destiny, for he is not really American and no longer Spanish. Thus the Mexican, the compulsive imitator, considers himself an inferior being. One concentrated expression of Mexicanness is identified by Ramos in the uneducated, poor urban male known as "*el pelado*," the manifestly aggressive and macho persona who affirms the values that are assigned him.

Ramos conceived his book as a therapy: he suggests that the young race of Mexico should be aware of its complex so as to avoid possible negative effects on its development. For Ramos, the Mexican resembles a developing child who feels an emptiness in his being that demands fulfillment; as a consequence, he now must begin to acquire the mature personality that he lacks. Mexican *machismo* is, for Ramos, not in fact a Mexican essence, but rather a pathology. Not an essential part of his being, it is instead a fiction created by the Mexican to compensate for the accidents of his history and his collective childhood.

After Samuel Ramos, many Mexican philosophers approached the subject of "the Mexican being." The Spanish philosopher José Gaos—who lived in Mexico, where he taught and wrote about the history of ideas—exerted an enormous influence. For the young Octavio Paz, however, the reigning interpretations were insufficient to explain the Mexican. Following the principles of psychoanalysis, under each accepted notion he looked for another existence. "There is an unknown person who dwells within each one of us," explains Paz, "and, in this sense, *El laberinto de la soledad* was an attempt to bring to light that unknown person who inhabits me. An attempt to unearth my remains and to look at myself, and through myself, to look at the face of my fellow men." The book was, in his own words, "a confession, a quest, and a declaration of love."[8] Mexico was his object, his concern, his collective face in the mirror.

Whereas Adler and his theory of neurosis were the basic reference for Ramos, for Paz the Freudian principle of an unconscious existence was only a means to arrive at a moral and historical critique. The rich repertory of images, desires, hidden impulses, dreams, and inhibitions he finds buried in the soul of his "ideal Mexican" is simply the path toward a very personal approach to the history of Mexico. As he sees it, "History is situated between science and poetry. The historian sets forth descriptions as a man of science, but he has the visions of a poet. . . . History paves the way to understand the past and, sometimes, even the present."[9] At the beginning of the book, he says that the Mexican is not located in history; he *is* history itself. We are not simply the eyewitnesses of change; we ourselves are the changes.

During the time in which he wrote *El laberinto de la soledad*, some of the major intellectual influences on Octavio Paz were the French philosophers Roger Caillois and George Bataille, and particularly their teacher, the anthropologist Marcel Mauss. They wrote extensively about the meanings of the *fiesta* in traditional communities, and Paz identified their descriptions with his experiences in Mexico with the celebration of the Day of the Dead. These French thinkers had also examined the meanings of sacrifice, the difference between sacred and profane time, the importance of the ritual gift, the meanings of the ritual mask, and the phenomenology of loneliness. These are but a few of an entire gamut of analytical instruments that Paz integrated into his own examination of the Mexican, as any reader of his book will notice.

For Ramos, the Mexican hides behind a mask invented by his inferiority complex. For Paz, the Mexican does not *hide* behind a mask; he *is* a mask. And that mask is a totality of gestures to be deciphered. It constitutes a cultural and anthropological phenomenon.

It is important to note that this approach to cultural analysis implies that all world cultures are masks: that being a mask is not exclusive to Mexicans, but rather that all cultures don their own masks, or to be more precise, that each culture constitutes a different mask.

Thus, the same notion could be applied in the analysis of the culture and character of the ideal Canadian or the ideal American. What kind of mask does the inhabitant of the United States concoct? What kind of mask is fashioned by the inhabitant of Canada? Perhaps to believe that specific cultures can be seriously described in terms of *values* is a prominent feature of the Anglo-Saxon mask.

In a conception like the one described by Octavio Paz, values *are* masks. His methodological approach goes even farther: it suggests that there is much more at stake in the defense of "values," as any psychoanalyst would readily detect. Values are principally related to the dimension of the superego—the world of moral duties and laws—only one of the three Freudian dimensions in the individual psyche. From that perspective, a mask proves to be much more integrated and complete: it is an aesthetic fixation in the world of beliefs and in that of the personal ritual duties within the community. It is simultaneously a gesture surfacing from the dimension of the id, the world of instincts. As opposed to values, the mask speaks more deeply and more eloquently about cultural character. Values constitute a mode of representation that fails to take on any symbolic nature. From its beginnings, the mask acknowledges its symbolic existence. The Anglo-Saxon who believes that he lives in a skeptical world of values, with no blemish of the id or strain from the instinctive forces of the unconscious, is simply hiding himself, his inner being, behind values: in short, symbols disguised as non-symbols.

As concerns values, when different people wish to share a common life, they do indeed construct common values. But it is inconceivable for entirely different cultures to share a common mask. To do so would be highly spurious and ultimately false, of no use at all for an authentic common life. What *can* be enacted, however, is a new ritual—I would even venture to call it a dance—in which different masks may well participate together. Not to avoid differences, but rather to invite them to participate in the choreography of an utterly new dance. Our new challenge (in North America and the world at large) is to share our differences, our national identities.

Sharing National Identities

For many years, efforts to understand what it means to be Mexican have been attempts to define a presupposed national essence. Being a writer, and not a philosopher or a sociologist, I have followed a different path. Even in my essays, I always appeal at first to situations and images, as opposed to concepts and definitions. These come later, if at all. Literature is a way to say things that can only be expressed in literary situations. That is why literature exists: its fiction tells us truths in its own ways. And the essay is a literary act in which an author essays himself, experiments with himself in a theme.

Maybe that is why, instead of discussing my personal idea of the essential Mexican and his core values—or my idea of the essential American or the essential Canadian—I would like to propose a principle of relativity regarding national identities.

Let us consider the classical theological image of the demon as multifaceted. In the Bible, the demon is asked, "What is your name?" He answers, "My name is Legion, I am many." As our modern demon, national identity can also assume many bodies, many faces, and many personalities within each person. Which of these is chosen or worshiped by each group, community, or individual? Which side suits others, and which facets fail to harmonize with others?

From a cultural point of view, we are not only what our passports tell us we are. Each one of us is a kaleidoscopic identity.

To my mind, national identity is not an essence but a contrast, a situation. This is because we are also constituted by the ways others think of us as foreigners, by the ways we think of ourselves in our differences with regard to others, and by the ways we affirm, deny, extend, or lessen those differences. National identity is a geometry, an art of distances. And therefore it is a challenge of tolerance toward ourselves and others, toward the others' closeness.

As a child living in a suburb of Mexico City, I experienced the phenomenon of the "distant neighborhood." The family next door was American. Not far away lived a Swedish family, and next to them a family of Arabs. In all those houses lived children my age. But there was also the family of an old Belgian colonel; and several other families were of Spanish and French origin. There was an old village nearby, and that added another facet to my local gallery of particularities. Furthermore, my family was clearly identified as having come from the north (my mother and my father were born and raised in Sonora), and other families had come from Veracruz, Monterrey, Colima, Puebla, Yucatán, and Chiapas, or had moved out from Mexico City.

Suburbs like the one I grew up in are frequently human quilts. They are also places where people do not stay for long. More than towns, they are places of passage. It was evident that many prejudices regarding nationalities circulated in that neighborhood. Even the smallest problem between children or adults was immediately attributed to the participants' national identity. For each family, the term was not *prejudice* but *core value*: different conceptions of what a family is, of what privacy means, of work and leisure, rights and duties, loneliness, and everyday life. There were different attitudes toward nature, race, religion, money, politics, health, food, music, adolescence, weapons. Within each family there were differences, of course. But even between the most contrasting families, there were also shifting alliances.

Anyway, disapproving judgments became the hinge for explaining everything in our life of different values. Some of the most common prejudices affirmed that Europeans in general were stingy with others and with themselves; Americans were spoiled and selfish; Mexicans, of course, were lazy and dirty; Arabs were too traditionalist, and they ate too much; the

Swedish were too cold and reserved; the Spanish were stubborn and disdainful; the French were just disdainful and dirty; people from Veracruz were too noisy; those from Puebla, too conservative; from Monterrey, greedy; and from Mexico City, vulgar and conceited.

There was almost never a recognition of positive national values. An emotive approach to another person, the beginning of a friendship, often started by establishing an exception to the rule. A child might say: "That American boy is not so selfish." Or a teenager might realize: "That Swedish girl is not so cold." And so forth.

Relativity is fundamental to seeing and understanding the map of values in which we lived: the American family was considered too liberal for Mexicans, who in turn were too liberal for the Arab family. At the same time, Swedes were too liberal for Americans. Everyone was too much of something.

Very soon I discovered that even if we were all foreigners in the eyes of others, we were more or less false foreigners. Once, when some Americans came to visit us, we introduced them to our next-door neighbors thinking that they had a lot in common: a national identity, a language. But our American neighbors were considered almost pure Mexicans by our American visitors. The same was true regarding all the national differences existing in our neighborhood. The Spanish were not considered Europeans by those who came directly from Spain, and even my northern family was not considered Sonoran at all by our uncles and cousins in that region. I experienced this relativity myself because I lived for more than two years in Ciudad Obregón, Sonora. While living there, I was never accepted as a member of a northern family. And coming back to Mexico City, the opposite happened.

This constantly equivocal situation exists when differences come into contact, be they of a national, economic, or sexual nature. National identity is also a movable feast. In any community, our values, even core values, are always shifting in the eyes of others. People always want to have, acquire, or get rid of some values, as if there were a stock market of national values. This is not so easy. And even if we want to think of our values as solid and immovable, they don't belong exclusively to any individual. Rather, they are valued in a group, and they only function in a collective situation.

Paradoxically, the best moments of that common life for me as a child were not when some people recognized in others a part of themselves, but when someone tried to share his or her particularity with others. The effort to share a difference was stronger and more binding than an established commonly held belief or attitude that differentiated two people from others: a French woman giving cooking lessons or recipes to her housewife friends, a child sharing his imported toys, teenagers exchanging new record albums. To share is one of the most difficult aspects in life; it is the main challenge posed to different national identities of those intending to forge a common life.

Naturally each family had a different history and evolution; but, again, it was interpreted as a result of each national identity: the American couple divorced after one of their sons died of an overdose of drugs and another committed suicide. Most of the families coming from different regions of Mexico went back. Even if one family became very rich and another very poor, national identities were considered to have played a role in that. From this point of view, national identity is also a destiny. An idea of past and future is implicated in the presupposed national values of each group.

From this kind of interpretation, it is very easy to deduce a doctrine like the one developed in the United States in the nineteenth century (but still active today under another name). I am referring to Manifest Destiny, which indirectly affirms that one nation has the right to invade another, to show it the proper path toward law, order, and progress, or democracy. Its logical complement is the idea of the other country—perhaps the neighbor—as an eternal rebel, potential invader, permanent menace. This is the other side of Manifest Destiny, and a historic dissonance between national identities thus emerges.[10] It is at such a moment that the art of relativity, which should define a national identity as an art of contrasts and varying distances, becomes instead an art of arrogance.

My very small suburban situation, my travels, and the nearly eight years I lived in Paris taught me the absurdity of considering my national identity the only one of value. But it also taught me the absurdity of considering any other national identity the most desirable. How to be proud of what we are without turning that pride into arrogance or intolerance? How to fight against prejudices and stereotypes? How to accept our national identity with a certain degree of relativity?

Some of the answers to these questions are implied in the way we solve this additional question: how to accept the idea of the Other in our life? The Other, Otherness, is the radical limit of who we are. Then, how to accept our limits, demonstrated to us by the compelling existence of the Other? For many cultures, the Other automatically means savage or barbarian. This attitude has been so resistant and permanent that we still call the use of words derived from other languages a *barbaridad*, or "barbarism."

In this century, the Greek poet Constantine Cavafy responds to this permanent stereotype in his poem "Waiting for the Barbarians." There a voice, in an ancient city, cries out, "The Barbarians are coming." Everyone panics and waits and waits, and in the end, they, the citizens, and we, the readers, discover that the Barbarians are already in the city because, the poet says, the Barbarians are us.

How to accept the existence of the Other within us? How to accept the many voices each one of us utters? And by the same token, how to build a nondestructive image of the Other in our collective life?

Many years ago, when I was around twenty, I made a trip to the coast of Oaxaca. A beautiful unspoiled beach lay about half an hour's walk from the closest village. It was a place of pilgrimage for many young Americans, and even more so Canadians, but for very few Mexicans. It was known as a nudist beach, which meant, in the terms of the post-hippie culture of the time, that it was considered a place of freedom, beyond the establishment's reach. For many young Americans and Canadians, Mexico itself was precisely that: an escape from what they considered a rotten civilization, an imaginary island of ideal primitiveness. At the time, that idea seemed naive to me, but full of charm. I considered those post-hippies very innocent people, as I did the Europeans who believed that the world was done with in Europe, and that only in Third World countries was there hope for humanity. But my surprise had no limits when I discovered that those same erstwhile hippies considered me, the Mexican city boy, not just very naive, but very primitive as well.

And Mexico had its preconceptions about me, too. Before arriving at the beach, I had a conversation in a small Oaxacan village with an old man, who praised me for speaking Spanish so well. When I responded that the praise was totally unmerited, that I was Mexican, he immediately affirmed, "Yes, you are a Mexican from the Mexico on the other side of the border." "No," I said, "I am from the Mexico on this side of the border." He answered without hesitation, "Yes, but you say this side of the border because you are looking over from the other side."

At that moment I understood that it was useless to insist on my Mexicanness because for him I was not a Mexican. I was a complete stranger speaking Spanish. The many cultural differences between the two of us were real and present, far beyond our common language. We were linked by words, but the meaning of our words set us apart. Even my strongest desire to lend precision to a very simple phrase was thwarted by the weight of cultural differences. For my interlocutor, the simple expression "this side of the border"—used by both of us—clearly described opposite sides of that border: same passports, same language, different identities.

A catalogue of differences inside any country, from races and regionalisms to historical and economic factors, has no limits. The more global, heavily populated, and comprehensive a national identity tries to be, the more ideological, and even mythical, it becomes. Even the idea of a nation as a whole, as an absolute coherent entity, is more or less always a kind of forgery. In fact, the cultural characteristics of only one region or one group almost always become emblematic of the nation.

In Mexico, many characteristics of a central region, Jalisco, with its tequila and *charrería* (rodeo around which a regional elite culture has evolved), are considered national ones, and they are not. I am no less Mexican because I don't use a charro sombrero or because I am not short. In Spain, many years ago, someone told me, half jokingly, half reproachfully, that I was no real Mexican because I did not play the guitar and sing macho songs. For eight months of the eight years I lived in Paris, I stayed in the Mexican students' house at the Cité Universitaire. I was practically forced to abandon it because I could not stand to wake up every day hearing the same songs, "Amorcito Corazón" and "El son de la negra," rising up over the smell of cornmeal fried in oil, *la fritanga*. (By the same token, a Frenchman is no less French because he arrived late for an appointment the other day believing that I would arrive late because I am Mexican.)

All these misunderstandings with regard to national identity recall the story of the ivory noses that invaded New Spain during the colonial period. As it happened, a man lost his nose in a battle. Having seen the ivory figures made in the Philippines, he asked a merchant to have a nose made for him, what we now call a prosthesis. Delighted with the results, he ordered another one. The ivory artisan in the faraway Philippines, on receiving the second order, happily imagined an enormous market for noses in the Americas and made a hundred of them. Initially, he was not disappointed: the noses were so rare, so faithful to the idea of Oriental exoticism circulating in New Spain, that they sold well, particularly after the story of their origin became known. But subsequent large shipments of noses did not do so well, no matter how eager the artisan and merchant were to succeed with this lucrative product. Their idea of the nasal identity of Americans was, to say the least, excessive. Fortunately, there were no diplomatic implications involved in this misunderstanding, and so we don't have in our history of exchanges with the Orient the War of the Noses.

How many times do we attribute "a certain need for noses" to other nationalities? How many times do we attribute "a certain need for noses" to our own nationality? From a cultural point of view, "nation" means a need for coherence, a need for a nose sufficiently representative for everyone. Some historians assert provocatively that even the idea of nation is relatively new, a recent invention. Though it emerged to name a reality, in this century the term has usually become a modern ideology, an ideology used to replace the historical reality in the minds of the people. And more than once it has become the "fire in the minds of men" because the idea of war is of a piece with the idea of nation. After all, there is no nation without a proud readiness "to make its defense against any enemy." National anthems of many nations sing it loud and clear. And many times, for many people, a nation means a fortress.

In this epic state of mind, national identity is something that needs to be always, urgently, defended. A neighbor is either a menace or an ally. For people who think this way, we are what we were able to rescue from the dangers of life in the past.

In Mexico, many intellectuals are afraid of NAFTA, believing that the trade agreement is a menace to our culture, and especially to our language. They don't realize that our culture is already a mixture of cultures, that a quarter of the words in our language are of Arabic origin, that life is movement, and that true living culture everywhere changes a bit every day. Nor do they consider the fact that, in cultural terms, the value of each gesture changes and is always seen from different points of view simultaneously.

Those suffering from cultural panic in the face of change would do well to recall the story of the Jesuits in China, whose difficult mission was to convert the Chinese. They learned the language, they dressed like the Chinese, acted like them, lived like them. Some of the missionaries became respected in their Chinese communities, and a few even belonged to the Mandarin court. They translated the Bible in literal Chinese terms. Since there was no ideogram for God, they used the closest one: Heaven. After a few decades, an important part of Catholic theology was alive in China. The Jesuits were proud of the results of their mission and came back to Europe to show their work to the Western world.

They arrived dressed like Chinese, speaking with a strong Chinese accent, behaving and praying like Chinese. And they brought with them some brilliant young Chinese whom they had managed to convert. When they explained all their efforts and works and methods, instead of being received with the deep admiration of the Western world, they were accused of the heresy of having been converted by the Chinese. The truth is that they were not Chinese, but neither were they exactly what they were before; they had built a new religious culture, a third one.

We can never simply conserve our culture or merely adopt someone else's. We are always building a new culture based on the one we have, if we are lucky enough to still have one. And maybe it is a third one, or a fourth, or a fifth. In the case of Mexico, I do believe it is always in the process of creation. Ours is a syncretic culture—old, with millennia of history behind us and a long colonial past, young in the capacity to adapt, borrow, and internalize. Thus, in the more complex, pluralistic Mexico of today, more than ever we must reject attempts to locate an essentialist identity, whether based on core values or *mestizaje* or on a shared sense of collective lessons from the past. Rather, following Octavio Paz, we ought to accept the fact that Mexicans are not putting on masks, that they are masks, offering a totality of gestures to be deciphered. In this sense, as I have argued, all cultures are masked, including Canada and the United States. Each culture is an anthropological phenomenon, presenting masks rather than a list of core values.

I would like to end with a question that, in its own way, is a conclusion, or a paradoxical, never-ending conclusion to these reflections on the relativity of our national identities. Is it possible to build a new conception of identity that also assumes our natural Otherness, our multinational nature? If so, what is needed now in North America is a dance of the masks, based on listening, understanding, and complex signaling among the three. Our challenge is to share our differences and our national identities.

PART TWO

Group Identities and Interactions

Pluralism and Ecology in Canadian Cities

DAVID CROMBIE

The question of "whither North America?" must necessarily begin in its great cities, for who can envision a North American future that ignores the quality of life in Mexico City, Los Angeles, Chicago, Vancouver, or Toronto? Moreover, these great city-regions harbor within them new insights that, in comparative analysis, can shed light on the changing society of the continent.

Mexico has placed the environmental rescue of Mexico City high on its national political agenda, as well it should. One of four Mexicans live in Mexico City, broadly defined. And they live in a colossally polluted capital whose very geography combats the most ingenious and far-reaching environmental laws and enforcement techniques. The convergence of pollution problems, especially air-quality issues, has produced a natural affinity with Los Angeles, where over one million Mexican nationals live today.

Yet Mexico also has 40 other cities of populations of 300,000 or more. This little-known fact inscribes urban policies and development even more deeply into the Mexican national agenda. Perhaps these cities can become a kind of relief valve for Mexico City's overflowing satellite cities (some of which run into the millions), or perhaps the same problems that afflict Mexico City may come to afflict the others.

In the United States, urban centers have been hollowed out for decades, with "white flight" abandoning the cities proper to the poor, minorities, and a variety of ethnic newcomers. In economic terms, the "region" in a city-region frequently has become more important than the core "city" itself. Less expensive real estate, excellent highways, and lower tax rates have drawn major industries and jobs far from downtown. Former U.S. Senator Charles McC. Mathias sees danger in this:

There is an obvious and potentially destructive component to this metropolitan evolution. In fact, economic vigor continues to drain from its core of the metropolitan area to the new communities on its edges. The bulk of the population on those edges is of European descent. The inner city increasingly has become or is becoming the home of Americans not of European descent. To a notable extent, poverty and concomitant crime are becoming the hallmarks of the inner city. A vicious socioeconomic circle has become operative.[1]

Yet it is wise to remember that all cities are different. As political and social places they are shaped by their particular histories, laws, and founding moments, carrying the past forward in their customs and habits. In short, they have different identities.

Furthermore, there are marked differences in the urban experience among nations. Canadian metropolitan regions bear little resemblance to their Mexican and American counterparts: they lack the network of small cities that is characteristic of both of their southern neighbors, the level of pollution that plagues the Mexican capital, the kind of inner-city underclass that marks all cities of size in the United States.[2] Strung out along the border East to West, Canadian cities are historic centers, nodes of national life that are paralleled only by Monterrey in northern Mexico.

While it would be comforting to assume that cities can be approached generically on the basis of any one or two of them (which, at the very least, would ensure easier urban policy making), the reality is that only centralizing bureaucracies, built on the myth of urban homogeneity, really believe standardization is possible or desirable. Indeed, it can be argued that since the Second World War, millions of dollars have been wasted by attempts to apply new urban visions, based on academic generalizations, to the practical level.

Not only does each city or city-region have its own personality, rooted in the history and the needs of the people who live there; it has its own imaginings, its own challenges, its own experience of place.[3] One must be respectful of the immense differences in the diversity of civic cultures. It is neither helpful nor useful, let alone fair, to assume that all cities are the same: that if some are in trouble, so must they all be. For example, Detroit is clearly in trouble, as is Mexico City, as well as significant parts of New York and Los Angeles. We all have our lists of those in trouble. But we should also remember that we can go to such places as Seattle, San Francisco, Portland, Cleveland, Montreal, Pittsburgh, and Philadelphia for some lessons on how to do some things better. A city's history and civic culture matter because they allow you to understand the place and consequently what you need to do to repair, regenerate, and sustain it.

The purpose of this essay is to focus on the experience of Toronto and, to some degree, of other Canadian cities that share a civic ethos arising from the shared aspects of their history. Because of their social, multicultural, and linguistic diversity, Canadian cities offer interesting ideas about how cities work and the way they express and support social values and identity.

Despite travel-poster images of untouched mountains, wild rivers, vast plains, and empty spaces, of Canada as the Great White North, and the plethora of patriotic poems to wilderness, wind, water, rock, and trees, about 80 percent of all Canadians live in cities—most in large metropolitan regions. Nor is this a recent development: beginning with the 1921 census, more Canadians were urban than rural dwellers.

Canadian cities are usually described as clean, safe, and livable. They are seen as having learned the secret of maintaining a vital, safe, healthy downtown core in the face of suburban expansion, and they have absorbed waves of multiracial, multicultural migrants without succumbing to the pox of racism and the deadening grip of a permanent economic and social underclass.

But whatever their similarities, each of Canada's three largest cities has a distinctive character. Vancouver has become a Pacific Rim city with the busiest West Coast port in North America. It is experiencing strong migration from other parts of Canada and other parts of the world, especially Asia. Montreal, with its energy and style, where mandating which language to use may make a political statement, is a city expecting to reap major benefits from NAFTA and market integration. And Toronto, declared by the United Nations to be "the world's most multicultural city," is the country's media, banking, cultural, and financial center.

Yet Canadian cities in the aggregate share qualities that set them apart from even those just across the border, as visiting Americans discover in many ways, starting with the notices against bringing guns into Canada that now adorn the major airports and border crossings. The inner cities are more diverse; metropolitan regional authorities have more power; and cities on the whole seem to work better by comparison.

Some observers explain these "successes" by saying that Canadian cities were lucky enough to lag behind those in the United States and, therefore, were able to fight off the more destructive urban forces and policies of the past 50 years that so disabled many other metropolitan areas. Others point to a Canadian instinct to look for the middle: the balance that sometimes yields merely the mediocre but more often protects most of us from the indulgences of extremism. Reality is somewhat more mixed, and more complex, making the subtlety and pervasiveness of factors that shaped the growth and development of Canada's largest cities worth considering, however briefly.

First, one should never underestimate the influence of Canadian history on Canadian cities. Despite the significant differences among them, Canadian cities share a civic ethos that conditions their perspectives and responses to change and challenge. Canada's post-aboriginal history begins with Louis XIV and the French Empire, of which Canada was a part for some 150 years. Only with the Peace of Paris in 1763 did it become part of the British Empire, "upon which the sun never set"—until, of course, it did.

Canada itself took shape largely through the exploitation of such staples and resources as fish, fur, forests, wheat, and precious metals, organized and controlled by imperially supported companies, organizations, and governments linked to large metropolitan centers, both domestic and foreign. Indeed, most Canadian cities owe their beginnings and their growth more to trade, commerce, transportation, and government and military establishments than to agriculture and agrarian settlement.

Moreover, as the Canadian historian J. M. S. Careless notes, compared with the United States,

Canada produced far fewer middle-sized cities and country towns. Its urban net did not become so thickly beaded and many-stranded, its country population remained much smaller and less broadly distributed. Hence the influence of a limited number of major cities was strongly, plainly manifested across the Canadian landscape—cities which became notably larger for Canada's total population and were in no way inconsiderable within North America as a whole. Behind the rise of frontier, hinterland or region in Canada lay the power of the metropolis.[4]

An understanding of the Canadian experience, Careless underscored, must take account, first, of "the directing power of cities; above all, of the metropolis, the preeminent urban place." But it is important to note also that these cities were not all of a piece: from the start, metropolitan-based forces in Canada's five geographical regions built their own identities in a unique counterpoint with, first, the imperial power, and then the national government.[5]

To sum up, a few directing cities in Canada's resource-based economy were the core of a communications system carrying goods, people, ideas, orders, and money. Under British colonial rule in Canada, social diversity was tolerated, but everything was connected to everything else, and the Imperial Writ ran throughout.

Canadian cities, therefore, became the primary sites for inculcating "peace, order, and good government"—the specific overriding values set out in the British North America Act of 1867, the country's founding contract, and retained in the Confederation Act of 1982, by which Canada's Constitution was "patriated" (i.e., brought entirely within Canadian law and regulation). Interestingly, all three elements speak to "us," not to "me" or "them," and they form a thread that runs insistently through all aspects of Canadian society. This fundamental dynamic of Canadian history has profoundly shaped the civic traditions of Canadian cities.

By connecting the regional frontier to the power of the metropolitan center, "peace, order, and good government" provided a coherent, interdependent context for communities from wilderness to the primitively rural to the most urban. All people were understood to be part of the whole, and this engendered an appreciation of community, social order, and public behavior that still informs the standards and expectations of life in Canadian cities today. Traditionally, we've understood the connectedness of things, not just in nature, but in human ecology as well.

This has helped develop a strong sense of loyalty and obedience to law and civil authority among Canadians; culturally, it legitimized the educational, intellectual, and moral styles, trends, and standards of the day, mostly dedicated to the personal virtues of industriousness, responsibility, and respect for property.

While some of this sturdy public morality has, perhaps, eroded, it is nonetheless clear that there has been a remarkable persistence in Canadian civic traditions: the "us" has proved, generally speaking, stronger than the "me" and the "them." For evidence that this is so, one need only look at responses to major public issues. Seemingly insignificant in themselves, they show how, over time, small, incremental, step-by-step willingness to change pays substantial dividends of social peace.

Public Order

Both the law and public opinion in Canada tend to deal harshly and unequivocally with those seeking to push their own agendas by fomenting public disorder. For instance, after the original Rodney King verdict (exonerating Los Angeles policemen charged with beating a black man), what had been a traditionally peaceful protest in downtown Toronto degenerated into a melee, in which windows were smashed, stores looted, and people threatened. Did Toronto, too, have a race problem? It quickly became clear that a few hoodlums, who happened upon the march, were using events for their own gain. The entire incident was over within three hours; there were no fires, no fatalities. Culprits were quickly apprehended and held in custody; though some were later released, those with prior records received jail sentences. The very fact that the event attracted so much attention—U.S. media assumed it was parallel to the widespread rioting and destruction that took place in Los Angeles—shows that, small as it was, the incident was totally out of character for a city in which a million people poured into the streets to celebrate 1993's World Series victory, with only one person harmed.

Learning how to keep public order in an increasingly multicultural society required redrawing and redefining the limits of public order and public behavior, so that the customs and habits of a "new" public would be served, while order was maintained. None of this involved legislation, but it did mean that everyone—especially politicians, the police, and members of the media—had to learn more about others, understanding how different communities organized themselves, and recognizing and respecting differences.

For example, in the years since the Second World War, some half-million Italian immigrants have settled in Toronto. In areas where they clustered, this led to great concern about the presence, late into the night (and especially in summer), of "hordes" of Italian men, seemingly standing around on street corners. In time-honored fashion, police officers would come along. "Break it up; break it up" became their usual order. Over time, however, police, and the society they represented, learned that Italians had brought with them, not just a marvelous cuisine, but certain traditions—including the tradition of males gathering on the streets, especially on Friday evenings, to play bocce.

Other cultures have flourished in Toronto neighborhoods as well. For the past quarter-century or so—in a city where only the military, the Orange Order, labor organizations, and Santa Claus had usually paraded—there has also been Caribana. To this day, it is one of the largest, brightest, most popular exhibitions of Caribbean culture anywhere in the world. A city in a country that, even in the 1950's, had only a minuscule black population had become, by the late 1960's, a center in which there was strong support for celebrations of sister Commonwealth members' culture.

Today, Caribana attracts hundreds of thousands of people from all parts of the world, who come to dance in the streets, in magnificent costumes, before crowds that sometimes reach nearly a million residents and visitors. Here, too, police and citizens are reminded that what is different is not, by definition, threatening. Caribana is a matter of local pride—and, not incidentally, an economic boon of some CN $200 million annually.

The change in attitude in these, and in other matters, was common sense: if we were going to maintain anything close to our traditional belief in public order, it could not be on the basis of "us" and "them." In that direction lay an unstable community; only by ensuring, at a minimum, that "they" and "us" could cohabit could the imperative for peace and order be fulfilled.[6] There could not be separate kinds of public order: the result would be an unannounced state of civil war, sporadic and debilitating. Peaceful public order must be rooted in a belief in the value and legitimacy of the social order: if it depends on the use of force, the emphasis is on "order," not on a public sense of what is implied in "peace, order, and good government."

Gun Legislation

Though Canadians have picked up the American phrase "gun control," it is a misnomer for our existing laws. Canadian legislation not only goes far beyond the Brady Bill enacted by the U.S. Congress in 1993, with its five-day waiting period between purchase and the receipt of the firearm; it is far more restrictive than even the strictest law in any U.S. jurisdiction.

Under federal legislation, rifles are permitted for hunting, but the ownership and use of other firearms—handguns, automatic weapons, whatever—is sharply restricted. A person must submit an application to own such arms and then must apply separately to use them.

Reasons for wanting these permits must be given: membership in a gun club, for example. The Firearms Commissioner, a local official delegated by the Commissioner of the Royal Canadian Mounted Police, receives the application, which is forwarded to the police in the division where the person lives. They in turn assign an investigator to look at the applicant's background to ensure that the gun is needed for a legitimate reason and will be properly stored and maintained, and to recommend for or against approval. The process can take several months and might more accurately be described as "gun permission" rather than gun control.

These differences between Canadian and U.S. law flow from sharply differing assumptions: rather than deciding who ought *not* to be permitted to own a gun, the Canadian premise is that the law defines who *should* be allowed to have one. We arrived at our principle as the result of both history and common sense.

Historically, it was the Crown and its officers, rather than individuals, who were charged with the responsibility of maintaining and ensuring individual rights in the context of the community's peace and order. In fact, it is worth noting that many Canadian cities were founded as military posts and bastions of empire, under the auspices of the Crown. Peace and order on the "frontier" were ensured, not by dint of competing firepower between individuals, but by the officers representing the Queen's law, the Royal Canadian Mounted Police. (The peaceful use of guns by farmers, hunters, sports enthusiasts, and others was, of course, lawful but was never confused with some "right" to use a gun against other human beings.) The question of who should bear arms and who had the right to command behavior by the use of force was settled very early: the Crown held that as a monopoly. Americans are still grappling with an issue that Canadians have long since resolved.[7]

Health Care

While the complex history of health care in Canada is well beyond the scope of this chapter, it is possible to say that there is nothing in the history of Canada's social legislation that is more cherished or more fiercely protected. The health care system has become fundamental to what we understand as "being Canadian."

Canadians have enjoyed a national, publicly funded, portable, universally accessible health care system for more than 35 years. It originated in the provinces (most particularly, Saskatchewan), some of which organized public resources to create cooperative hospital and medical care well before the 1930's. The idea that essential health services should be a public responsibility gained strength as families were wiped out by sickness, particularly when epidemics ravaged cities.

Like the right to education, the right to health care came to be seen as fundamental to equality of opportunity, and it quickly moved out of local, municipal, cooperative, and labor negotiations to the top of the public agenda: people should not be expected to suffer and die because they could not afford the costs of care, any more than personal finances should decide who is educated and who is not. Moreover, some partners in the Commonwealth (the organization of former British colonies), notably Britain, Australia, and New Zealand, had established national health plans that were closely watched and widely admired in Canada.

As an increasing number of Northern European countries likewise adopted such plans, Canadians were eager for the reforms in health care that, together with educational reforms, would allow them to break the ancient grip of class, by which the poverty, illiteracy, and poor health of one generation was, inevitably, visited on the next.

In the 1970's and 1980's, it seemed that only the sky was the limit when it came to funding health care. In the sober 1990's, even as governments—federal, provincial, and municipal—go through painful cuts in costs and services, the strength of Canadian devotion to medicare is unwavering: whatever else goes, the principles of Canadian health care will remain, and only the most obtuse politician or bureaucrat would suggest otherwise. This, too, is an expression of "us," rather than just "me."

Certainly, individual Canadians are determined to avoid the kinds of horror stories that come out of the experience of the some 37 million Americans who have no health insurance. This is especially so because money is not the issue: health care costs in Canada account for close to 9 percent of the Gross National Product, compared with more than 13 percent for the United States. But, beyond that, there is a strong sense in Canada that something would be very wrong with a public philosophy that accepted the need for protection of consumers against misleading labels but did not understand the crucial importance of universally accessible health care to people's life chances.

To a largely unrecognized degree, Canadian cities have benefited immeasurably from the contribution that publicly funded health care makes to the equality of opportunity. The ability of diverse people to live harmoniously with one another is powerfully supported by public expenditures on that most personal issue, one's own health, and by the resulting individual sense that the system really works—and that the system works for *them*.

Canadian experience shows that a solid, stable health care system leads to thinking about health in broader terms, and that it significantly influences public policy making. Antismoking and environmental planning confirm this point. From a standing start some fifteen years ago, when the first limitations on smoking were adopted in Toronto and Ottawa, smoking has now been banished from the workplace, from the marketplace, and from virtually all other places where people congregate. In fact, smoking is increasingly seen as private behavior.

In Canada, environmental and planning issues are being articulated through the prism of individual health. City dwellers are beginning to regard the presence of the automobile more critically than ever before and are looking for policies that will expand the already substantial stock of public transit facilities found in most Canadian cities. In Toronto, the Healthy City Office, which uses a comprehensive ecosystem approach, has published a major report on criteria for measuring air pollution, noxious fumes, soil contamination, and other things affecting the quality of life.

It bears repeating that the role of history and the physical environment of the North have reinforced our tendency to look at policy in ways that will work in cities, and from cities out to vast, sparsely populated regions. With most Canadians living in a thin band of cities strung along the U.S. border, we have long associated "society" and "city" in policy terms, and we are not so given to Jeffersonian agrarianism or Mexican centralism.

Our approach to public order, gun control, and health care has made an enormous contribution to the "peace, order, and good government" of the Canadian city. But for many, it is the Canadian encounter with multiculturalism that has commanded the most attention.

Urban Multiculturalism

In their comparison of U.S. and Canadian cities, the economist Michael Goldberg and the geographer John Mercer note that "multiculturalism has been enshrined in Canadian federal public policy, and publicly supported cultural pluralism is manifest at both provincial and local levels." Like many Canadians, they are somewhat skeptical of the reality, and in fact polls show that a majority of Canadians believe multiculturalism is an artifact of government policy. "Whether or not this is simply good politics," they continue, "and devoid of real meaning or a true reflection of an important dimension of social life is for the specialists to debate."[8]

As the former Minister responsible for multiculturalism in the Mulroney government, I speak from experience as well as conviction. The second half of the twentieth century has been characterized by an increasing worldwide movement of peoples—from rural area to city, from country to country, from hemisphere to hemisphere. This has brought with it an urgent necessity to deal with the challenge of living in close quarters, in the same geographic space, with diverse races, languages, cultures, and religions.

Not surprisingly, the Canadian view of multiculturalism is rooted in our history, and the American and Canadian approaches are, on their face, very different. In the words of the historian Arthur Schlesinger, Jr.:

The United States had a brilliant solution for the inherent fragility of a multiethnic society: the creation of a brand-new national identity, carried forward by individuals who, in forsaking old loyalties and joining to make new lives, melted away ethnic differences. [The immigrants] *expected* to become Americans. Their goals were escape, deliverance, assimilation. They saw America as a transforming nation, banishing dismal memories and developing a unique national character based on common political ideals and shared experiences. The point of America was not to preserve old cultures, but to forge a new *American* culture [emphasis in the original].

Schlesinger then goes on to discount the Canadian experience: "it is so vulnerable to schism [because] as Canadians freely admit, their country lacks such a unique national identity."[9]

This is an unfortunate misreading of Canadians and Canadian history, and it may even be a misreading of the American experience. It seems to me that New York governor Mario Cuomo comes closer to the real America when he says: "Most Americans can understand both the need to recognize and encourage an enriched diversity as well as the need to ensure that such a broadened, multicultural perspective leads to unity and an enriched sense of what being an American is, and not to a destructive factionalism that would tear us apart."[10]

Schlesinger notwithstanding, life certainly does not hold only two possibilities for us: segregation or assimilation. Indeed, Canadian history and experience clearly show a third way, not easy to sum up in a single word. But the word that comes closest to describing it best, I think, is "cohabitation." (Though in recent times, the word has taken on a more limited meaning, it comes from the Latin "to dwell together.") The strength of "cohabitation" is that it does not imply either ignoring or embracing those different from ourselves; it means only learning to dwell peacefully with them. Even now, with a separatist party from Quebec occupying the position of the official Opposition in the House of Commons, Canadians seem content to allow the historic lessons of cohabitation to come into balance and to pursue their country's traditions as "the Peaceable Kingdom."

Because cohabitation was a fact of city life in Canada long before the idea of multiculturalism became the subject of government policies, we cannot properly appreciate the influence of multiculturalism without placing it in historical context, which is to say, in the context of our involvement from the start with the purposes and practices of empire. As colonials, Canadians grew accustomed to the idea of belonging to a global sort of citizenship, one that included the many nations, languages, cultures, religions, and races that owed allegiance to the British Crown and made up one-quarter of the globe. We identified with all those splashes and dots of British red on the map of the world that hung on the wall of every classroom. We were all British subjects, resident in our *particular place*, united by our allegiance to the Crown.

To be sure, there were hierarchy, racism, classism, and constant, continuing colonial struggles and wars of empire, but empire *did* give the Canadian psyche a more flexible understanding of citizenship and immigration. It allowed us to feel a part of people and events beyond our borders. In fact, Canada did not have its own citizenship until 1947; before that time, "Canadians" were British subjects "resident in Canada."

Within our borders, we became more local and regional in our loyalties. The Canadian literary scholar and critic Northrop Frye articulated that instinct: "Culture," he said, "has something vegetable about it that increasingly needs to grow from roots, something that demands a small region and a restricted locale. Culture is not a national development, it is a series of local and regional ones."[11] Canadians, therefore, needed to develop policies to deal with these matters that would reflect the reality of their own situation: a small country made up of separated settlements in a vast land with many languages and cultures and traditions.

Our constitutional heritage, which supported and reflected our practical experience, insisted that language, culture, and community were local and place-related, and that we had significant—even supreme—loyalties that were, officially at least, located beyond our borders. We had to become a political house of many mansions, a place in which we could make substantial room for multiple loyalties and a maximum acceptance of individual and community differences.

The British government laid down the principle of separate legal, linguistic, and religious rights in the late eighteenth century in a series of Imperial acts (the Quebec Act, 1774; the Proclamation Act, 1763; and the Constitution Act, 1791) giving separate rights to French-speaking Québécois and aboriginal peoples. These laws were anathema to the expansionist Americans, with their unitary, revolutionary, and civic ideology. In fact, the concept of laws applying to specific people and specific places rendered the principle of assimilation impossible and many years later would make the American melting pot approach unattainable.[12]

Instead, we were to be a "coat of many colors" woven together so that the original strips of cloth need not disappear. Or, to use another analogy, we were to create a "beef stew" in which all the chunks would contribute to the whole without necessarily losing their identity. This approach makes sense to Canadians because it is consistent with our history, geography, practical experience, and general understanding of who we are.

It must be clearly noted, however, that Canadians were not looking to be mere celebrants of unrelated particularisms. We have always understood that our divisions need to be rooted in common ground, and that the price of continuing diversity is the endless search for unity.

To J. M. S. Careless, the cities were a critical factor in this search, performing a constantly shifting brokers' role between local interests and the nation. "The upshot was a very Canadian condition . . . in which views of national identity were limited by regional perceptions, and regional by national in turn." Thanks to this process, he continues, "there is a distinctive Canadian coexistence of identities wherein the balances can shift over time but the conjunction has endured." [13]

Indeed, as the unifying vitality of the Crown and Empire faded, as British strength diminished and the American presence expanded, Canada was faced with the necessity of finding more of that common ground within its borders. The symbols and touchstones of national identity became much more important. The Citizenship Act of 1947; the Maple Leaf flag that replaced the Union Jack in 1965; the Official Languages Act of 1970; the acceptance of *O Canada* as a national anthem; and the adoption of the Charter of Rights and Freedoms in 1982 became rites of passage to nation-state status.

Yet even these solid symbols of normal nation-building were careful to respect our historical bargains: the need for diversity and multiple loyalties. In the words of the Charter's author, the then Prime Minister Pierre Trudeau:

Canada's multicultural composition and the moderation which it includes and encourages, makes Canada a very special place, and a stronger place as well. Each of the many fibers contributes its own qualities and Canada gains strength from the combination. We become less inclined—certainly less obliged—to think in terms of national grandeur; inclined not at all to assume a posture of aggressiveness, or ostentation or might. Our image is of a land of people with many differences—but many contributions, many variations in view—but a single desire to live in harmony.

On a planet of finite size, the most desirable of all characteristics is the ability to cohabit with persons of differing backgrounds and to benefit from the opportunities which this offers. [14]

This powerful message endowed the idea of the Canadian mosaic with a compelling sense of purpose and extended the legitimate limits of diversity. It welcomed the distinctiveness of newcomers and minorities and provided them with a sense of belonging.

Whatever the consequences for national unity, this "mosaic" approach emphasizes and legitimizes our inclination for the global, the regional, and the local, and allows immigrant communities to merge into Canadian society with a minimum of tension and violence. People are able to pursue old cultures, develop new identities, and participate in the general society in a more relaxed way. In cities, this is worked out through the experience of cohabitation in the neighborhood.

The Ecology of Neighborhoods

Around the world, people in cities understand the fundamental importance of their neighborhoods: "I'm from Brooklyn"; "J'habite au premier arrondissement." Neighborhoods are not just physical places where people live; they are psychic spaces where human personalities are formed, identities learned, and the rudiments of survival absorbed. Here, dispensed on a daily basis, are early practical responses to cosmic questions such as, who am I? What do I believe? How do I behave? Where do I belong?

In Toronto, the power of the neighborhood instinct has been strong enough to repel expressways, succor languages and cultures, inspire civic reform, discipline the use of cars, and compel the loyalties of politicians and public servants. It is even understood that groups, cultures, and generations have a claim on the place, while respecting history, revealed through the street signs with their historic neighborhood names ("the Annex," "the Village of Yorkville," "Leslieville"). They register the history of successive waves of immigrants. In some areas the street signs themselves are bilingual: English and Chinese, English and Greek, and so forth.

In neighborhoods where race, ethnicity, and the immigrant experience are dominating or determining characteristics, the answers to questions of personal identity will be refracted through the light of particular kinships and particular cultures. Everybody wants and needs to know what life is about and his or her role in it.

Distinctive settlements in the city emerge in response to human need. They allow for a sense of kinship where particular customs, habits, and languages can be expressed and the warmth of familiarity experienced. They usually become places where work can be found and where housing and transportation are cheap and convenient. They are dependable islands of human touch that offer some coherence and predictability and a web of helpful relationships to combat an often alien and sometimes hostile world.

In *Gathering Place*, his excellent history of Toronto neighborhoods, Robert Harney describes them as places that become the home, the yard, the marketplace, the town square, the social club, the defensible turf, and the playground all in one. Here people exchange gossip, fight for points of view, meet and mate, organize social events, make important personal decisions, and share collected wisdom. The neighborhood itself, with its increasingly familiar streets and institutions—the settlement house, the school, the cafe, the corner store, the places of worship and of recreation—as well as the web of relationships, becomes the "base camp" from which newcomers can reach out into "contested terrain" to pursue their dreams. In doing so, they learn to "negotiate their ethnicity, and make those constant adjustments of style and thinking which are milestones in the process of learning to live within the larger North American setting."[15]

Through this process, newcomers begin to devise their own internal, biographic map of the city—both spatially and psychically. The map tells them where home and friends can be found, where danger lurks, and where places to be avoided are located. It contains practical points of information about daily routines and regular social and sporting events. It also locates other places and people: an uncle in Chicago, a cousin "up north," places where work can be found, places where "they" won't hire. This map represents the newcomers' sense of space. It links them physically and psychically to all the things that are important to their known world and their future.

According to Hugh Brody's *Maps and Dreams*, the same phenomenon is to be found among the Beaver Indians of Northwest Canada. Brody illustrates with a number of maps that, to the untutored, seem to be mere squiggly, incoherent, spaghetti-like meanderings. They are actually biographic land-use maps the tribe follows in identifying trap lines, berry-picking places, hunting and fishing sites, and locations for camps. The maps are not static or written down: they evolve according to what is known, what is learned, and what is dreamed. Far from being obscure, they represent patterns of activity and behavior that "constitute a persistent basis for the material well being and therefore the cultural strength both of peoples and of individuals." In short, they are keys to individual and group survival.[16]

Cities: The Habitat of Choice

Despite the ways in which Canadian cities, and cities in general, have nourished people and their dreams, they have always been demonized. In fact, historically, the very idea of the city has had to overcome an extraordinarily negative bias. The agrarianist Thomas Jefferson, for example, regarded the growth of American cities as "pestilential to our future," and

much of American literature and social comment has continued to reinforce that imagery. Our daily news media steadily feed us a rich diet of
stories and pictures about an urban milieu whose main ingredients are
crime, violence, drugs, poverty, mendacity, and indifference. Movies, television, and magazines generally reflect and magnify these perceptions.

To be sure, the city has always had its critics. To them, cities were
crowded, unhealthy, fearful, vice-ridden, ugly places that spawned plagues
and epidemics; they were places where taboos could be broken and moral
instruction ignored, and where foreigners with strange ideas and customs
could tempt and corrupt the unwary.

Cities housed the "dark satanic mills" of Blake, exploited Marx's increasingly impoverished urban proletariat, and condemned them to the
frightful squalor of Charles Dickens's Industrial City. In *Sister Carrie*,
Theodore Dreiser's heroine loses her moral way as soon as she reaches
Chicago. In our own time, the critics have convicted cities of being unfix-
able, crime-infested, race-ridden financial and environmental disasters that
should be avoided in favor of more bucolic surroundings—small towns,
suburban enclaves, and rural landscapes. Put simply, the City is a bad place
where bad things happen. The countryside is a good place where good
things happen, a place where people are more human and God is more
knowable than on city streets.

Although it is clear that the city-bashers have had their way, cities have
not been without their defenders. Throughout history and around the
world, cities have also been idealized and extolled. Great works of archi-
tecture, vast schemes of city building, and triumphs of literary imagination
have offered the city up as a temple to the power, wealth, ideology, or
spirituality of many dynasties, empires, and civilizations, ancient and modern. The City of God, the City on a Hill, the Holy City, the Garden City,
the City Beautiful, the Radiant City evoke the divine mission of cities, the
places where, Lewis Mumford contends, "the separate beams of life" and
the "issues of civilization" are brought into focus.[17]

But for the millions and millions of ordinary people who for centuries
have gone down the road to the cities of the world, the City has always
meant freedom and choice. To them, cities are centers of trade and commerce, places of opportunity where they can build, change, and transform.
To them, cities are places where the real mingles with the imagined, and
"you can try to be what you want to be"; where fame, fortune, and future
are ripe for the picking; and where, if you're lucky, you'll find a sense of
community that will serve your needs, shape your day-to-day experiences,
give focus to your freedom and meaning to your hopes.

Whatever the bias, it is increasingly clear that we can no longer ignore the needs of our cities and their burgeoning regions. Whether people in North America can achieve a higher degree of economic, environmental, and social well-being will depend directly on our ability to comprehend how our large urban places work and what must be done to regenerate and sustain them.

North America today is dominated by large urbanized regions that sprawl across municipal, provincial, state, and even national political boundaries. These vast, multi-connected places include within their ambit cities, towns, villages, farms, forests, wetlands, rivers, and valleys, with millions of people living and working in them. They have become *the* human habitat of choice, and *the* social fact of North America and the world. Characterized as "plug-in cities," they can span hundreds of miles and connect people to places where they live, work, and play in a web of roads, highways, rail, jetports, telephones, faxes, radio, computers, roof-top satellites, and television—all dependent on an evolving urban ecology that we are only just beginning to understand.

Often competitive with one another, these urban regions have also become great centers of extraordinary change as human migration, the technological revolution, and new global perspectives combine to significantly alter our economies, our landscape, and our way of living. They are heralding new values, overwhelming traditional local jurisdictions, pushing aside old boundaries, and insisting on transnational influence and status.

Our North American economy is being restructured and our society reshaped as we struggle to give birth to a new economy based on information technology and try to salvage what we need from a shrinking old economy based on selling off natural resources and symbolized by the industrial smokestack.

Nuala Beck, a Toronto economic consultant, has documented the broad outlines of the national and regional transformation in the United States and Canada. As evidence of the extent of the change, she notes the following:

- The U.S. health and medical industry has become larger than oil refining, aircraft, autos, auto parts, textiles, steel, and mining combined, and will employ one in ten Americans by the end of this decade.
- The aerospace industry employs more people than the auto and auto-parts industries combined.
- More Americans make computers than cars. More people work in the computer industry as a whole (hardware, semiconductors, and computer services)

than in the auto, auto-parts, steel, mining, and petroleum-refining industries combined.

- The software industry, which was barely a dot on the economic map before the 1980's, has been growing at the astounding rate of almost 25 percent a year and in 1992 accounted for $42 billion (U.S.) annually.
- In Canada, which is supposedly stuck in the woods and the mines and the oil fields, more people work in the sophisticated electronics industry than in pulp and paper—even in forest-rich British Columbia.
- More Canadians are now employed in communications and telecommunications than in mining and petroleum combined, and almost as many people work in the computer services industry as in the entire air transport industry.
- More Québécois work in health and medical care than in construction, textile, clothing, furniture, and mining combined; more Albertans work in financial services than in oil and gas; and more Nova Scotians work as teachers and professors than as fish processors, miners, forestry workers, pulp and paper workers, and construction workers combined.
- More Americans make semiconductors than construction machinery, and more of them work in data processing than in petroleum refining.
- More Americans work in accounting firms than in the whole energy industry. The number crunchers employ three times more people than the entire mining industry.
- More Americans work in biotechnology than in the entire machine-tool industry.
- The U.S. movie industry employs more people than all the auto industry.
- The U.S. travel-service industry is bigger than the petroleum-refining and steel industries combined.
- Twice as many Americans make surgical and medical instruments as make plumbing and heating products.

"In no way, shape or form," says Beck, "are these developments unique to North America. The trends sweeping North America are also transforming the economics of Japan and Western Europe." [18] These economic transformations are fundamentally linked to a movement in North America (*all* North America) away from raw materials and heavy industry toward knowledge-based industries and high technology. This means quite clearly that urban life on this continent is entering a new phase where we have a chance to maximize the benefits of social interactions and minimize environmental degradations.

Governments are reorganizing their policies and programs; corporations are rethinking their strategies and priorities; and community and individual responsibilities are being redefined in response to such major issues as free trade, deregulation, global competitiveness, skills development, debt reduction, and environmental responsibility.

Work shapes a city, and it is in the communities, neighborhoods, and workplaces of great city-regions that the actual change is taking place and that real people are being affected. The city is where jobs are lost, and new skills and interests are pursued. In the city, new values are tested and beliefs recast. Here, also, is where fear and hope contend, and where individuals, races, ethnicities, and languages jostle for a place in the new order of things.

In the process, much more is changing than just the physical appearance of the city, suburb, and countryside. The nature of the workplace, patterns of leisure, politics, art, music, public tastes and manners—all are being affected as well. Walk down any busy street, visit the local parks, playgrounds, workplaces, malls, restaurants, cafes, wedding halls, subways, and other places where people congregate, and you will see and feel the change.

How do we plan for the new metropolises, these new expanding city-regions? How do we provide for their evolving ecology? How do we take account of the historic movement of peoples, the revolution in our technological and economic life, and the environmental imperatives requiring our attention? In the face of these transforming challenges, our governments seem geographically fragmented, jurisdictionally gridlocked, and bureaucratically and politically divided. In consequence, our public policies, programs, and initiatives are experienced as episodic, inconsistent, and uncoordinated.

Traditionally, we have planned and managed our urban places in a piecemeal fashion, treating economic, environmental, and social issues separately. But we know that in real life these are related, and that decisions in one area will affect matters in another. Clearly, then, what is needed is a more comprehensive, integrative approach. That is why, in the past few years, the idea of using an ecosystem approach in planning and developing cities is gaining stronger acceptance in Canada and around the world.

As the writer and critic Jane Jacobs puts it:

At some point along the trail, I realized I was engaged in studying the ecology of cities. . . . By city ecology . . . I mean something different from, yet similar to, natural ecology. . . . A natural ecosystem is defined as "composed of physical-chemical-biological processes active with a space-time unit of magnitude." A city ecosystem is composed of physical-economic-ethical processes, active at a given time within a city and its [region].

The two sorts of ecosystems—one created by nature, the other by human beings—have fundamental principles in common.[19]

The fundamental philosophical basis of the ecosystem approach is that everything is connected to everything else. Therefore, it focuses on *relationships* and insists that we have a responsibility to ourselves, to other people, to other generations, and to other species. It is highly compatible with the Canadian civic ethic discussed above.

It reminds us that hydrology, topography, and climate set the fundamental conditions of human habitation, which, through design, can give each of our human places unique style and character. The ecosystem approach incorporates the principles of stewardship, carrying capacity, resilience, and sustainability, and insists that economic growth, environmental health, and social well-being are not mutually exclusive but mutually interdependent.

Finally, ecosystem planning is evolutionary: there is no perfect city. Inevitably, our generation's changes will be changed in turn by those who come after us. And change, which is inevitable, comes as a better friend when it occurs within an overall context of continuity and community.

This applied multidisciplinary, multijurisdictional approach to planning will differ from one city-region to another as each area reflects its own particular history, tradition, cultures, and habits. But cities will also discover some common organizing principles of ecosystem planning. Seven principles, in particular, seem to me critical, namely, recognizing the primary importance of natural features and natural processes; understanding the mutual interdependence of economic and environmental health; integrating land use and environmental planning in public process and law; integrating urban and rural planning to link the City with its region; creating concurrent, rather than consecutive, planning processes; integrating capital budgets of all government departments and agencies to ensure coherence, economies, and financial strength; and recognizing the increasing importance of designing places and spaces that allow people to feel a part of nature while they enjoy the immemorial human pleasures that only cities can offer.[20]

In Jane Jacobs's words:

We human beings are the only city building creatures in the world. The hives of social insects are fundamentally different in how they develop, what they do, and their potentialities. Cities are, in a sense, natural ecosystems too—for us. They are not disposable. Whenever and wherever societies have flourished and prospered, rather than stagnated and decayed, creative and workable cities have been at the core of the phenomenon; they have pulled their weight and more. It is the same still. Decaying cities, declining economies, and mounting social troubles travel together. The combination is not coincidental.

It is urgent that human beings understand as much as we can about city ecology—starting at any point in city processes. The humble, vital services performed by the grace of good city streets and neighborhoods are probably as good a starting point as any.[21]

The question of styles and values of urban life in separate nations is in some senses an intimate one and should remain so. The stones and breezes speak different languages when you wake up one morning in Quebec and the next morning in Miami. But North American interdependence enjoins us all to respond: is there some ethos common to life on this continent, wherever it is lived, some recognition that we are all multiethnic, all creatures of the shared natural environment, all believers in sufficient public order to guarantee both individual liberty and social cooperation?

A single city like Toronto, closely examined, may contain the seed of an answer to this question, but surely the full harvest can be found only in the study of a broad array of cities and their regions. Perhaps interdependence's greatest virtue is that we now can—and perhaps must—look beyond our borders for a greater range of answers than ever before. As we do, the Canadian experience suggests that the cities will respond, and there we will find the most concentrated examples of how policy and practice interact in the context of continental integration.

It is no coincidence that Toronto, this essay's focal case, is Jane Jacobs's adopted home.

The Dynamics of Assimilation in the United States

RICHARD ESTRADA

> The question America confronts as a pluralistic society is how
> to vindicate cherished cultures and traditions without breaking
> the bonds of cohesion—common ideals, common political in-
> stitutions, common language, common culture, common
> fate—that hold the republic together.
> —Arthur M. Schlesinger, Jr., *The Disuniting of America*

Few events since the Second World War have more graphically demonstrated the need to reflect upon the meaning of assimilation in the United
States than the Los Angeles riots of 1992. Misperceived by many Americans as yet another expression of traditional black-white conflict, these, the
deadliest and most destructive riots in U.S. history, were in fact illustrative
of a more complex and troubling social reality.

The list of explanations that were offered for the riots' 50 or more
deaths and $1 billion or more in property destruction was long and occa-
sionally contradictory.[1] Some analysts focused on the hopelessness and
frustration bred by poverty in the inner city. Others insisted that it was
not a matter of dollars and cents, but that a poverty of values was to blame.
The roles of television, liquor, and drugs were explored. Experts stressed
that the conflict in Los Angeles could easily break out elsewhere in the
country. Though less widespread, numerous riots had in fact already occurred since 1980 in Miami, New York City, and Washington, D.C. A
nationwide debate ensued as politicians attempted to fashion an appropriate policy response. On one point there was virtual unanimity: the disorders revealed that the fabric of the country's assimilationist ethic had
become dangerously frayed.[2]

Nearly a quarter-century after the Civil Rights era, charges of racism—
particularly "institutional racism"—are multiplying on college campuses,
in public schools, and in workplaces, churches, and halls of government.
According to a 1993 report, 25 years after the National Advisory Commis-

sion on Civil Disorders' Kerner Report warned of racial separation and inequality in the nation, U.S. cities are not only beginning to experience civil disorders once again; they are also "resegregating."[3]

Countering the cries of "racism" are mutterings of "reverse racism." More and more members of America's majoritarian community are disturbed by what they perceive as a tendency to allege racial and ethnic discrimination without any proof other than statistical differentials, and often not even that. This has given rise to majoritarian suspicions that such charges are often attempts to invoke cloture on public policy debates whose stakes include the disbursement of public funds and government jobs. Affirmative action policies are often viewed as unfair to European Americans in general.

At any given time, perhaps five different explanations are offered to explain growing ethnic strife in the United States. Such conflict is portrayed as (1) a response to massive population growth that replicates among humans the conflicts observed among laboratory specimens forced to interact in unusually crowded conditions, (2) a response to racist oppression and repression by the Euro-American majority against everyone else, (3) the product of mere cultural misunderstandings, (4) the product of an ideological push for diversity and multiculturalism above all else, buoyed by the demise of common external enemies, and (5) the product of traditional socioeconomic competition among different groups, exacerbated by economic recession and structural shifts in the economy.

Reasonable observers may disagree about why social and ethnic conflict is on the rise in America today, but there is no disagreement that a lack of comity increasingly characterizes the debate. In Milwaukee and Dallas, minority elected officials threaten to take up arms if their political demands are not met. In Houston, white police officers are following the lead of black and Hispanic officers in seeking their own police association. In North Carolina, certain congressional districts are found to be drawn solely on the basis of race, leading a U.S. Supreme Court justice to express fears of "political apartheid."[4]

Caught up in the forces driving this strife, an increasing number of ethnic groups—or certain elements within those groups—no longer believe there should be a dominant culture in U.S. society. Especially for ethnic activists and politicians—and for their liberal, libertarian, and neoconservative allies—the melting-pot metaphor is properly giving way to others that underscore the concept of greater separateness, and perhaps even separatism. These benign-sounding metaphors include the "salad bowl," the "patchwork quilt," and the "cultural mosaic." Far from being

concerned about any danger to national unity stemming from ethnic fragmentation, minority political leaders and activists accuse those who do
raise such concerns of exaggerating the potential problems and of trying to
impede the progress of "people of color." Libertarians who exalt freedom
above all else appear to see the debate as irrelevant, persuaded that free
markets will tend to resolve this and perhaps all other problems as well.

Has either side fully confronted the underlying issues here and their
portents for the United States, especially in an ever-more-interdependent
North America?

Immigration and the Assimilationist Dynamic

Whether the United States takes nearly as many immigrants and refugees for permanent resettlement as the rest of the world, or, as some
believe, twice as many as all other nations combined, no other nation, with
the exception of Canada, is so powerfully committed to making room for
newcomers.[5] Indeed, immigration has been among the most important
features of the national identity since the earliest days of the republic. This
has been true not just in terms of the ethnic and racial groups that physically make up the American people, but also in terms of a psychological
openness to the idea of ongoing demographic shifts from abroad. Time
and again since the eighteenth century, this propensity to accommodate
ethnic pluralism has been the object of excited commentary and even
amazement by visitors from abroad.

As great as the commitment to immigration has been, however, it has
never been absolute. As increasing numbers of Germans came to the new
country, for example, both Benjamin Franklin and Thomas Jefferson expressed concerns about the creation of large enclaves of non-English-
speaking immigrants along the eastern seaboard. Such worries arose not
because the newcomers were not of English stock. Rather, Franklin and
Jefferson were worried that the non-English-speakers' preference for their
own language would have deleterious implications for society as a whole.
In Pennsylvania, these immigrants preferred to speak German in their
homes; they also wanted to send their children to German-language
schools instead of public schools. That they often refused to take oaths
and to serve in the military reinforced concerns about the possibility of
national political disintegration.

Some critics have portrayed the concerns of Franklin and Jefferson as
exaggerated, revealing the darker, less noble side of the Founding Fathers.
They note that German Americans went on to become the most thor-

oughly assimilated of all U.S. immigrant groups. Yet the critics overlook the heuristic value of the historical counterfactual. What would have happened if massive, impoverished German immigration had continued to spiral upward instead of taking on the quality of an ebb and flow? This question must be addressed if modern-day Americans are to be able to decide whether the concern over separatism was really a red herring nurtured by intolerance and xenophobia. It is relevant to note that at least one historian of the U.S. immigration experience has pointed to reduced influxes from the period after the end of the Revolutionary War to the end of the War of 1812 as having been an important factor in the creation of a national consciousness.[6]

Though unwritten, a covenant between newcomers and the citizens of the American nation has long existed: in return for full membership in the polity and the right to retain the culture of the newcomer's homeland, the immigrant was supposed to learn the language and civic culture of the United States. A measure of how well this understanding worked is that Americans of German or Irish origin, groups that were once near the bottom of the social, economic, and political ladder, are today virtually indistinguishable from those of English origin. Indeed, even U.S. citizens of southern European origin, whose forebears were the targets of considerable discrimination, have become part of the American mainstream. Italian Americans are the salient case in point. The U.S. success in assimilating the vast migration of French Canadian Roman Catholics to New England at the end of the nineteenth century from contiguous Quebec is another case in point.

The oft-heard argument that the United States willingly embraced massive immigration from Europe in the late nineteenth and early twentieth centuries, but today balks because newcomers are increasingly from Latin America and Asia, is misleading. It is of course true that there is a racial element to the objections of some modern-day opponents to immigration.[7] But it is also true that concerns are being raised among ethnic minorities and immigrants themselves, not to mention a growing number of voices that have long been affiliated with progressive political causes.[8] Moreover, the fact is that the great wave that entered during the late nineteenth and early twentieth centuries was not willingly embraced at all, but on the contrary, was perceived as harming the interests of the American people—so much so that laws curtailing the influx were passed in the early 1920's. Though the restrictionist movement was at the time suffused in undeniable racism, this does not preclude the existence of legitimate grievances relating to the competition for resources, including jobs.

An end to the constant large-scale replenishment of the labor market through immigration was a plus for those already here during the Great Depression. During the Second World War, women and blacks in particular were the beneficiaries not only of the military draft that took millions of traditional workers out of the labor pool, but of the low rates of immigration. Of course, the labor force as a whole, including returning veterans, benefited from the postwar manufacturing boom, but it is likely that low rates of immigration provided more job opportunities and better wages and working conditions for U.S. workers than if the immigration floodgates had remained open.

There were concerns about how the returning veterans and newly enfranchised groups would all be accommodated, but the postwar boom enabled a powerful middle class to arise, comprising the children and grandchildren of turn-of-the-century immigrants. Even the status of African Americans began to rise, and by the early 1960's, the Kennedy administration was talking about ending poverty in America. It was thus during a period of prosperity and civil rights activism that U.S. immigration laws were relaxed and reformed in 1965.

Since the late 1960's, the United States has been experiencing another huge wave of immigration. One of the most obvious features of this, the "Fourth Wave," is its high degree of concentration. Perhaps 75 percent of all immigrants settle in just six states: California, Texas, Florida, New York, New Jersey, and Illinois. Between 1970 and 1980, the number of Hispanics in Los Angeles jumped from 1.05 million to some 2.07 million, and by 1990 the number had climbed to 3.35 million.[9] Florida annually receives more political and economic refugees per capita than any other state, including California.[10] Within these states, immigrants tend to settle in a handful of large urban areas—Los Angeles and New York City being only the most popular. Other destinations include the Standard Metropolitan Statistical Areas of Miami, Houston, Chicago, Washington, D.C., and San Francisco. This concentration has resulted in a disproportionate impact, and as such the phenomenon has often been underappreciated by citizens in other parts of the country. Taking into consideration the numbers of legal immigrants on the one hand, and political refugees on the other, the number of lawful permanent resettlers in the United States may soon average around a million or more a year.

Though long-term economic forecasts are often inaccurate, most economists concur that a structural shift in the economy has abolished millions of the well-paying manufacturing jobs that did so much for Americans in the 1950's, 1960's, and 1970's. Job creation since then has shifted into services. While many of these positions are desirable, they require higher levels of skills and education than were demanded by traditional manufacturing jobs. And yet the skills and educational levels of large numbers of immigrants today are roughly the same as those possessed by newcomers at the turn of the century. Thus, the challenge of replicating the historical experience of the previous wave of immigrants would appear to be greater.

As Peter Skerry and Michael Hartman note, this fundamental difference is routinely swept under the rug:

In part we have not faced these questions because there has been a conspiracy of silence among liberals and conservatives on the subject of immigration. . . . On the one hand, free-market enthusiasts and their neoconservative allies have refused to acknowledge any problems created by record levels of immigration. On the other hand, liberals have been eager to identify problems, but trace them to racism, not to immigration. Hoping to win Hispanics as political allies, liberals depict them not as immigrants but as oppressed racial minorities in need of social programs and affirmative action.[11]

Though the proponents of massive immigration often allege that crass racism explains the motives of those who wish to curtail immigration, an increasing number of America's most distinguished commentators argue otherwise. The recent observations of George F. Kennan are timely:

Actually, the inability of any society to resist immigration, the inability to find other solutions to the problem of employment at the lower, more physical, and menial levels of the economic process, is a serious weakness, and possibly even a fatal one, in any national society. The fully healthy society would find ways to meet those needs out of its own resources. The acceptance of this sort of dependence on labor imported from outside is, for the respective society, the evidence of a lack of will—in a sense, a lack of confidence in itself.[12]

What, then, does the national interest require us to achieve? A stringent enforcement of the rule that jobs must go to U.S. citizens or authorized green card holders or valid temporary contractees? Good laws and clear guidelines promote dignity and respect. Yet Americans have shown little stomach for enforcing them, and without immigration reform (see below), even these steps would fall short.

Language and Assimilation

Because a person's ability to speak more than one language is an important advantage in life, it follows that a society that promotes a multilingual citizenry is giving itself a competitive edge. In a modern era featuring accelerating levels of global trade, the ability to command more than one language is more valuable still.

The European experience is a case in point. National societies gradually coalesced around this or that language not because linguistic unity was forced on them, but rather because the social and economic benefits of mastering a certain language were self-evident.[13] Yet the different countries of Europe have long had special incentives to learn other languages. Competing within the confines of a cramped continent (unlike the spacious, almost insular United States), educated European elites repeatedly have proved their willingness to learn whatever languages they needed to facilitate commerce, trade, and diplomacy. In the last century, French was often recognized as the common language of the educated across much of Europe and beyond; today, English is ascendant.

The evolution of the global village means that the United States is destined to become less insular, more cosmopolitan. There is every reason for Americans to learn not just French and German, but also languages once considered "exotic," such as Japanese and Chinese. The passage of NAFTA certainly promises enormous new opportunities south of the border. U.S. entrepreneurs will only be able to fully capitalize upon them by learning Spanish.

Increasingly, however, the commonsensical view that linguistic cosmopolitanism is good is being introduced out of context. Advocates are attempting to justify the accommodation of the linguistic preferences of masses of newcomers through government-sponsored programs that ultimately do more to maintain the language and culture of the newcomer than to promote assimilation. In other words, the real issue in the current U.S. policy debates over language is not so much whether the American people should try to expand their knowledge of foreign languages as whether they should expect those who choose to join their ranks to command the traditional language of this country—English.[14]

To elaborate, vigorous debates are being waged on such issues as whether English should be the official language of the nation, whether federal funds should continue to be spent on "transitional" bilingual education, whether or to what degree a knowledge of English should be required for aliens seeking to naturalize, and whether legislation providing for bilingual ballots should be extended. Yet after decades of federally funded programs designed to help newcomers integrate themselves into the linguistic mainstream, problems of linguistic alienation have not only failed to recede, they have grown enormously.

A common language is almost always cited among the most important features of a nation-state, and indeed all Latin American nations require the primacy of Spanish or, in the case of Brazil, Portuguese. Language is a cohesive factor that facilitates social, economic, and political interaction among the residents of a community, among different towns and cities and, indeed, among regions. "Without some common language, a tower of Babel emerges," notes the immigration scholar Barry R. Chiswick, "[thereby] increasing transaction costs and decreasing economic welfare."[15]

The argument that immigrants should learn English, or that English should reign supreme as the official language of the nation, is constantly repeated by native-born Americans, and even by many naturalized citizens. Such exhortations are often misinterpreted by newcomers as an implicit criticism of themselves, of their very heritage. They evidently feel that when citizens exalt the English language, they are denigrating all other languages. Yet, as we have seen, there are legitimate reasons to be concerned about language conflicts.

Consider the current situation in Los Angeles and Miami, cities where the heavy immigration of recent years has promoted linguistic maintenance instead of linguistic assimilation. This is not to say that many immigrants are not learning English rapidly and successfully; a great deal of linguistic assimilation is in fact taking place. Rather, it is to point out that the growth of huge linguistic ghettos in many cities has resulted in a limited but increasingly significant amount of nonassimilation. Ethnic diversity is among the most attractive features of American society—but is the fact that a Spanish-language radio station in Los Angeles has now captured the largest market share of all radio stations in southern California a uniformly positive development?[16] Does the recent repeal by the Board of Supervisors in Dade County, Florida, of an ordinance making English the county's official language reflect traditional assimilationist patterns? These questions deserve serious, comprehensive, and ongoing discussion.

The Role of Ethnic Group Leaders

The existence of a large mass of unassimilated people—whether native-born citizens living on the margins of society or ethnic newcomers seeking to improve their own socioeconomic status—will inevitably produce political leaders from within that group. People naturally gravitate toward those of the same ethnicity. Such a phenomenon is not necessarily racist, as the term is commonly understood. Especially when they are at a socioeconomic disadvantage, the members of a particular ethnic group will tend to congregate or network with one another. Group solidarity is an important strategy in climbing the ladder of success. Though it is often assumed that ethnic political leaders therefore will work for the benefit of those whom they represent—particularly in helping them to assimilate into the society at large—the truth is more complex.

In a democratic society guided by the principle of "one man, one vote," ethnic political leaders will inevitably identify their own best interests with the arrival of as many newcomers from their own ethnic group as possible. This is an important dynamic in and of itself. Though the recently arrived are not allowed to vote, they are nonetheless desirable to ethnic political leaders and their liberal, neoconservative, and libertarian allies in the majoritarian community because of the constitutional provision stating that "all persons shall be counted" in the national census. The census is in turn used as a basis for drawing congressional districts.

Naturally, professionals in the ethnic community will also appreciate an expansion in the size of their clientele. To be explicit, it is generally assumed by outside observers and ethnic leaders and service providers alike that newcomers will prefer to conduct business with those of their own kind. As the group continues to increase its population share, the dynamic of the situation will unfold further in the tendency to create new jobs in order to "meet the needs" of the community. Social workers will tend to be in high demand, along with bilingual education teachers, bilingual police and fire personnel, telephone operators, bank tellers, clergy, and so forth.

In our liberal democracy today, it also seems to be the case that political representatives of the majoritarian community must genuflect before the argument of "proportionality." This argument says that because X percent of the population of a political entity hails from a particular racial or ethnic group, then X percent of all political posts—both elected and appointed—should be held by people of the same ethnic origin. This interpretation is particularly valuable for today's ethnic politicians because it conveniently avoids any reference to the legal status, age, and voter participation rates of newcomers qua constituents.

Seldom noted is the fact that tension often exists between ethnic political leaders and the groups from which they spring. The reasons are often not apparent to the outside observer, perhaps because they are hidden in the nuances of class interest, or because they are overshadowed by the more obvious commonality of ethnicity, which is presumed to uniformly galvanize the members of the ethnic group as they engage in group politics. It is also often assumed that ethnic political leaders will work for the benefit of those whom they represent—particularly in helping them assimilate into the society at large.

The deeper, more complex reality, as John Hingham, a historian who has emphasized contradictory tendencies in the role of the ethnic group leader, points out, is that an underprivileged group "is likely to choose leaders whose economic success or professional attainments make them relatively acceptable outside the group." In fact, leaders often do not spring from the most representative segment—or "socioeconomic core"— of their followers. Though they go to great lengths to identify with the poorest elements within their group, ethnic political leaders are often motivated by a fundamental desire to "leave" their constituents in a socioeconomic sense.[17] In a situation where leaders and followers need each other in order to attain goals that may be alternately symbiotic and mutually exclusive or divergent, tension and outright disagreement are more common than might be assumed.

Curiously, the very ethnic group leaders who have become the most assimilated—in terms of being able to articulate their ideas fluently in English and being able to operate within the nation's traditional civic culture—are typically among those who most vigorously advocate cultural maintenance and, in some instances, the nonassimilation of the groups they lead. The irony of those who have the most in common with the majoritarian society attempting to keep their ethnic brethren from achieving the same degree of assimilation is reinforced by the fact that many of these leaders are only superficially familiar with the source language of their ethnic group, not to mention its traditions, customs, and history. "For [Hispanic American leaders]," conclude two students of developments in the United States, "the Hispanic cultural renaissance ends where the irregular verbs begin."[18]

That ethnic leaders of this stripe may well be out of step with the mass of Hispanic Americans is the implication of recent survey research by the political scientist Chris Garcia and his colleagues. According to them, assimilation is what the great majority of Hispanic Americans—citizens and noncitizens alike—want.[19]

It is important to stress once more that if mass immigration plays a role in creating ethnic group leaders, those leaders have a considerable political stake in perpetuating mass immigration. The symbiotic bond forged in an earlier day, when the ethnic politician pled the needs of the newcomers at city hall or the statehouse or on Capitol Hill, and they in turn served as a power base for him, may be substantially weaker. Even so, a constantly increasing number of immigrants continues to be highly prized by those bent on leading them.[20]

Free Trade: Boon or Bane to Assimilation?

At this writing, one of the most energetic debates to grip the United States in years has just been decided in favor of NAFTA. Whereas the United States signed a free trade agreement with Canada in 1988 with little public notice and still less public interest, the asymmetry between the U.S. and Mexican economies has raised serious concerns that NAFTA might actually undermine the best interests of the American people. The rhetorical volleys are still flying over a raft of issues. Will free trade with Mexico create more jobs than it will cost? Will it improve the environment or degrade it further? Will it debase labor standards? Will it change societies in both countries for the better, or will it provide each with the worst features of the other?

The answers have been mostly contradictory. As the official negotiators have often said, NAFTA is a trade bill. Its objective is to promote gross efficiencies within North American markets. While jobs are vital aspects of those efficiencies, they are not tied down in the hold of a fast-moving, rocking, continental-sized ship. Mexico is generating 800,000 potential new entrants into the workforce each year. Will NAFTA create 800,000 new jobs for them in Mexico? No one thinks so. Are the environment and labor side agreements likely to help in this? Not much thought has been given to using them in this way (although there is a potential to do so). From the U.S. trade union perspective, in fact, the object is to minimize job flight to Mexico, with little thought given to job creation in that country.

The impact of NAFTA on human beings, therefore, is ambiguous, aside from the unimpeachable data substantiating trade expansion's positive impact on economic expansion in general. Yet this will not be enough in itself. Immigration issues are being dealt with by not being dealt with. As the shortfalls of the last major overhaul of U.S. immigration law in 1986 suggest, a focused and tightly coordinated effort to address immigration on its own terms remains necessary. Otherwise, NAFTA or no NAFTA, the unregulated movement of peoples across U.S. borders will continue.

There need be no fear that affluent or upwardly mobile immigrants will be unable to handle the demands of adapting to a challenging environment as a consequence, let alone lose their family values. U.S. history has repeatedly demonstrated that the possession of human resource capital upon arrival in the country has greatly increased the possibilities of success for both individuals and groups. But the skills and educational levels of immigrants vary greatly even within waves of the same national origin— the emigres from Cuba in the early 1960's were often better prepared to compete and succeed in this country than were subsequent groups of Cuban newcomers. Refugees from Communist Europe in the 1950's possessed far higher levels of education than immigrants from Europe at the turn of the century.

So is optimism justified today in the case of millions of impoverished immigrants who are continuing to arrive from developing nations? The issue being raised here has nothing to do with race or ethnicity. Rather, it relates to the massive social and economic challenges posed by rural-to-urban migration—challenges that countries such as Mexico have grappled with for years. In turn, this spills over into transborder migration. Indeed, the pressure from residents of poor countries to enter rich countries will remain a major policy challenge to governments for the foreseeable future.

If Americans consider their own farm-to-city social experience earlier in the century, they will remember that traditional family values came under great strain as (mainly) black farmhands moved to urban areas. Social problems such as alcoholism, prostitution, and family abandonment became rampant. While prejudice against the group abounded, this probably owed as much to class-based snootiness and economic competition for jobs as to racism pure and simple.

If only 25 years ago the migration of rural workers to America's cities was mainly from the South, and mainly African American, today's rural workers often hail from south of the border. This is not to equate Hispanic migration with the movement that produced an impoverished inner-city class left behind by economic change. However, the current phenomenon does require an acknowledgment of the legal dimension of the issue. Legal U.S. migrants, like U.S. citizens, have every right to move about the country at will, but undocumented immigrants from other countries are by definition not even supposed to be on U.S. soil in the first place. While many pretend to minimize the significance of immigration laws, the consequences of nonenforcement can be severe. To pretend that such laws are meaningless represents a virtual abandonment of U.S. society's right to establish its own identity in the future.

As for the impact of external migration on the marginal elements in U.S. cities, there is growing evidence that those who migrated from the South years ago are now being displaced by the newly arrived. The Census

Bureau has noted that for the first time in the twentieth century, more African Americans are moving back to the South than are leaving it. Doubtless, many blacks are leaving states such as California simply because of local economic downturns, but to fail to consider the impact of heightened immigrant competition in the areas of jobs, affordable housing, and social services is indefensible.

The issue is even more troubling at a time when the creation of low-wage, low-skill jobs is as inadequate as the availability of training and education for high-wage, high-skill jobs. Add to this the fact that the skills deficits of millions of newly arrived workers often include the inability to speak the language of the host society, and the challenge to integrate them only makes the challenge of integrating America's own dispossessed greater still.

None of this is to imply that impoverished newcomers with low educational levels cannot acquire desirable skills. Clearly, they can, and legions of them have done so. Yet such an observation must be accompanied by specific explanations of how long it will take, and how much it will cost the country as a whole, as well as the costs to its most disadvantaged social elements. Decisions of this kind will be extremely important to the ongoing evolution of American identity.

Free or freer trade will tend to change the culture of our North American societies in fundamental ways. The accelerated expansion of business and commercial trade across international boundaries will necessarily alter, to one degree or another, traditional national identities. For example, more Mexicans than ever before will learn English, and more Americans and Canadians will learn Spanish. Already inundated with U.S. cultural exports, Mexico will almost certainly find itself becoming more Americanized in its tastes. In all likelihood, Mexico's influence on U.S. culture will be less significant, at least for the foreseeable future.

But a danger lies in the fact that cosmopolitanism will not necessarily permeate the lower socioeconomic classes of the continent. Far from learning new languages, there is a danger that many will continue to experience difficulties in gaining an adequate command of their own national language. Before giving in to the euphoria of the rapid cultural change that may accompany free trade, policy makers would be well advised not to confuse the linguistic needs of the affluent or the upwardly mobile with those of the popular classes. The privileged of North America will intuitively grasp the benefits of learning other languages, and indeed, so too may the not-so-privileged classes. But such an awareness will not necessarily be sufficient to transcend the circumstantial barriers to achieving their educational goals, including poor schools made poorer by the waves of Mexican children flooding into them.

In sum, the logic of those who argue that free trade will eventually improve the lives of a greater number of people across national boundaries is compelling. The brave new world of free trade should be the destiny of the United States and its two neighbors. But policy makers must keep in mind that the generalized benefits promised by free trade will be savored only after a drawn-out process. The expected desideratum will not be the result of a single event.[21] During the interim, there will be enormous capacity for socioeconomic harm to workers and taxpayers unless the implementation of free trade is accompanied by policies designed to offset collateral harm in such areas as the environment, labor standards, and job loss and retraining.

Burdened with exceptionally high welfare costs in the face of a military-industrial downsizing that has caused severe economic dislocations and recession, California is perhaps the first state to reconsider its policies toward what has till now been a loosely monitored flow of peoples. Whether the topic is immigrants or part-timers in the labor market, Californians are beginning to draw the line, and, increasingly, that line is their border with Mexico.

The Mexican Americans: A Special Case?

In 1848, the Treaty of Guadalupe-Hidalgo ended war between Mexico and the United States and brought about the transfer of much of northern Mexico to its expansionist neighbor. Almost a century and a half later, millions of people of Mexican descent have successfully assimilated into U.S. society. Not only have they served in the Senate, the House of Representatives, and presidential cabinets; they have served with distinction in the nation's wars, have made their mark in the arts, and are beginning to distinguish themselves as writers and commentators on the national scene.

Yet over the years and down to our own day, some scholars have believed the modern dynamics of the U.S.-Mexican border, including the rapid growth in the Mexican American community, should give pause. For them, the future assimilation of people of Mexican origin in the United States is not guaranteed. Not only are the skeptics concerned with the ability of the Mexican immigrants' experience to replicate that of previous European newcomers, but they also fear what they see as a challenge to the very integrity of the American nation. In effect, they say, the assimilation of one group of Mexican Americans—no matter how large—should not blur the nonassimilation of other members of the same group. The fear is the greater, for some, because that group, unlike others (the Canadians excepted) resides in an area directly contiguous to its country of origin.

Peter Skerry has reminded us of the opinion once expressed by the late Morris Janowitz, for many years a distinguished sociologist at the University of Chicago:

Mexicans, together with other Spanish-speaking populations, are creating a bifurcation in the social-political structure of the United States that approximates nationality division. . . . Thus, the presence of Mexico at the border of the United States, plus the strength of Mexican cultural patterns, means that the "natural history" of Mexican immigrants has been and will be at variance with that of other immigrant groups. For sections of the Southwest, it is not premature to speak of a cultural and social irredentism of sectors of the United States which have in effect become Mexicanized and therefore under political dispute.[22]

Does this mean the Southwest will become another "Quebec"? Skerry himself downplays the idea. However, one of the most difficult truths to grasp is that many, even most, of the recently arrived may assimilate and not assimilate at the same time. Good public policy, accordingly, should build on that split-level impact (or bifurcated effect, if you will), promoting assimilation, while recognizing that the proximity of Mexico creates a unique kind of reinforcement that works against change. In fact, the chronic cultural replenishment from south of the border often serves as a type of "rein" on disadvantaged Mexican Americans trying to assimilate into U.S. society, who find themselves lumped with, and balked by the racist attitudes of some Americans toward, Mexican immigrants.

What makes things harder still is that such prejudice can cut both ways. Along the border, a Mexican American who is unfamiliar with the culture or language of Mexico is likely to be saddled by his fellows with the pejorative term *pocho*. Even when that is not the case, the Mexican American who dares speak or write English too well—that is, on a par with the average Anglo American—is derided as *agringado*. (Mexican *fronterizos* have their own views of these cultural and linguistic tags, as Jorge Bustamante points out in his essay below.) Likewise, a Mexican American may be held up to opprobrium if he or she adheres to the Anglo ethic of individualism at the expense of the Hispanic sense of communitarianism.

The obvious point of such ridicule is to whip the "offender" into line with the rest of the group. To the extent that such ploys are successful—too often the case among the poor—they delay or impede social, political, and economic assimilation. For all the genuine linguistic assimilation that is occurring in the Southwest, it should be noted that among a certain element of the Mexican American population, the knowledge of English and Spanish alike is often superficial. The fact that upwardly mobile Mexican Americans do not want to be tainted by this phenomenon, along with the disinclination of Anglo observers, especially liberals, to make uncomfortable observations about superficial assimilation should not keep truth seekers from exploring the possibility that a minority within the minority is "neither fish nor fowl." The upshot is that those Mexican Americans who persist in following a full assimilationist trajectory are often obligated to leave the border region.

In many cities with large concentrations of Hispanic newcomers, numerous unfortunate incidents have occurred because of the inability of immigrants to speak or at least understand English. Tragic deaths have been blamed on the inability of law enforcement officers or fire department personnel to communicate with newcomers in their own language. Yet instead of leading a campaign to control massive illegal immigration and, simultaneously, teach newcomers English, many political leaders in the Mexican American community have chosen to demand that local governments accommodate the newcomers by forcing police and firefighters to learn Spanish. In many instances, Mexican American political leaders have fiercely opposed laws to enshrine English as the official language of the United States. These trends could lend credence to Morris Janowitz's observations that Mexican culture is in some instances displacing traditional American culture. The demand for the use of other languages, of course, has by no means been limited to the Mexican American community, but given the size of the Mexican immigrant group, and the chronic nature of the influx, developments within that community must be taken seriously.

Some prominent Mexican American leaders, including Henry Cisneros, the U.S. Secretary of Housing and Urban Development, have argued that Mexican Americans represent a unique ethnic group in U.S. society because they were here first. To the extent that Mexican Americans acknowledge their European origins, they were presumably "here" before all other European groups; and to the extent that they stress their Indian origins, they rank alongside the Native Americans in seniority. Even though this claim of seniority is almost never explicitly analyzed, its value to those who invoke it may lie in its potential to cast aside the demanding constraints of a democratic meritocracy based on the worth of the individual, in return for guaranteed group preferences based on blood lineage and a vague quasi-irredentism.

Separate and apart from the issue of whether Mexican Americans or any other group should be afforded special considerations for having been "here first" (a premise that may come under growing challenge as the majoritarian community invokes the equal protections guaranteed by the Constitution), there are problems with the historical accuracy of the claim. When the United States took over the territories formerly belonging to Mexico, perhaps 100,000 Spanish-speaking people resided there.[23] The majority of the 14 million or so persons of Mexican descent who reside in the United States today are the descendants of immigrants who came after the turn of the century or are themselves newcomers. To a large extent, then, Mexican Americans are very much like other immigrant groups in the United States, and the claim of seniority for the group as a whole is exaggerated. Implicit in the claim of having been "here first" is a disdain for the international border. With chronically high levels of Mexican immigration to the United States and the growth of an alienated minority within the minority, it is difficult to see how traditional pluralism will not come under increased strain.

Perhaps the most significant factor in the Mexican immigrant experience relates to the difference in size, rate, and duration of different waves of immigration. The wave that occurred after the turn of the century through the Mexican Revolution of 1910 has now been eclipsed by the wave that began in the late 1960's or early 1970's and continues to this moment. One measure of the contradictory tendencies in assimilation for Mexican Americans and other Hispanics in the Southwest can be found in the fact that today, one in four adults in Texas is not a U.S. citizen; the figure for California is an even more astonishing 50 percent.[24] Whatever outward signs of assimilation they may show, these people are politically disenfranchised because citizenship is a prerequisite for voting rights.

While most Mexican American leaders may fiercely contest any argument that links Mexican immigration to problems in assimilation, their stand on the issue is contrary to that group's leadership for several decades beginning in the 1920's. As one Mexican American scholar put it some time ago, "time and time again, just as we have been on the verge of cutting our bicultural problems to manageable proportions, uncontrolled mass migrations from Mexico have erased the gains and accentuated the cultural indigestion."[25]

The California and Texas data confirm that, in human terms, the trade-oriented framework of NAFTA is dwarfed by current realities. They also cast some reasonable doubt on other single-faceted approaches, such as doubling or even tripling the size of the U.S. Border Patrol, or cracking down on the traffic in fake documents. A comprehensive approach to the continental labor market would have to be the starting point for a new policy. The point is that immigration policy must be comprehensive, and it has to be hammered out on its own terms, not as an adjunct to policies focused on other objectives. Such an effort will require great political will and capital and close coordination with the other two governments. But there are grounds for hope that a fresh mix of policy instruments can be forged that will address the array of causes and consequences of persistent, massive immigration, much of it illegal.

Conclusion

Understanding the process of assimilation is perhaps best compared to viewing and understanding a motion picture. Stopping the movie in order to analyze an individual frame—that is to say, a particular point in the assimilation process—can be useful. Yet if we try to infer too much from a single frame, a distorted view of the story line may result. For a fuller comprehension, it is important to see as much as possible of the preceding and succeeding frames. Where no succeeding frames exist, it is important to use past experience and intellectual reasoning in order to try to anticipate what the "sequel" will be like. As mentioned above, the historical counterfactual can occasionally be used to advantage in this regard. What would have been the outcome for the United States if mass migration from Europe had not been interrupted in the 1920's?

The traditional proponents of massive immigration might argue that an uninterrupted flow of newcomers would have created more prosperity. Skeptics, on the other hand, might respond that such a scenario would have been disastrous, that it not only would have added to the 25 percent unemployment rate at the height of the Great Depression, but might also have intensified nativism still more and perhaps even spawned social revolution.

The difficulties plaguing the assimilation debate in the United States today include the inherent limitations of language, the narcissism of class, and the natural sensitivity—sometimes hypersensitivity—of ethnic groups. For example, the debate over immigration is often needlessly polarized when the policy alternatives are said to be those of either "opening" or "closing" the nation's door. Both images effectively encourage polarization and the maximalist position of "all or nothing." Simultaneously eclipsed are more sophisticated conceptualizations and policy options, such as that of a prudently generous immigration policy versus an imprudently generous one.

The fact remains, however, that assimilation in the United States today is being powerfully affected by the phenomenon of immigration, and more specifically, by the highest levels of immigration in the country's history. In proportion to the total population, this current flow is smaller than earlier immigration surges in the nation's history; but given changes in the labor market and easy transportation from nearby sending nations, the impact may be greater, and it is destined to grow. A recent report by the U.N. Population Fund states that cross-border and rural-to-urban migration is occurring in higher numbers than ever before in human history. Approximately 100 million people now live outside the land of their birth. A key difference between old and new patterns is that old-fashioned circular migration is declining; people are resettling permanently in other countries. Industrialized and developing countries alike are being adversely affected. With more and more claimants struggling for economic resources that are either declining or growing at an insufficient rate, "the growth of a global economy has emphasized rather than reduced inequality between nations." The phenomenon, concludes the U.N. report, "could become the human crisis of our age." [26]

As the premier receiver of immigrants and refugees in the world, the United States is under special obligation to ponder the implications of this startling development. The time for debate—sustained, honest, and rigorous—is clearly upon us. Though the impact of immigration from all sender countries should increasingly be taken into account and discriminatory policies should be eschewed, the fact remains that immigration from the Caribbean Basin, including Mexico, requires special monitoring as a practical matter. Though allegations of discrimination will inevitably be heard, the legitimate reasons policy makers will have for such vigilance are to be found in tradition (the channels of migration have already been dug deeply over several decades), demography (those nations are experiencing unusually high rates of labor force growth), and geography (they are either contiguous to or are especially close to the United States). [27]

What is needed is a frank assessment even of close neighbors whose best interests are often, but not uniformly, in our own best interests. The simple fact that the Mexican labor force is projected to double in size over the next fifteen or twenty years could by itself pose a major challenge to U.S. policy makers. Most observers concur that free, or at least freer, trade will accommodate some of the new job claimants, and it is true that job creation in Mexico will favor social and political stability. But experts also suggest that the job-creating benefits of free trade will not sufficiently manifest themselves for another generation. In the meantime—that is, in the short to medium term—free trade may actually *intensify* northward migration. The obvious lesson for U.S. policy makers is that they should continue to resist the argument that the free movement of goods and services should be accompanied by the free movement of people.

Otherwise, should more and more newcomers in fact flood into the United States in the short to medium term—that period before free trade and the peaking of labor force growth begin to relieve migration pressures—the benefits to be derived from free trade would increasingly be dispersed among a growing number of claimants. The competition for jobs, social services, and affordable housing would intensify proportionately. The end result could be that those U.S. citizens who were initially promised that their sacrifices in the early stages of free trade, including sectoral job losses as certain operations move to Mexico, would be rewarded with greater job creation would have sacrificed in vain. Such a scenario could accelerate socioeconomic polarization in American society, intensify schisms along ethnic and political lines, and, last but not least, stimulate a backlash against a free trade regime.

Though the economic plight of U.S. residents cannot be the sole criterion in setting immigration policy, it must nonetheless be a very important one. U.S. immigration history appears to show that reducing immigration tends to promote assimilation, and that a lax policy tends to yield the opposite result. While it is certainly true that immigrants who in the past entered during a period of laxity went on to assimilate, it is also true that waves of immigration have traditionally been followed by periods of curtailment—the all-important ebb-and-flow effect that is too often neglected or underappreciated by students of the U.S. immigration experience.

As the United States contemplates its identity today and in the future, the issue should never be viewed in terms of the presumed superiority of one culture over another. For Americans to see the debate over national identity as a Manichaean struggle between good and evil or between progressive and conservative is to miss the point: because of the country's tradition of immigration and because of particularly dramatic and increasingly accelerated changes in the world economy, the national identity is bound to change continuously regardless of what ideological, political, and tribalist opponents desire.

The real issue is often lost in the din of the debate, a debate too often enjoined by those furthest removed from the adverse consequences of any possible policy error. Specifically, given that social and economic change is inevitable, at what rate will the change occur? And what is the relationship between the different possible rates of change and their respective costs to the common welfare of living, breathing citizens of the United States?

As I write, two leading nations as diverse as the United States and Germany are saying "no" to further massive flows of foreigners, while paying close attention to upgrading the complex relations of interdependence with the labor-sending countries in their regions. It is true that Germany, whose industrial "miracle" was achieved with the help of Turkish workers, has a citizenship policy undisguisedly based on race and rarely grants citizenship to even fully assimilated German-born and -educated persons of Turkish extraction. Yet it is under similar pressures from poor neighbors who want in.

While Germany attends to Eastern Europe, it is in the national interest of the United States to promote the growth and development of Mexico and the Caribbean Basin through free trade, while tightening up and specifying the conditions under which labor from our neighbors will be welcome. Again, good rules and clear guidelines promote dignity and respect among peoples.

Once here, immigrants should be asked forthrightly to subscribe to the traditional American covenant: in return for full membership in the polity and the right to retain the culture of their homeland, they should learn the language and the civic culture of the United States. Assimilation on these terms is at once generous and historically grounded. All nations need myths and symbols: the covenant with assimilation's historic benefits to nationality is dear to Americans, and fundamental to our polity.

So, yes, we are sustained by generous instincts and traditions with respect to immigration, but we also need to specify what is required to uphold our traditions and our institutions, so well set forth by Arthur Schlesinger at the outset of this essay.

In the end, there is reason to hope that the United States can continue to absorb the newcomer, even as the newcomer contributes to the evolution of the American identity. For all the problems that arise in maintaining the world's premier pluralist society, this traditional symbiosis remains among the most inspiring and stimulating features of daily life in the United States. And while it is true that some racism persists in U.S. society, alongside daunting economic challenges, so too does the willingness of citizens of various ethnic origins to enrich their own lives by viewing their experiences through the prisms of others.

One of the most capable proponents of assimilation in the United States, the writer Richard Rodriguez, was once asked how he, born a U.S. citizen to a Mexican immigrant family of modest means, and now a Ph.D. in English literature pursuing a successful journalistic career, viewed himself. Musing over the question briefly, the longtime resident of San Francisco answered wryly and with a profound insight into the reality of his country. "I think I am increasingly Chinese," he said.[28]

Mexico: Culture and Identity in the Information Age

ALEJANDRA LAJOUS VARGAS

Fear of the Americanization of our culture has been present for many decades in Mexico. In 1955, Manuel Montes Collantes, a well-known newspaper columnist, wrote in *Excélsior*: "Film, radio and television, important media that might have been employed to reaffirm our national identity through the propagation of our typical customs, have in fact become enemies of our country, conspiring to exalt whatever is foreign. . . . If we do not put a stop to this ignoble effort and rapid loss of Mexican identity, in a few years our country will become a hybrid nation without tradition and personality."[1]

Nowadays, with the signing of NAFTA, scholars and politicians have begun to focus their attention even more on the impact of highly sophisticated information technology on Mexican culture and identity. How are media like television, film, and radio enhancing or detracting from Mexico's experience of interdependence in North America? Do they bring Mexican society closer to U.S. society? Do they highlight diverging values and priorities? Or do the powerful market forces behind them simply make the diverse information media unmanageable and unpredictable agents of change? These are some of the questions that, in a pragmatic way, address the effects new technologies may have on the culture and identity of the Mexican people. As such, they deserve a straightforward answer, offered in the first part of this essay. To further support and elaborate my vision of the present, however, in the second part of this essay I will briefly analyze the historical elements that make Mexican culture so singular and provide the foundations of our current experience of change. Finally I will speculate on what this cultural base will mean to Mexico and its North American partners as interdependence on this continent intensifies.

I

In order to approach the subject of culture and identity in the Information Age, we first have to make a clear distinction between the technology itself, that is, the instruments used to convey information, and the content that is relayed through them, the "software," so to speak, which is a cultural product.

The modern technological tools of development, information, and communication, such as the telephone, fiber optic cable, fax machines, satellites, VCRs, and computers, as well as other common household appliances, are already a part of global culture. Their use, per se, does not imply the "Americanization" of Mexican culture. Some years ago, Mexicans jokingly referred to modern, sophisticated gadgets and appliances as "un invento del hombre blanco y barbado" (bearded white man's invention), perhaps a grim reminder of the impact the Spanish conquerers had on the Native Americans in the sixteenth century.

Today we could more accurately describe these technologies as "yellow man's invention," but nobody seems to be worried about Oriental influence on Western culture and identity. It is therefore absurd to defend our national identities against the widespread use of technological tools, tools that have in fact enabled many millions of people around the world to live more efficiently and comfortably.

Marshall McLuhan's technological determinism, crudely applied to media and other widespread and standardized instruments of the Information Age, does not properly take into consideration the broad array of historical, social, and economic factors that affect a particular society. Cultural products, the *content* conveyed by these media, can take many different forms. Television programs, for instance, are produced with technological instruments, but their content is a people's cultural expression, their own way of viewing and accepting life. That is why television programs are not easily interchangeable in the global market, especially between widely differing cultures, such as the Mexican and the Anglo-American.

Yes, it is true that the strength and dynamism of the U.S. arts and entertainment industry, particularly film and television, has enabled it to export its products widely, conveying different representations of American values and lifestyles to countries all over the world. Thousands of hours of American television programming are available for export, amounting to about $2.3 billion annually in recent years. More than half of the 300-plus satellite-delivered TV services around the globe emanate from the United

States, including "super channel" MTV, reaching hundreds of millions of households, and CNN, which is seen in 137 countries.[2] The volume is overwhelming and undoubtedly poses a great challenge to local cultural industries worldwide.

In this context, how can we explain the fact that some developing countries have extremely strong arts and entertainment industries of their own? Take India, for example, which has a film production output—hundreds of films a year in several different regional languages—that is the envy of many northern, industrialized countries. Brazil's O Globo chain of broadcast and news media is among the most profitable in the world. Much closer to home we find the giant Televisa, a corporation that was 100 percent Mexican prior to its recent public offering on the stock market. Besides owning most private TV stations in Mexico, Televisa has strong commercial interests in radio broadcasting, recording, publishing, entertainment, film, and tourism, as well as cable TV and sports.[3] Its recent reacquisition of a large share of Univision, the Spanish-speaking U.S. network, which strengthened its position in a market where it already owned Galavision, one of Univision's Hispanic TV competitors, will probably make some Anglo-Americans fear for their own "cultural identity." Of course, the rapid expansion of Hispanic television north of the border is just a reflection of the increasing population of Latin American origin. All together, the three main Hispanic networks in the United States serve an estimated 15 million Spanish-speakers.[4] Aside from that, American television is quite homogeneous, with very little foreign—European or Asian—programming.

But the point is that in these three examples, Brazil, India, and especially Mexico, it is clear that strong arts and entertainment (cultural) industries have successfully appropriated foreign media technology while turning out products that respond closely to their national values, beliefs, and traditions. In the case of Mexico, these products have been exported, with great success, to many other countries in the world, including China, Russia, and, of course, the United States.[5]

Mexico's major export, the *telenovela* ("soap opera"), represents many important traditional viewpoints on life, notably, the value of the extended family; marriage and motherhood as supreme female aspirations; conservative sexual mores; mobility in the class structure; poverty as a trial to be endured; solidarity between neighbors; and religious devotion.

Although some segments of Mexican urban society have discarded a few of the more conservative values and have adopted lifestyles closely resembling those in First World countries, the fact is that the general population overwhelmingly prefers to watch Mexican fare on TV. Nationally produced soap operas, along with game shows, variety shows, situation comedies, local sports, and even old black-and-white films are among the highest-ranking programs in Mexico. This definite preference runs across age and social boundaries in both urban and rural communities. It is quite common for schoolgirls, coeds, and professional women to sit every evening around the dinner table, along with housewives, and even their grandmothers, to watch the tribulations of María Sorté portraying an unwed mother in *De frente al sol* while ignoring the kind of modern American feminism embodied by Candice Bergen in *Murphy Brown*.

U.S. television networks, confronting fierce competition among themselves and with increasing numbers of cable companies, would certainly envy the ratings most of Televisa's soap operas get in prime time: 40 or 50 points, 60–70 percent of the audience share. By contrast, even the most popular American programs offered in Mexico, though enjoyed by large segments of middle- and upper-class audiences, rate less than 15 points.[6] It is important to point out that language does not constitute a barrier in this case, since American programs are regularly dubbed into Spanish for nationwide broadcasting.

The only households that have direct access to some American television broadcasts in English are those of the 450,000 cable subscribers, 800,000 MMDS antenna (Multivision) subscribers, and about 200,000 satellite dish owners. Thus, exposure is limited to an elite who have been close to American culture, to people who already share some cultural characteristics with their northern neighbors, or to those who are interested in American news because they feel the Mexican market is deeply tied to the United States.

Broadcasting on radio stations presents a similar pattern, although radio is less monopolistic than television in Mexico, distributed as it is by numerous companies and institutions. Far and away most of the music broadcast consists of popular tunes sung by Mexican, Latin American, or Spanish artists, in a wide range of styles: tropical (Caribbean) rhythms, folk, ballads, romantic *boleros*, and even rock 'n' roll.[7]

The adoption in Mexico of rock 'n' roll, an unmistakably American musical expression, illustrates an important point. When the form was introduced to Mexico's youth by record companies in the mid-1950's, and popularized a bit later by Elvis Presley films, local musicians quickly adapted Spanish lyrics and mainstream Mexican values to the music of major U.S. hits. A generation of young singers and musicians rose to fame with a local, "Mexicanized" (and quite tame) version of rock 'n' roll, which was superseded in the 1970's by the global popularity of American and British rock groups. Through the years, however, Mexican, Latin American, and Spanish singers have prevailed upon the popular taste, sharing the radio dial with the less successful foreign rock music.[8]

The development of the film industry in Mexico further illustrates this dynamic of cultural adaptation and transformation. Mexico has always been quick to appropriate and use sophisticated media technology; radio broadcasting began in the early 1920's, and television was available at the end of the 1940's. Cinematography, introduced almost 100 years ago, in 1896, reached its peak as an industry during the Second World War. Organized on the Hollywood model, with American film technology, several big studios, and even a local, burgeoning "star system," the Mexican film industry became immensely productive and in the 1940's exported movies throughout the large Latin American market, neglected during those years by the more powerful American film industry, which was busy making propaganda films for the war effort.[9] But again the context of Mexican films was distinctively national in perspective. By far the most popular genre was the *charro* film, which featured a curious type of character combining toughness and virility with extraordinary singing abilities and a keen sense of honor. This character, although initially modeled after the typical cowboy of Hollywood westerns, gradually came to represent the true Mexican male spirit.[10] To local and foreign audiences alike, charros are emblematic of the Mexican people. Here we have an example of how not only a foreign technology but also a genre (which is a cultural product) can be completely assimilated and transformed into an integral part of another cultural legacy. As I will describe below, this phenomenon has occurred constantly in Mexican history. Over the millennia Mexico has received and absorbed many messages from abroad; in the process, it has re-created these messages as well, transforming them and incorporating them into the dynamics of our vital society.

It would be misleading to give the impression that Mexican society has not changed since the onset of the Information Age. Exposure to American films and television programs, as well as the effect of massive advertising of American goods and services, have altered many Mexicans' tastes and patterns of consumption. This process, which could be accurately described as a rising uniformity of tastes and patterns of consumption—especially among youth—occurs all over the world and is irreversible. Its main cause, however, is not the media, but the worldwide distribution of standard products manufactured by multinational enterprises so sweeping that these products are found in the most remote corners of the planet. I discovered this myself 25 years ago when I journeyed to a small village on the coast of the rural southern state of Oaxaca. After many, many hours of traveling on almost impassable roads, I finally arrived, starving, to find that there was nothing to eat except for warm Coca-Cola (there were no refrigerators) and Twinky Wonders, little cream pastries wrapped in cellophane. This tiny village had not been exposed to any media: there were no radios, televisions, or newspapers, not even good roads. Nonetheless, the villagers had ready access to the same industrially processed food products available in the large urban centers.

More than "cultural imperialism," a technological revolution and entrepreneurial prowess have created a global market in which everyone— thanks to excellent marketing and low prices—has access to U.S. fast-food chains, Japanese electrical appliances, and German apparel designed in Italy and made in Taiwan. The person who benefits from this consumer-oriented economy does not modify his view of the world; he merely uses these objects according to his own way of life. That is why these goods are much more frequently the object of transaction than cultural products. However, we do find one change of attitude, or at least consciousness, in the consumer who is familiar with and demands international products: sooner or later, his purchasing and consumption decisions make him aware that he is participating in and, ultimately, competing in an international market. In this regard, the goods of this interdependent world are much more fungible than ideas and values.

In the final analysis, to be afraid of the Americanization of Mexico as one fears a possibly devastating storm, for which one feels unprepared, is absurd. The Americanization of Mexico and the Mexicanization of the United States are evident aspects of reality in both countries. Perhaps as much as 10 percent of the Mexican population already lives "on the other side" (of the border), and our markets are saturated with foreign goods. But can we really say that this means Mexicans are less Mexican or that Americans have become "Latinized"?

The journalist Alma Guillermoprieto recounts the following experience in an article in the *New Yorker* as a way of illustrating that Mexico can indeed survive free trade with an economy 25 times its size:

A big mustachioed truck driver I fell into conversation with one evening at the Tenampa [Bar] in Garibaldi [Square, in Mexico City] reminded me that this is not an unreasonable hope. "I'm from the north, from the state of Chihuahua!" he shouted over the din of competing mariachis. "And, unlike those of you from farther south, I know what it is to be intimate with the United States, but does that mean that I don't look Mexican? As for trading with the gringos, I can tell

you that's nothing new. Remember *fayuca?*" He meant contraband. "There's always been trade between Mexico and the United States. The only difference is
that, before, it wasn't free." He rubbed thumb and forefinger together to indicate
the bribes that were paid to bring anything from nail polish to cars. "I'm for the
free trade treaty," he declared, and then, to make clear that he did not suffer from
any lack of patriotism, he called a mariachi over and sang "Mexico Lindo" with
them for me.[11]

II

In August 1982 the Mexican government was forced to acknowledge
its inability to continue payments on its foreign debt. Thus ended the
dream of self-sustained development. Further, the ensuing uncontrollable
exodus of capital proved that no measure, not even nationalizing the
banks, could alter the natural market forces along an 1,800-mile border
with the richest nation on earth. Reality was imposed on us, and changes
were forthcoming. The new government of Miguel de la Madrid, although emerging from the same political party that had developed an
economy based on import substitution, now proposed and established—
unilaterally—an open-door commercial policy. This change brought about
other, equally important, ones. As a whole, these changes not only have
enabled Mexican society to weather a severe crisis but have also fostered a
positive attitude generally toward something we have all been made aware
of in this Information Age of ours: that "opening" is essential to facing
and dealing with the processes of globalization characterizing the end of
this century. Nonetheless, it should be emphasized that these changes were
possible only because we Mexicans know, as a result of our historical experience, that we have the cultural resources required to assimilate external influences and to create, from these inputs and our existing reality,
something new—something syncretic—that we recognize and accept as
our own.

To understand Mexico's capacity for assimilating and managing change,
we must review Mexican history and analyze the forces and experiences
that are the ancient foundations of a modern nation. Mexico is a multiethnic and multicultural nation in which the State has historically played a
decisive role promoting integration and social change. In fact, where classical theory would have the State emerge as the legal representative of the
nation, in our case, as well as that of many other countries, the State came
first, organized by an elite, and only much later did the inhabitants perceive themselves as a nation. It is important to point out, even so, that this

Mexican nation was consolidated through the amalgamation of very different elements, creating, in the process, a strong and distinctive identity.

About 1000 B.C., many cultures developed in the central and southern part of Mexico. They were groups organized by lineage or *señoríos* that protected families, territory, language, and religion. The Olmecs, Mayas, Zapotecs, and Teotihuacans were the most important. At the height of their civilization, they developed urban centers inhabited by large populations. Each capital had its own ceremonial center and marketplace. These cultures developed arts and sciences in their own written languages. But in spite of their differences, they shared many characteristics: agriculture, local commercial exchange and trade with faraway places, and political and social organization through the señoríos. All of them developed calendars, writing, and a knowledge of astronomy, as well as their own religion and art forms. Ball courts and human sacrifice were another common trait of these cultures.

Between A.D. 700 and A.D. 900, for reasons still unknown, the great Mesoamerican cities were abandoned. Less-civilized peoples from the north took over, the most prominent being the Toltecs and the Mexicas (better known as the Aztecs). Both were warlike groups that absorbed the knowledge of the cultures with which they made contact even as they extended their hegemony over them by force of arms or alliance. As a result, several languages were spoken and different cultures coexisted in Tula, the capital of the Toltecs. When the Spaniards arrived, in 1519, the Aztecs had managed to dominate all of the other cultures in Mesoamerica.

Warlike groups like the Toltecs and Aztecs became less barbaric in time as they assimilated elements of the cultures on which they imposed their rule. Their military and commercial power neutralized the centrifugal forces produced by a constellation of ethnic groups under their dominion. The diversity and complexity of Mexico in those times are reflected in the fact that today 56 ancient languages are still spoken among the Indian population.

The destruction of the Aztec Empire and the conquest of the lands it had previously dominated was an extraordinary Spanish military feat, achieved as an extension of Spain's retaking its own territory from the Moors in what has been called the Reconquista, or Reconquest. As in Spain, it quickly became necessary to control territory, establish cities, redistribute land, and compel the local population to observe a way of life defined and governed by Castilian institutions. A profoundly hierarchical society arose, but the Castilian custom of permitting local populations to designate their municipal authorities—a practice first applied in territories recovered from Islam—was eventually applied to land conquered from the Indians. Much of the organization and administration of city-states in the pre-Hispanic period was accordingly preserved. With the towns of New Spain essentially simply grafting Castilian laws to local practice, distortions and adaptations occurred that virtually transformed Castilian municipal rule into the original indigenous model.

Spanish settlement in remote locations followed this colonial form of organization and contributed to ethnic intermingling, already a common occurrence between Moors and Castilians and among the Mesoamerican cultures. Thus was born the ethnic phenomenon that, in time, would become dominant in Mexico, the Mestizo, the offspring of a Spaniard and an Indian woman. Black Africans, imported by the Spaniards to perform the hardest labor, also added to New Spain's racial mix. Consequently, an elaborate caste system arose, which, at least formally, had sixteen divisions based on the various racial components of each individual. The result was a social pyramid, with the light-skinned Spaniards at the top.

Achieving an ideological integration of such complex social realities was painful. By destroying the indigenous peoples' temples and exterminating the priesthood, the conquerors assaulted the Indians' ancient belief systems and wisdom. In the process of conversion to Christianity, ancient Indian gods were mixed up with angels and saints. This syncretism achieved its most intense and powerful expression in the eighteenth century in the worship of the Virgin of Guadalupe, who united the matriarchal values of the ancient goddess Tonantzin with the yearning of the American elite—pure-blooded but Mexican-born Spaniards known as Creoles—to be credited as the only and legitimate heirs to the New World. In the Creoles' view, their preeminence was ratified by the presence of a new kind of Virgin, a dark-skinned one, who was hailed as the queen of the Americas.

But the Creoles were not destined to preserve either political or cultural hegemony in New Spain. Those roles, over the centuries, fell to the Mestizos, the Mexicans whose blood is Spanish and Indian at the same time. As Octavio Paz recounts, Mexican unity was created through the massive clash of contradictory forces and inclinations:

The ambiguity of the Mestizos duplicates the ambiguity of the Creoles, although only to deny it, at the end. Like the Creole, the Mestizo is neither Spanish nor Indian, much less a European in search of permanent roots. He is a product of the American soil, the new product. The sense of belonging sought by the Creoles through religious and historical syncretism is achieved by the Mestizo in a concrete and existential way. He is a social outcast, rejected by Indians, Spaniards, and Creoles; in a historical sense, he is the fulfillment of the Creoles' dreams. His relationship with the Indians is marked by the same ambivalence: he is their executioner and their avenger. The Mestizo in New Spain is both bandit and policeman; in the nineteenth century, he is guerrilla fighter and leader [*caudillo*]; in the twentieth century he is banker and union leader. His ascent is that of violence in the historical horizon, and his figure embodies the endemic civil war. The Creole dream and project were accomplished through the Mestizo, but they came about through violence that, until 1910, did not have its own historical project. For more than a century, we Mestizos have lived off the leftovers of European and North American intellectual banquets.[12]

Nineteenth-century Mexican history is the history of the creation of an independent national State. But it was not the kind of State envisioned by the Creole elite, who believed it was possible to transform New Spain into an autonomous nation without altering the organization and values of Spain. The Empire originally proposed, as well as the centralist and federalist endeavors that followed, never quite succeeded because between the Creole dream and the reality stood the majority of the population, the Mestizos and Indians, who were not given the predominant role that demographically they deserved. To pretend that it was feasible to fashion a State in the European or U.S. style was as hopeless as trying to blot out the sun with an outstretched finger.

Half a century of political instability—1821–76—did not alter the life of the Mexican people in a significant way. They remained in their villages, often unaware of the revolts organized by elites intent on shaping the State. They only reacted to the extreme circumstances brought about by the French invasion in 1860 and Benito Juárez's struggle against it. In their widespread outrage against foreign leadership can be seen the first real inklings of a solid basis for modern Mexico's emerging national identity.

But the Mestizos' insistence on being considered the center of gravity of the new nation was not satisfied even when one of their own, Porfirio Díaz, came to power and remained there for more than three decades, until 1910. Porfirio Díaz's image remains disgusting to Mexicans to this day, even though he is credited with a role in shaping and modernizing the nation, and with bestowing on Mexico its first 30 years of political stability since the War of Independence. The bitter feelings aroused by Díaz are due not only to his authoritarianism, but also to the deep-rooted cultural and social insecurity that led him to adopt a contrived and superficial French refinement. His pretensions were never accepted by the local bourgeoisie, which always considered him a social climber whose weak character led him to betray his own roots.

The Mexican Revolution that dispensed with Díaz also dispensed with influences on Mexican identity that lacked solid historical grounding. Advocated by the nascent middle classes rather than the elites, the Revolution enabled a continuous flow from the past to the present and the future in ideological and cultural terms. It also fused the peasants' and Indians' struggle with the desire of middle-class Mestizos to improve their standing in national life by giving all groups a voice in the national debate. Its triumph is a victory for Mexican identity and reflects the awareness that the Mexican people were strengthened by examining and celebrating their own values rather than by trying to import values from abroad. The external synthesis of this deep emotional commitment to Mexico's own experience and perspectives can be found on all sides. Mexican mural painting reflects Mexican national identity, as does the phrase of José Vasconcelos that is the National University's motto: "Por mi raza hablará el espíritu" (My spirit shall speak through my race). In time, the Mestizo, although initially ashamed of his lack of identity, had achieved the necessary demographic mass and cultural integration to become the gravitational axis of the nation. Vasconcelos's "cosmic race" was the loftiest expression of the Mestizo's prominence and dominance in determining his own fate.

The culture that arose from the Revolution made every Mexican into a moral Mestizo. This concept is as widespread as twentieth-century education. The new gospel was spread by teachers—especially rural teachers—and has been well received because it rescues and legitimizes everyone.

Before a so-called socialist education was offered in Mexico (1934–40), or the first free and compulsory official textbook came into being (1960), the leaders of post-Revolutionary Mexican culture had already realized the importance of a collective consciousness—a consciousness on which, nowadays, the whole development of the Information Age is based. Reaching deep into Mexican history, they well understood the example set by missionaries in our colonial past, who by launching a "spiritual conquest" achieved more durable feats than their military counterparts.

A good example of this post-Revolutionary insight is the famous speech by Plutarco Elias Calles, *jefe máximo* of the Mexican Revolution. Speaking in Guadalajara in 1934, he explicitly stated the importance of ideas, attitudes, and common understandings to national identity: "We must enter a new revolutionary stage I would call the psychological revolutionary period; we must go in and seize the children's consciousness, the consciousness of youth, for they are already a part of and must belong to the revolution. . . . The child and the youth belong to the community, and it is the revolution's duty to dispel prejudice from their minds and shape a new national spirit."[13]

But the pendulum swang too far. The reaction to foreign influence and prestige in the nineteenth century developed into a struggle to isolate Mexico from the rest of the world during the better part of the twentieth. In terms of the economy, we closed our borders with the idea of developing on our own, regardless of what went on in the rest of the world. The growing shortcomings of our import-substitution policy, in force until 1985, proved that this was impossible. Mexico's isolationism had its chance and failed: the policy not only did not produce wealth; it almost drove the country bankrupt. Fortunately, we were able to emerge from this crisis free of the ideological excesses brought about by isolationism. In the end, we saw that pride in belonging to the Third World only led us to accept the impossibility of reaching beyond the limits of inferiority.

Neither "cosmic race" nor inferior human beings, at the end of the twentieth century we Mexicans know that our future lies in participating in the process of globalization. We trust our new vitality because we are aware that Mexican culture, forged by assimilating the external and merging the heterogeneous, has a density and a uniqueness that make it very solid. We are conscious of the fact that external influences have the power to change us, but understand also that, once digested, they can become a valuable component of our own culture. Mexico has opened up with conviction, rather than fear. Who can deny that our country, led by President Carlos Salinas de Gortari, has been the main advocate for the North American Free Trade Agreement?

III

In the Information Age, Mexicans know they must have access to as many new technologies as possible: thousands of computers are being sold here every year, mainly to large and small businesses. Fax communications and electronic mail are readily available throughout the country, and databases are regularly employed by bankers, government agencies, and academics at the large universities. Their use does not imply, in any sense, a betrayal of our cultural identity. In fact, the best guarantee any nation has of maintaining its identity is continuing its development and encouraging competitiveness in a world built upon global exchange.

Our past has shown us that a national identity cannot be understood as something static; at the same time, our present is proof that Mexican national identity is not opposed to the concept of interdependence. Both past and present suggest that, for us, exchange is a source of enrichment. A national identity is the vital experience of a collective entity whose strength lies in surviving and assimilating changes and, through them, being able to express itself anew.

Certainly much of what is identified today as Mexican will cease to exist, but new forms of Mexican identity will appear. Cultures do not disappear—they evolve and change. Therefore, as Mexicans, we must focus our attention on improving the welfare and living conditions of our fellow countrymen. This will further their chances of making themselves heard. Confronted by the prospect of global change, we must appropriate emerging technologies and methodologies with the certainty that these will enhance our capacity to create new cultural products as we have always done in the past.

As Mexicans, we are approaching the end of this century well disposed toward change and with the clear perception that our association with Europe and Asia will be bolstered by our relationships within North America. Likewise, we are conscious of the fact that North America will consolidate its relationship with Latin America through Mexico. Thus, for us, the twenty-first century heralds a fascinating new frontier. In the dynamic Information Age of intensified interdependence, Mexico can once again relive the "encounter of two worlds."

PART THREE

Regional Perspectives

Quebec in the Emerging
North American Configuration

DANIEL LATOUCHE

The resilience of Quebec as a distinct national entity in a challenging cultural and physical environment has been the source of some puzzlement and occasional admiration. Oblivious to this attention, the descendants of the only "vanquished" European settlers in North America (Mexico's defeat in war with the United States excepted) have gone through a number of identity crises as they embarked on what has turned out to be a rather more difficult venture than initially expected: preserving and enriching one's cultural distinctiveness in a world where the forces of homogenization (education, lifestyles, telecommunications) threaten to overcome those exclusionary mechanisms (borders, unilinguism, religion) traditionally so important for a group's identity.[1]

Now we add to the list of challenges North American "interdependence" (including but not limited to trade). Is this multifaceted phenomenon providing a new strategic framework for Quebec's identity? The conclusion of this essay is yes. As in the case of all identities, the Other is a critical factor, and now for Quebec the Other may be changing. The emergence of new possibilities in North American civilization is freeing Quebec from some aspects of its problematical links to English Canada, while this, in turn, poses English Canada with its own identity crisis. In fact, it is not just North America that provides the new contextual Other for Quebec but globalization itself.

But before approaching the contemporary context, it is prudent to take a critical look at some of the reigning explanations of the many instances of "nationalism-outside-the-nation." Having reviewed these traditional cultural and developmental explanations of nationalism, we will be in a better position to suggest a more strategic perspective and then test it against the changing geopolitical environment provided by the ongoing redefinition of the North American commercial space, both within the Canadian-American Free Trade Agreement (FTA) and within its North American successor (NAFTA).

Of course we must realize that to even think of nationalism in political and theoretical terms is not an easy task, especially in North America, where the pretense of political universality and correctness is the norm. Yet taking this detour is not only a necessary precaution on the way to practicing "safe theory"; it also reminds us that social scientists have yet to develop the necessary instruments and vocabulary to study what is fast becoming a very indeterminate and evanescent phenomenon.

Clearly, nationalism offers unlimited prospects to all groups, large or small, bent on making a legitimate claim on a national status of sorts. It also generates much uneasiness. For those who object to the survival of the "nationalist era," one way out has been to suggest that although nationalism is unlikely to disappear entirely, it will only persist, as E. J. Hobsbawm believes, "in subordinate, and often rather minor roles."[2] "Nationalism is a declining force," writes John Breuilly.[3]

Other explanations, more reconciled to the continued existence of nationalism, have had to face the contrary dilemma, having to explain why nationalist movements do not always get their due—there are still more nations than there are states—and appear quite willing to engage in questionable warlike practices with ethnocentric overtones, thus making it difficult to fully rehabilitate nationalism as both a permanent and a decisive force for change. Even when nationalism remains a peaceful and progressive force, it often appears incapable of following through to its logical nation-state conclusion. For example, why is it that the Québécois seem unable to make up their minds and opt out definitively from the Canadian federal union or that Scotland is so hesitant about translating its well-established national identity into institutional terms?[4]

Could it simply be that even in the age of globalization and interdependence, nationalism remains somewhat of a mystery to us all?

Figuring Out Quebec

Until Quebec underwent its so-called "Quiet Revolution" in the 1960's,[5] French-Canadian nationalism, as it was then called, was seen as the ideological embodiment of a set of social structures and a value system that presumably isolated the province from the modernization process and from the rest of North America. This "insulation" was said to have al-

lowed the descendants of fewer than 10,000 French pioneers to "survive."
With French-Canadian family and religion at the core of identity, Quebec
came to organize itself around a clerical, rural, and agricultural system of
beliefs.[6] This self-projection was considered resolutely past-oriented and
unconcerned with the outside world. French Canadians, it was said, were
withdrawn upon themselves, at best oblivious to what was happening
around them.

This vision of what is broadly referred to as "conservative," "pessimis-
tic," or, more generically, "traditional" nationalism has rarely been ques-
tioned and is generally supported by an apocalyptic vision of pre-1960
Quebec society.[7] At best it is conceded that nineteenth-century French-
Canadian nationalism could have followed a different path if the 1837 rebellion against British colonial rule had been successful. This aborted
rebellion, coupled with clever manipulative policies of the British political
and economic elites, propelled the clergy into a position of authority from
which it could successfully impose its reactionary vision.[8] Although commentators differ on the extent of the clergy's power or the extent of the
support it could find among those who simply defined themselves as inhabitants, a majority see traditional Quebec nationalism as a closed, im-
permeable, and organic system of ideas, supported by effective institutions
and selected segments of the intelligentsia.[9]

There have been few similar culturalist interpretations of post-1960
Quebec nationalism. Among Quebec sociologists, Fernand Dumont has
been the most insistent on seeing nationalism strictly as an ideology and
making use of an ethnic-based national identity.[10] Richard Handler has
aptly summarized Dumont's unique vision of Quebec nationalism as a
constant dialogue between the individual and the collective, as well as
"the creative manifestation of self, the imposition of self onto the external
world."[11]

Léon Dion's vision is certainly not as "idealist" as Dumont's, but it
too involves a somewhat tormented search for the Quebec soul, a continuing dialogue, he claims, between the individual and the collectivity, between oneself and the "others" that make up the Québécois's imaginary
world.[12] Marcel Rioux, another sociologist, has talked of "Homo Quebe-
censis," the human specimen found in Quebec, for which he coined the
much-used label "Latin of the North."[13] None of these cultural visions of
Quebec identity and nationalism deny the important socioeconomic transformations that have reshaped the immediate worlds the Québécois live
in. But all would concur that these transformations are primarily the end
result of a unique personality, a mixture of obstinacy and audacity, bold-

ness and prudence. The other central theme in this culturalist perspective is that of the schizophrenic and dualistic nature of the Québécois's character, which is alternately considered the secret weapon or the Achilles' heel of Quebec.[14]

Structural explanations of Quebec nationalism are so rich that one hesitates to even try to summarize the developmental mobilization arguments in this abundant literature.[15] One such version explains nationalism as a consequence of an ongoing ethnically based division of labor that over the years has come to assign Francophones and Anglophones to different niches in an increasingly hierarchical and segmented labor market.[16] Nationalism is thus not only a verbal protest against a situation judged to be unacceptable, but an attempt to change the "rules of the game" by making it easier for Francophones to have access to jobs that had traditionally been closed to them either because of their poor qualifications or because of straightforward prejudices. This is probably the best-known structural interpretation of Quebec's unrest.[17]

But recent data on total revenues earned by Québécois seem to indicate that in Quebec, at least, nationalism has little to do with a closed labor market, since within the short 1970–85 span the revenue gap between Francophones and Anglophones declined from 44 percent to 16 percent.[18] In fact, total revenues of bilingual Francophones have overtaken those of bilingual Anglophones.[19] Those who expected Quebec nationalism to die down as the Québécois caught up with the economic status of their English-speaking compatriots have clearly been disappointed.[20]

Closely related to the division-of-labor explanation is the class interpretation of Quebec nationalism, according to which Francophone elites cleverly manipulated the symbols and discourse of nationalism to consolidate their own position within the Quebec class structure while acquiring more "elbow room" vis-à-vis the dominant English-Canadian bourgeoisie.[21] By clearly demonstrating "working-class" support for the Parti Québécois (PQ), however, voting studies have shown the limits of an interpretation that assumed nationalism could only exist as a political fraud.[22]

A more political explanation of Quebec nationalism insists on the breakup of the consociational compact that had characterized Canada since the mid-nineteenth century. No longer able to co-opt the new intellectual and economic Quebec elites in their Canada-wide system, English-Canadian elites could only stand by almost helplessly as they fell victim to a strictly Quebec nationalist discourse, powerless to overcome the advantage of an unambiguous message that could serve as a more cohesive bond.[23] One of the most diversified versions of the developmental explanation of Quebec nationalism has been the dependency hypothesis. However, its early depiction of Quebec as a semicolonial society responding to political oppression and economic dependency in much the same way as a Third World society has been widely criticized.[24] A. G. Gagnon and M. B. Montcalm have reformulated the original explanation into a more political and continental one, suggesting that post-1945 structural changes in the world economy are the main "culprit," not foreign control over the Quebec economy and its local comprador elites. Thus, peripheralization and not dependency is the main reason for Quebec nationalism. First, they observe, as the Canadian economy has become increasingly integrated into the American one, traditional East-West links have been rapidly replaced by North-South lines of force. All Canadian provinces and regions have been subjected to this continentalization, although some have been able to benefit more than others from American economic hegemony. Second, the growing importance of the energy sector favored an investment shift in favor of the country's western provinces, exacerbating an already dislocated Canadian economic space. And finally, the rise of the services sector, coupled with the North-South and East-West realignments, has accelerated the transformation of Toronto into the financial and industrial capital of Canada.[25]

By 1960, it had become clear that the combined effects of these three sets of forces would pose a major threat to the social, economic, and political survival of Quebec's cultural distinctiveness. As the central government tried to halt the peripheralization of Canada as a whole, it worsened matters for Quebec by implementing policies that were devised either to consolidate the economic core of Canada (i.e., Toronto and Ontario) or to bring the outlying regions (i.e., the West and Atlantic Canada) more in line with the development levels of the rest of the country. A central element of the English-Canadian progressive explanation of the rise of Quebec nationalism has always been the belief that the continentalization of the Canadian economy and the failure of the federal state to oppose it constitute the real reason why Quebec resorted to nationalist agitation. Quebec found itself losing on all grounds. In a typically Canadian fashion, these attempts only half-succeeded and aggravated the sense of isolation of Quebec elites, who realized that the policies of Ottawa, successful or not, could only be expected to further peripheralize Quebec within an already peripheral Canada. The stage was set, they concluded, for a zero-sum game where each federal initiative, whatever its internal merit and logic, ran afoul of the many programs devised by Quebec's own elites, now in full control of a dynamic but resource-starved provincial state apparatus.

Although Gagnon and Montcalm focus on peripheralization as the major process at work, there is no doubt that the central actor in the Quebec national drama has been the State. The State-centered vision of Quebec nationalism has now reached a status of quasi-hegemony among the many structural explanations that have surfaced over the years. On the whole, cultural factors and the ethnic substrata of the previously mentioned ethno-revivalist school have been pushed aside.

But which State, the Canadian or the Quebec State? The many divergent answers to this rather simple question have furthered our understanding of the workings—especially of the institutional format—of the State in modern societies, as well as its relationship with the other "sacred" object of our secret desires, the Nation.

Oblivious to the fact that the Quebec State is but a provincial or regional administration, a number of authors have adopted what could be referred to as a "managerial-pluralist" perspective and have stressed the societal push for statist intervention in order to accelerate or at least regulate the modernization process.[26] Nationalism is presented here alternatively as the ideological representation of the State as a totality, as a policy output of the same order as health or economic policies, or as an attempt to reinforce one's collective identity following the tensions created by the state-building process.[27]

This elite-technocratic vision of the Quebec State stresses the various ways in which elites have made use of a national vision and nationalism to create a polity that not only would further their own interests and "represent" them, but would also organize State-society relations along lines that reduce contradictions and tensions between opposing factions. In its search for social hegemony, the new middle class has used nationalism to establish systematically its own "technical" competence to run Quebec and to provide Québécois with a definition of themselves that would facilitate the reproduction of their ideological control.[28]

As we can see, Canada and the Canadian State are completely absent from such interpretations. Some Anglo-Canadian students of the State have reacted to this omission by making the Canadian State, or more appropriately the failure of the Canadian accumulation process, the major culprit for province building in either its Quebec national form or its regional manifestation in other provinces.[29] There have been few Quebec takers for this strictly Canadian perspective, although in the late 1970's a group of Marxist Quebec analysts decided to bring Canada back into their understanding of Quebec by defining it as a regional manifestation of Canada's social formation. "Quebec distinctiveness," according to Gérard

Boismenu, "is in part a function of its insertion into the overall Canadian reality." As a result, the economic, political, and ideological aspects of this distinctiveness, including the nationalist discourse, "can only be understood as peculiar manifestations of the class struggle within the regional space of Quebec."[30]

Recently, earlier proponents of strict class analysis have felt the need to "bring the society back in." Thus, according to Anne Légaré and Nicole Morf, Canadian federalism seeks to "make Quebec into a regional space, a region like all the other regions in Canada," while proposing itself as the permanently re-created synthesis of the country's many regions. Quebec's civil society, they argue, holds the key to either becoming a nation or falling back on its regional status. The more autonomous, the more dynamic, the more activist Quebec society is, the more national its outlook.[31]

All such developmental interpretations of Quebec nationalism agree on the crucial role played by the Quebec State and its ongoing battle with its Canadian equivalent, both in the formation of, and the constant fine-tuning of, the Quebec identity. Periodical stocktaking of Ottawa-Quebec relations would seem to confirm how much the nationalist discourse emanating from Quebec, as well as its many transformations, is dependent on the twists and turns taken by Ottawa-Quebec relations.[32]

With the exceptions of the postal system and defense, one is hard pressed to find a single area where Ottawa and Quebec do not operate competing programs. In recent years, television violence, tobacco advertising, the ozone layer, pay equity, day-care centers, manpower training, illiteracy, reforestation, urban infrastructures, and acid rain have joined such "traditional" issues of contention as consular offices, economic development, R&D, welfare, unemployment, communications, and energy. In short, every possible new form of State intervention has been rapidly integrated into the Ottawa-Quebec conflict.[33]

In the early 1980's, Quebec's attempts to form a social pact aroused some opposition in Ottawa, which not incorrectly saw in the succession of European-like tripartite socioeconomic summits run by the PQ government an attempt to mobilize both labor and business against the neoconservative agenda coming out of Ottawa and the very idea of an Ottawa-led economy.[34] Although limited in their successes, these neocorporatist policies alarmed the federal government, which immediately proceeded to institute its own version of neocorporatism.

When the Parti Québécois was replaced by the pro-business and anti-interventionist Liberal Party, a new set of conflicts emerged, this time on the extent and direction that deregulation and what was called "de-statism" (privatization) should take. Ottawa feared that Quebec-based banks and financial institutions could take advantage of deregulation and thus provide still further ammunition to the growing nationalist discourse in the business community. Some observers went so far as to suggest that the special kind of "market nationalism" espoused by the new Quebec entrepreneurial elites constituted a more serious threat to the Canadian federal experiment than the emotional discourses of an earlier generation of poets, students, and other nationalism-prone groups. Whether this "Balzacian" bourgeoisie can become the most potent single threat to Canadian unity remains to be seen.[35] Controversy swirls over whether or not this business bourgeoisie provides the nationalist movement with the security and consensus it needs to present its sovereignty option as a "project" for all of Quebec. One view is that the forces of the world economy are having the same destabilizing effect on the Quebec economic actors, notably the trade union movement, as they have had in the rest of Canada, turning Quebec into a mere copy of the other provinces or even of Canada as a whole.[36]

On the basis of the surprising consensus arrived at during the Bélanger-Campeau Commission set up in the wake of the Meech Lake fiasco, others have argued that the unified front of the Quebec bourgeoisie, until now solidly aligned behind the most antinationalist positions, has crumbled and can never be reconstituted. Following the rejection of the Meech Lake compromise by two English-Canadian provincial governments, the Quebec government set up a special parliamentary commission made up of not only elected members but also "representatives" of various interest groups to consider future constitutional options for Quebec. As expected, the Commission could not arrive at a single plan of action but surprisingly concluded that if Canada's constitutional system could not be "profoundly" revamped, political sovereignty was a viable and acceptable solution. Business representatives concurred in this analysis.[37]

Limits and Criticism

Taken together, these interpretations do in fact "explain" some or even most aspects of the persistence of Quebec's cultural distinctiveness. The contrary would be quite surprising. But what do they explain, and what is missing?

Cultural explanations of the Quebec identity cannot be entirely off the mark. If it is true that Quebec is an imagined community, then it is clear that its imagining powers are very strong indeed, for few other groups have been given so many opportunities to disappear through assimilation and migration. And yet the Québécois have chosen not to take this road.

Part of the Quebec identity is the Québécois's own belief that they are not and never have been indispensable, a fact that has never stopped them from trying to become so. This "unbearable lightness of being" certainly does not correspond to the image—not to say the cliché—of endurance, obstinacy, and solidity that emerges from the culturalist vision of Québécois distinctiveness. True, Québécois have an identity, but mostly in the form of an identity problem.

Even a superficial overview of Quebec's history will reveal that in no way can its identity be considered a primordial attachment. Yes, the Québécois have been given many chances to "exit" History—one could even say they have been shown the door on a number of occasions—and have refused to do so. But they have also been given an equal number of chances to put their historical presence, what has been called the "Quebec fact," on a more solid political and institutional footing, and have just as stubbornly refused to do that either. In fact, their "loyalty" to their own distinctiveness is certainly not above suspicion, and most of the time their "voice" is a confused one.

Permeating the Quebec identity is the apparent wish to be somebody else, somewhere else, a very curious primordial identity if there ever was one. Québécois writers have gained fame and some recognition talking of exile and self-dispossession as if alienation were Quebec's raison d'être. Thus, the Quebec identity is certainly a soft one, and this softness is not captured by the primordial culturalist approach and its insistence on specifying the molecular structure of identity. As I will note, interactions between such an identity and a new North American context are complex and not easily captured by simplistic cultural explanations.

The various structural explanations are also somewhat lacking. Salary differentials, job market segregation, dependency, and class structure tell us *something* about the Quebec story. But one has the feeling that these interpretations, even when combined, miss some of the mixture of "extraordinary" and "ordinary" that has characterized the Quebec saga through its various incarnations. As we have said, the Quebec identity is soft and built on a form of civil indifference. It also tends to forget the rationalities of well-conceived explanations. For example, the vast majority of French-speaking parents in Quebec send their children to French schools because it is the normal and ordinary thing to do. This is what you do when you are French-speaking parents in Quebec. But occasionally, these same parents will go down in the streets, a very un-ordinary thing to do, especially in midwinter weather, to protest the intention, or so they think, of their provincial government to give them the right to send their children to English schools, which they are already supporting with their taxes. At the same time, these parents will go to great lengths, not to mention expense, to have their children learn English through private lessons, summer programs, and the like. (Members of the Quebec English-speaking minority can send their children to English or French schools at their option.)

The Missing Link and the New Environment

What is missing from both sets of explanations is a more strategic perspective on the nation. For it to exist, the nation must make sense of itself in relation to its environment.

How to deal with the "other" and the "outside" is central to understanding nationhood. Nationality is but a relational construct that seeks to organize on its own terms a system of differences to which it assigns meanings. "Nations are forever haunted by their various definitional others," writes Andrew Parker and his colleagues.[38] How each nationality chooses to treat this dream defines the style of each nationalism.[39] Thus, more important than the list of distinctive elements—language, religion, beliefs, and institutions—is their salience, which becomes "real" only as a result of the perceived need to make sense of what is happening outside the community. In this sense, a "national" identity is neither invented nor activated. Nor is it given. It is constructed, or more precisely, continuously reconstructed as external events and even the definition of what the "outside" really is are changed and, what is more important, are perceived to be changing.

Benedict Anderson is certainly right in stressing the "imaginary" aspect of any national community. His perspective falls short when he fails to explain the triggering mechanisms of this imagining process, yet he does note the preconditions that suddenly made it possible for the community to dream about its own existence. Three fundamental cultural conceptions had to lose their "axiomatic grip" before this could happen: the decline of sacred communities, the rejection of the dynastic realm as the organizing political principle, and the appearance of a simultaneous vision of time that allows us to be able to say "meanwhile." But is it sufficient to say that once these stumbling blocks had been eliminated, then the "search was on for a new way of linking fraternity, power and time meaningfully together?"[40] No doubt Anderson is correct when he suggests that "nothing perhaps more precipitated this search, nor made it more fruitful, than print-capitalism, which made it possible for rapidly growing numbers of people to think about themselves, and to relate themselves to others, in profoundly different ways."[41] But why do they suddenly all begin to dream at the same time or, to pursue the dream metaphor still further, how do they come to remember their dreams in such unison?

In this perspective, the "environment" of any national group plays an important and constitutive role in its formation and continued existence. It provides the ingredients of which the group's dreams are made. In other words, the environment, in both the sociological and the physical sense, is the sum total of those "others" and those "outsides" that the group has to reinterpret.

This perspective is a very subjective one. It assumes that the "out there" makes sense only from the viewpoint of the "in here." This is probably an exaggeration, but any national identity, even a very small operation like Quebec's, is necessarily subjective and always an exaggeration. But this very exaggeration helps focus the question: how can we characterize the "out there" from which Quebec dreams are made, when there are many dreams and still more ways to remember them?

The Quebec "out there" can be structured along several axes. First, the very existence of the "out there" and of its importance for Quebec has not only been recognized; it has come to occupy a central place in all Quebec dreams. Between 1960 and 1980, finding the internal configuration of the "new" Quebec society and the correct mix of ingredients needed to provide Québécois with a modern identity, one they could be proud of, was the obsessive preoccupation of all those who could claim to "speak" for the nation. Today, their conversation is not so much about the role of State corporations or the proper way to stimulate economic growth or redistribute its benefits as about the "out there." Second, North America has certainly become the most visible and talked-about element of the Quebec "out there," with both free trade agreements occupying so much attention. Yet there is more to North America, at least from the perspective of Québécois identity, than NAFTA.

While Quebec's relationship with its privileged Other, Canada, remains a central element of the Quebec imaginary landscape, it has lost some of its exclusivity while becoming more focused on an entity that certainly existed before, but to which the Québécois paid little attention. The rest-of-Canada or, to use its traditional name, English Canada, now shares the limelight with Ottawa and the federal government as the main *définisseurs* of the Canadian "out there."

Much ridiculed until as late as 1980, the Francophonie (which is to say, the global community of French speakers) has now become an important feature of Quebec's vision of what is happening in the rest of the world. France and Paris-based culture are still the dominant features of Quebec's French international connection, but they are not alone anymore.

Finally, Quebec's "out there" has not only taken a more important place in the Quebec imagination; it has, so to speak, "come home." Because of the combined effect of a prolonged demographic crisis (a low birthrate) and rising immigration of non-French-speakers, for the first time Québécois are forced to deal internally with "others" and the "outside." For the first time, Québécois are forced to come to terms with the very notion of nationality. The key questions have become, can one become a Québécois? Can the Québécois dream be shared?

Each of these changes in the environment presents challenges and opportunities for both Quebec's identity and its nationalism. Each will be briefly examined in order to illustrate how the new international environment is likely to be interpreted and gives rise to different "strategic" responses.

Globalization and the Quebec Identity

In Quebec as everywhere else, globalization and internationalization have stimulated new thinking. While in the 1960's the public discourse in Quebec was full of references to decolonization, neocolonialism, Sweden, or Cuba, it now makes full use of the new acronyms (GATT, NAFTA), the new concepts (regional blocs, strategic trade), and the not-so-new realities (integration, cooperation). This in itself testifies to the rapid integration of Quebec in the new syntactic order. The debate around Quebec identity and the best way to promote it has always had an international dimension; what is new is the content of this dimension and its saliency. The commercial and economic aspects of globalization have been extensively examined, and both the Quebec and the Montreal authorities have set up numerous task forces, commissions, and study groups to elaborate complex strategies to profit from the emerging New International Order (NIO).[42] Suffice it to say here that these strategies are not particularly original, insisting as everywhere else on the need to export more, to produce better, and to attract foreign investments. Compared with similar initiatives in Ontario, California, or even the Rhone region in France, the Quebec-based vision of the NIO differs only in its obsessive nature and its insistence on developing all-inclusive strategies incorporating commercial, cultural, immigration, R&D, and environmental concerns.[43]

More important is the impact of this "global obsession" and its related policies on the major features of what could be referred to as the "Quebec identity system."

Globalization has become an important issue area where the conflicting views of the Quebec and Canadian states are expressed with a renewed vigor. Because the Quebec government has generally agreed with the free trade position of its federal counterpart, these conflicting views have never gotten the same media attention as Ontario's ongoing battle with the central government over the FTA and NAFTA.[44] But the differences are no less real and in some ways go much deeper. Because both the FTA and NAFTA corresponded to its own ideological agenda, as well as its reading of the NIO, the Liberal government of M. Bourassa tended to support the various free trade initiatives of the Federal Conservative Party. But it did so in a quasi-diplomatic way and not because it followed the Canadian government's lead. At various points during the negotiations, Quebec sought to obtain special concessions, either in the trade deals themselves or in the ongoing constitutional negotiations. For the Quebec government and certainly a majority of its economic and intellectual elites, the "out there" includes both commercial relations with foreign countries *and* constitutional arrangements with the rest of Canada.

This attitude has not gained Quebec any points either in Ottawa or in other provinces, all of which objected strenuously to Quebec's insistence on judging the FTA and all other such international dealings essentially through its own optic. Not surprisingly, these diverging interpretations, even among governments that share free trade visions, only serve to reinforce Quebec's feeling of distinctiveness. Although Ottawa and Quebec agree on the positive effects of free trade, they differ on the best way to make use of its positive results and on how to deal with negative consequences as well. These disagreements have only served to put new life into long-standing quarrels about manpower training, R&D, economic restructuring, and regional development, to mention a few. Until recently, Ottawa-Quebec disagreements on these issues were somewhat technical, having none of the intensity of the traditional battles on language, education, and welfare. Globalization has made them much more important. The conflict over which government should decide on which professional program to finance—plumbing or automobile repair—is no longer a simple turf battle between overzealous civil servants eager to expand their sphere of authority, but a battle between competing "world visions."

Globalization has also changed the terms of the long-standing debate on whether Quebec truly needs to have an international "presence" of its own. Ever since the Quebec government signed its first international agreements in the early 1960's, claiming it had the constitutional authority to do so, Quebec's international activities have been the object of much attention, mostly constitutional, and some scrutiny, mostly political.[45] Many U.S. states and Canadian provinces now have such activities. Even cities have felt the need to acquire an international profile of their own.[46] This international activism by subnational governments everywhere has been taken as the indisputable confirmation of the growing difficulties experienced by nation-states and national governments alike in maintaining their monopoly over the international projection of certain traditional State responsibilities.

In Canada and Quebec, the debate over the future of the nation-state has taken a number of unexpected twists, all of which have served to confirm once more the distinctiveness of the Quebec situation. Paradoxically, those who share the vision of the coming demise of the nation-state have tended to be strong supporters of the Canadian federal system and of an active role by the central government in precisely those areas judged to have been escaping from its realm. On the other side, supporters of sovereignty for Quebec have tended to object to the image of the declining nation-state, presumably because they believe that without nation-state status, Quebec identity is eventually doomed.[47]

This is not the only paradox introduced by globalization. In the past, the argument for the necessity and inevitability of Quebec's sovereignty was couched principally in the language of statism and nationhood. The reasoning was simple: when a nation and a state exist side by side on the same territory, they tend to want to coalesce.

Increasingly, however, the argument for Quebec's sovereignty does not come out of the internal logic of the Quebec State or that of the Quebec nation, but out of the workings of the NIO.[48] This is a dramatic reversal, which will have important consequences not only for the political struggle between federalist and nationalist forces in Quebec, but for the national identity of Québécois. The "outside" is now an important element of who the Québécois are and how they should best make use of their new nationality. The most recent PQ electoral manifesto, *Le Québec dans un monde nouveau*,[49] clearly illustrates this reversal. Gone are the appeals to Quebec's uniqueness and the anger over its mistreatment by the central government. Serious doubts are even expressed about the dangers of ethnic nationalism in this era of interdependence.

Canada's Other National Identity

The community that, for lack of a better name, I have referred to as "English Canada" has always played an important role in the constitution of Quebec's own sense of national identity. To some extent, Quebec's nationhood is but a response to the "perceived" existence of this other Canadian national entity. In other words, part of the imagined Quebec national community has always rested on imagining another similar and parallel community "out there." So important has English Canada been to Quebec that the Québécois have gone to great lengths to construct an entity whose very existence has been rejected by English Canadians themselves.[50] In order to differentiate themselves from their "significant others," the Québécois have insisted on "inventing" a national identity separate and apart from their own. In fact, many of the central components of the Quebec identity have been given shape by making use of selected stereotypical views of "English Canadians." One could even argue that as the Québécois changed their perceptions of English Canadians and what "they" were up to, so they also changed their own self-definition.

It happens that the FTA has profoundly affected the English-Canadian sense of national identity. These changes have already had repercussions on the strategic environment in which Quebec's own identity is shaped. NAFTA will only add to this redefinition of what could be called the "imagining" environment. The more English-Canadian identity changes, or is perceived to have changed, the more the Québécois will be tempted, or even forced, to redefine their own identity.

In English Canada, the debate surrounding FTA clearly has been the most influential one in decades on what has been a relatively quiet ideological front. True, the 1984 election of a Conservative government and its somewhat feeble attempt to reshape the Canadian political agenda along the lines of Reaganism should not be underestimated, let alone, for that matter, such hot-button issues as gender and the proper constitutional arrangements needed to accommodate Quebec. Yet it is safe to say not only that the FTA debate brought life to a somewhat placid ideological field, but that it redefined many of the terms of these other debates. Suddenly, everything came together as, for the first time, Canada came close to experiencing a state of ideological warfare.

The major ideological fallout of the debate has been the public emergence of English Canada as a distinct national group and of English-Canadian nationalism as a legitimate ideological project. So public and consequential has this development been that much, although not all, of the traditional reluctance to acknowledge the existence of this "other" nationhood has been eroded. Until recently, the only form of nationalism that benefited from some form of public recognition by English-speaking intellectuals and political elites (in addition to Quebec nationalism, of course) was Canadian nationalism. Any attempt to suggest that this all-encompassing nationalism did not exist, or did not include Quebec, and the Québécois in it, was met with much derision or antagonism. Canadian nationalism existed, it was said, because Canada existed.

Since 1988, the idea that Canada has many nationalisms and thus has many "nations" within it has gained some ground. At a minimum, it is now recognized that what passed before as Canadian nationalism should be referred to as pan-Canadian nationalism.

Sylvia B. Bashevkin has defined pan-Canadianism as "the organized pursuit of a more independent and distinctive Canadian in-group on the North American continent, primarily through the introduction by the federal government of specific cultural, trade and investment policies that would limit U.S. out-group influences."[51] Going one step further than Bashevkin, I would argue that this pan-Canadianism is but another, more politically correct term for what is fast becoming "English-Canadianism."[52]

The elements of this new nationality are already visible politically and include at the core an Anglo-Canadian ethnic identity present at the "creation" of the community and around which the founding myths of the nation and the State have been established and spread to include other groups and other mythologies.[53] This single core has replaced the dual "founding nations" core of the traditional pan-Canadian nationality—a concept that in any case never caught on outside of Quebec and whose mere mention was sufficient to undermine both the Meech Lake and the Charlottetown constitutional proposals, both of which symbolically acknowledged this dualism with their recognition of Quebec as a "distinct society."

Other features also serve to characterize this emerging sense of "English Canadians." Traditionally, the role of out-group was held exclusively by the United States, the acknowledged nemesis of pan-Canadian nationalism. The lack of enthusiasm on the part of the Québécois for sharing in this anti-American vision has not only served to undermine the pan-Canadian ideology; it has also added Quebec to the select number of out-groups against which English-Canadian nationalists are increasingly defining themselves.[54] Although the Québécois have yet to be informed of this fact, they are now part of the "out there" of English Canadians.

English-Canadian nationalism can also be defined by its cultural project, that of multiculturalism; its insistence on territorial identity; its commitment to certain political institutions, notably the courts; and its vision of the Charter of Rights, which sees the only acceptable process of constitutional change as one where all provinces are treated equally and where debates take place openly. One is struck at how rapidly and thoroughly an "official" belief system has succeeded in equipping itself with a number of "values" attaining "star status": equality, policy responsiveness, democracy, social solidarity.[55] Even the high esteem that many Americans have openly professed for the Canadian health system has elevated Canadian medicare to the status of a national icon.

NAFTA itself will have little direct effect on the political and sociocultural institutions of English Canada (with the possible exception of television and the various literary industries), but it will reinforce most of these elements. Paradoxically, this agreement will further accentuate the replacement of pan-Canadian nationalism with a more restricted English-Canadian one.

Although Québécois have paid little attention to this changing "imaginary" environment, they will be directly and profoundly affected by the change of outlook. Clearly, their condescending vision of English Canada will have to change. As suggested below, both versions of Quebec nationalism will soon be confronted with a more intransigent and less insecure English Canada.

For the pro-sovereignty nationalists, the implications will soon become more apparent, including:

- As revealed during the 1992 referendum campaign, there is a widespread belief in English Canada that even if the Québécois would democratically and explicitly support the sovereignty option, violence and a Lebanese or Yugoslav scenario would almost be a certainty. Having repeatedly rejected anything even approaching a military solution in the past, advocates of Quebec sovereignty are for the first time confronted with the possibility of a violent reaction on the part of English Canada, whose sense of impotence and general lack of national "emotion" can no longer be counted upon.[56]
- Because of the almost mystical dimension that the integrity of the Canadian territory assumes in this new English-Canadian nationalism,[57] any attempt by Quebec nationalists to "take away" or "break apart" the Canadian territory will be met by much hostility and will have to be accommodated by territorial concessions.[58]
- The FTA debate showed very clearly that the traditional Quebec view of English Canada as a community dominated by commercial interests and run on strict economic considerations is no longer based on reality (to the extent that

it ever was). For most English-Canadian nationalists, the fact that a free trade agreement with the United States can be shown to bring economic benefit to Canada bears little weight when compared to the immense and irreversible damage the agreement is thought to have already brought to the cultural and social fabric of the country. For those in Quebec who continue to support the federal option, the FTA also marked an important turning point, whose consequences for their own vision of Quebec and its place within the federal compact are no less important.

- The "bilingual-within-a-multicultural" vision so central to the new English-Canadian nationalism runs contrary to the Quebec nationalists' plan of a unilingual Quebec, where multiculturalism, far from constituting an official cultural program, is at best recognized as a step on the road to integration and eventual assimilation within the French and Québécois majority.
- The vision of a Canada composed of ten equal provinces with similar, if not identical, responsibilities has already caused the derailment of two constitutional agreements, Meech Lake and Charlottetown. It is therefore difficult to imagine what an eventual federalist solution to the Quebec malaise would resemble. This series of defeats, first at the hands of English-Canadian provincial governments, and then at the polls, has given the pro-sovereignty definition of the Quebec identity an unexpected legitimacy.
- The belief in the supremacy of the Charter of Rights and Freedoms and the belief in the preeminence of the Canadian Supreme Court are now essential components of the new English-Canadian nationalism. In Quebec, however, these institutions severely limit the maneuvering room of those who argue that the Canadian judicial order provides Quebec with ample room to affirm its own distinctiveness.
- The belief in a powerful and effective central government with major responsibilities on all important issues, and most specifically, those related to culture, economic development, and social welfare, has also been shown to be yet another litmus test for any attempt to reform the Canadian federal compact. The problems for those who favor a strong Quebec provincial state but within the overall Canadian statist system are evident.

In short, the public emergence of an English-Canadian Other has profoundly affected the strategic calculus of those in Quebec, sovereignist and federalist alike, who until then had been happy to argue the merits of their respective option, as well as the essential components of the Quebec identity, in strictly Quebec terms.

NAFTA *and La Différence*

One of the major points of contention between the two sides is the cavalier way in which Québécois have tended to brush off English-Canadian reservations about first the FTA and now NAFTA. As mentioned, this lack of concern has served to reinforce an English-Canadian sense of nationhood. But what impact has the free trade debate, to the extent that it constituted a real debate, had on Quebec society, and to what extent can we expect the Québécois to modify their national outlook in response to a perceived difference in their strategic environment?

It is fair to say that few Québécois have expressed any worry about the negative impact of the new free trade environment on the specifics of their culture and identity. Many English-Canadian observers call this attitude sheer naivete. How could Quebec resist further American penetration when a good case can be made that Canada as a whole and even Ontario have legitimate concerns about this possibility? Beyond the fact that most Québécois tend to view free trade as inevitable, and the American presence as meaning their own acceptance within the North American family, there are a number of structural reasons why Québécois have expressed little concern over the likely negative fallouts from free trade.

NAFTA, either in its strictly limited trade sense or in its potential for developing into a wider pan-American integrative movement, has been perceived by most Québécois as posing very little threat to any of the core elements of their national identity. This perception, and more specifically the willingness of the Québécois to act upon it by actively supporting free trade, has become an important point of divergence between cultural nationalists on both sides of the Canadian linguistic divide. To a large extent, it made the establishment of a pan-Canadian anti-NAFTA front an almost impossible task.

The recognition of this impossibility has had important consequences for English-Canadian cultural elites but little direct impact on their Quebec equivalents, who never really considered a pan-Canadian common cultural front a viable alternative. Although Québécois have been unwilling or simply unable to see it, the impact of their own pro-FTA and pro-NAFTA choices on English Canada will seriously affect, if only indirectly, their own strategic environment in the near future.

To some extent, the failure of many Canadian cultural elites to fully support the constitutional agreement doomed Meech Lake. Without their active support for the anti-Quebec stand of native leaders and without their refusal to dissociate themselves publicly from the anti-French campaign that spread across English Canada following the Bill 178 affair (the furor over the banning of English-language signs), it is unlikely that the Manitoban government would have felt free to reject Meech Lake.

Many observers have marveled at the widespread pro-American sentiment among both the Québécois in general and the Quebec intelligentsia. Indeed, the Quebec nationalist movement is one of the few around the world that has eschewed anti-American rhetoric. The indignation of English Canadians over an attitude that seems to say the United States can do no wrong is understandable. But it misses the point. Quebec has always seen itself as an original founder of the North American compact, along with the Americans and the Mexicans (although until recently, the latter did not occupy a major place in their vision). For the Québécois, North America has been from the beginning a "tale" of three experiments, that of New England, New France, and New Spain. For generations, this is how they have learned to see their North American environment. They see themselves as cofounder and certainly as co-owner of the original American dream.[59] English Canadians, for their part, are seen as second-class North Americans, principally because of their presumed incapacity to differentiate themselves from Americans and because they rejected the American Revolution (as did Quebec, to be sure).[60]

To some extent, this "American dream" has continued to divide Quebec and English Canada, with Quebec seeing English Canada as unqualified to share in the dream. The more North American integration becomes a definite possibility, even as a simple trade liberalization scheme, the more it will become a wedge pushing the two linguistic groups apart. In large segments of English Canada, North America means the United States and, as such, is perceived as a threat to both English-Canadian cultural integrity and any reasonable chance at pan-Canadian nationhood. In Quebec, it is the United States that is seen as North America and as the natural stage for the Quebec difference to express itself. One cannot think of a more zero-sum-game perspective.

Francophone or Québécois

In December 1992, a major Paris-based publisher brought out a "French Quebec Dictionary" that included hundreds of anglicized words used only in Quebec to accompany hundreds of other English words used only in France ("shopping," "sponsoring," etc.). The uproar was instantaneous. In the 1970's the battle lines were between the nationalist intelligentsia favoring a "truly" Quebec language and a more federal-minded group, partisans of a nonlocal French. In 1992 the outrage was on opposite grounds. The dictionary was criticized for its "bastardization" of the Quebec language and was seen by many as another attempt by unnamed conspirators to prevent Québécois from playing an important role in the Francophonie.

Curiously, the simple possession of a distinct language—and Québécois can certainly talk in ways that only they will understand—is no longer seen as an attribute of nationhood. True, the Francophonie has yet to become an important international forum, though it has survived twenty years of France-Canada, France-Quebec, and, naturally, Canada-Quebec bureaucratic battles. Nevertheless, it is certainly part of the NIO, and its very existence has modified the traditional parameters of Quebec's linguistic identity. In order to be able to participate fully in the Francophonie, the Québécois have had to forget about their traditional anti-French resentment and recognize the cultural preeminence of Paris.

The Rise of a Québécois Cosmopolitan Nationalism

The major challenge to Quebec identity comes not from the United States, Canada, or France, but from Quebec's position as a successful North American society. The question is a straightforward one: can Quebec serve as one of the "gates"—even if it is to be a "side gate"—through which newcomers to the continent can go in order to insert themselves successfully into the social, political, and cultural fabric of North America? In short, can you be a North American while still being a Québécois, or in more mundane terms, "Can one play good baseball in French?"

If Quebec fails in this task, it will probably not disappear, protected as it is by its critical and much-concentrated demographic and political mass, but it will be pushed further aside on the periphery of North America and eventually will become an ethnic Disneyland. This final peripheralization could be accompanied by substantial ethnic and linguistic tensions, for a sizable number of the "old-stock" Québécois would certainly refuse to accept their minority status and use immigrants and newcomers as easy targets for their resentment.

This question is not only important for Quebec; it also is of some relevance to the rest of the continent and to French culture as a whole. If there is to be a North American civilization—along the same lines as we speak of a European civilization—then it has to be able to express itself in languages and cultures other than English and to provide an outlook on the world that is not limited to the outlook of the United States. We already know that North America speaks Spanish. But what about French? With 1.7 million Americans now speaking French as their first language (an 8.3 percent increase between 1980 and 1990), French's role on the continent appears to be growing.[61]

The major roadblocks to North American integration and cooperation are not commercial, economic, or even political. They are social and cultural. Paradoxically, if Europe "suffers" from too much diversity—2,000 kinds of cheese in France alone, as de Gaulle would point out—then North America, especially Canada and the United States, suffers from too much homogeneity. If North America is to succeed in its claim to universality, it must learn to recognize its differences. Not all non-nation-state "national" groups are the same. To treat them in a similar way is bound to fail.

If Quebec is to succeed in this task, its identity will have to be redefined in ways that many Québécois will find hard to accept. Newcomers are providing Quebec with a much-needed demographic boost, but they are also bringing with them values, orientations, and political agendas that do not necessarily coincide with those of the majority. Can the Québécois national identity move from an ethnic definition of itself to a more civic one, where a common language and respect for minority rights serve as the ties of a new nationality?

For the last twenty years, Quebec has been trying to define an immigration model that is different from the melting-pot approach of the United States, the multicultural mosaic of Canada, and the strict assimilation vision of France. This has not been easy, and so far elements of all three models have found their way into the Quebec "intercultural approach."

There appears to be a consensus, at least among Quebec Francophones and on both sides of the great political divide, that the French language should be the core axis around which to structure the active integration of newcomers. Of the many elements at the core of Quebec identity, French is the only one with any staying power and apparent capability to serve as the common denominator.

In its role as the core element of Quebec identity, French benefits from a number of advantages, but it also has to labor under an equally large number of constraints. French, like Spanish, is not just another distinct language. It is both a universal one—at least one with universal pretensions—and one with a long tradition of incorporating different national traditions. Through their use of this language, Québécois have a direct and privileged access to the rest of the world and to a strong cultural center (France and Paris). The fact that French and not ethnicity (although ethnicity continues to have impact) or race is the core of Quebec identity makes that identity more permeable to outside influences and less rigid. One can learn and acquire a language; one cannot do so with race.

The strategic environment of the Québécois is now increasingly being taken over by North American considerations. Canada has become part of a larger picture and is no longer the single reference point against which Québécois define themselves and assess their options. This new strategic environment raises questions of vital importance for all the minority or small national groups that find themselves suddenly being incorporated in supranational structures without the benefit of sovereignty and are thus incapable of negotiating for themselves their entry into those new super-structures. In Europe and the Americas, numerous other groups find themselves in this uncomfortable situation. The European nation-building experience is littered with national groups that almost made it through. Considering that NIO institutions are not particularly congenial to new-comers, especially if they are of the split-up variety, such questions are not just academic. Aboriginal peoples, Mexican Americans, Latinos, Catalo-nians, Basques, Slovaks, and Walloons will have their identity and their self-development prospects seriously affected by NAFTA and Maastricht. It is not sufficient, and it is probably wrong, to proclaim, as many do, that regional integration spells the death of national sovereignty and thus con-stitutes the "best chance" ever for those minorities to free themselves from the tutelage of national authorities.

Quebec obviously has had, and is continuing to have, great difficulty in translating its social and cultural identity into political terms. Should Quebec become a politically "distinct society" as a province within Can-ada, or should it opt instead for the status of a nation-state within North America?

Cascadia: The New Binationalism of Western Canada and the U.S. Pacific Northwest

PAUL SCHELL AND JOHN HAMER

> The global economy follows its own logic and develops its
> own webs of interest which rarely duplicate the historical
> borders between nations. . . . It is this borderless world that
> will give participating economies the capacity for boundless
> prosperity.
> —Kenichi Ohmae, *The Borderless World*

We do not yet live in a borderless world. Nor is such a world likely anytime soon. Indeed, since Kenichi Ohmae's insightful book was published in 1990, the world actually has seen a proliferation of new borders—witness events in the former Soviet Union, Yugoslavia, and Czechoslovakia.

And yet in some parts of the world borders are clearly breaking down, or at least becoming more porous. One such place is the vibrant region that many have begun to call Cascadia—also sometimes referred to as the New Pacific, the North Pacific West, the Northeast Pacific Rim, Pacifica, or Ecotopia.

Depending on how the area is defined, it potentially encompasses Alaska, parts of the Yukon and Northwest Territories, British Columbia, Alberta, Washington, Oregon, Idaho, and Montana. At the core of the region, and the focal point of cooperative activity, is the populous corridor that runs from Vancouver through Seattle to Portland. Some have called this stretch of geography VanSeaPort or Portcouver—though these awkward monikers have captured the imagination of very few residents.

I

Regardless of the name game, there is no question that a significant phenomenon has begun to evolve in this remarkable region. Something magnetic is drawing the region together and a political and economic environment for cooperation is developing out of this new identity, which both local and national media have been quick to analyze and describe:

The Pacific Northwest and western Canada may come to be known as the economic "nation" of Cascadia if some enterprising United States and Canadian visionaries have their way—and that dream is slowly becoming a reality. *Christian Science Monitor*, July 20, 1992

More than anything, Cascadia is a reflection of a new attitude, optimism and internationalism that is manifesting itself in Alberta, British Columbia and the U.S. Pacific Northwest. *Toronto Globe and Mail*, Jan. 25, 1992

Cascadia? It may never be found on a map. At least not yet. But visionaries in the Northwest are nurturing a dream of "erasing" the borders among five Northwestern states and two Canadian provinces to create a new economic powerhouse. *Boston Globe*, May 31, 1992

Media attention, while sometimes exaggerated, accurately reflects the regional evolution. Many people believe it is indeed time to reassess the boundaries of the U.S. and Canadian Pacific Northwest, lines drawn when the Pacific Coast was newly discovered by Europeans. Revising them requires no changes in allegiance to Ottawa or Washington. The lines imposed over 100 years ago have simply been transcended by contemporary cultural and economic realities. Consider a few facts and figures about the region:

- Cascadia, defined as the states of Alaska, Idaho, Montana, Oregon, and Washington, and the provinces of Alberta and British Columbia, is physically larger than the European Community. It ranks as the world's tenth-largest economy in terms of annual gross domestic product—an estimated U.S. $250 billion based on the combined production of the five states and two provinces.[1]
- The combined population is more than 16 million people, based on the latest U.S. and Canadian census data, and the figure has grown more than 10 percent in the last decade. The Seattle-Vancouver corridor, the economic and cultural epicenter of the region, has a greater population (6 million) than either the Boston or Washington, D.C., metropolitan areas.
- The region employs more than 8 million people, and employment has increased by nearly 20 percent in the past decade. In 1991, a year that saw the U.S. workforce fall by 1 percent, Washington's and Oregon's workforces grew by 1 percent and Idaho's by 3 percent. Montana and Alaska also recorded increases.
- The Washington–British Columbia border is the busiest of any along the 2,500-mile U.S.-Canadian border, with more than 30 million crossings in 1990.
- Cascadia boasts four major ports (Portland, Tacoma, Seattle, and Vancouver) and is the closest region in North America to Japan, Hong Kong, and China. Overall, it has one of the top ten port systems in the world.

- Vancouver shipped the largest volume of any port on the west coast of the Americas in 1990, with 66.4 million metric tons. Seattle is one of the leading container ports on the west coast, shipping more than a million containers for each of the last six years.
- The region is home to the world's largest aerospace industry, led by the Boeing company, which is the No. 1 exporter in the United States and employs about 100,000 people in the Puget Sound area.
- The region is the third-largest computer software development center in North America; Washington and British Columbia alone are home to more than 1,000 software companies, including the world's largest—Microsoft. Based in Redmond, Washington, Microsoft is now the most valuable company in the United States in terms of total stock value. Nearly 60 percent of its sales are overseas. Cascadia also is a growing center for environmental technology and biotechnology firms, with a total of at least 1,000 companies.
- Seattle was ranked the "No. 1 City in the U.S. for Global Business" by *Fortune* magazine in November 1992, although some local residents are skeptical of the ranking, citing the region's sometimes antibusiness attitude and relatively high tax burden.
- Tourism will soon be the Pacific Northwest's largest employer and generator of foreign currency, accounting for regional revenues of nearly $20 billion annually. Nearly 100 million tourists visited the five states and two provinces in 1990, spending a total of more than $15 billion.

All this economic activity—transport, technology, and tourism—ties Cascadia together in a multitude of ways. But for many, this development and the ever-growing interdependence of the region are a mixed blessing. As the saying goes, everyone wants progress, but no one wants to change. Much like the three nations of North America, the three major cities of Cascadia bring with them differing strengths, styles, and histories.

Portland, the smallest and weakest economically, fears domination from its Cascadian neighbors to the north (and the California megalopolises to the south). Vancouver, the nervous suitor, shares the traditional Canadian concern of creeping Americanization. Seattle, the most confident of the three, is still reluctant to share with its partners on the Interstate 5 corridor. And the other cities of the region—such as Anchorage, Fairbanks, Edmonton, Calgary, Spokane, Missoula, and Eugene, to name a few—have their own sometimes skeptical views on what it might mean to be part of a Cascadia largely dominated by its three major cities.

In addition, there have long been friendly rivalries among the states in the region. Washington and Oregon, the two most populous, are probably the most competitive in terms of the foremost economic activities—trade, foreign investment, and tourism. Meanwhile, Idaho and Montana residents sometimes view the other Northwest states with a mixture of envy for their economic strength and cultural attractions and dismay over their traffic, pollution, crime, and congestion problems.

Indeed, as Douglas M. Brown and Earl H. Fry have pointed out, there is some danger of a decoupling process connected to uneven development, "in which economically lagging hinterland regions harbor resentment against affluent international city sophisticates."[2] Panayotis Soldatos of the University of Montreal concurs: "This fear of imbalance in the development of cities and regions is reinforced by the fact that the high-tech and service economy as well as demographic concentration in cities and urban zones could create a risk of new 'oligopolistic' situations. The international development of cities could leave their hinterlands and other regions of the country lagging behind."[3] These concerns have also found graphic expression locally. "At worst, 'Cascadia' may be a conceptual Trojan horse," suggests a writer for Vancouver's *City Magazine*, "a construct which may facilitate the subordination and marginalization of Vancouver within a larger regional entity dominated by Seattle."[4]

On the other hand, the growing cross-border cooperation in Cascadia can be compared with a similar evolution in the eastern Canadian provinces and the New England states, which for about twenty years have undertaken various collaborative efforts under the organizational auspices of the NEG/ECP (New England Governors and Eastern Canadian Premiers). What began as annual conferences, conceived largely as informal exchanges, gradually gained considerable substance, contributing to important formal agreements such as the export of hydroelectricity from Quebec through the New England Energy Pool.

Martin Lubin of the State University of New York, a longtime student of the NEG/ECP, observes of this development:

Since the very first annual conference in 1973, the format has proven to be flexible enough to allow for a gradual building of a shared sense of common regional purposes. State and provincial political and bureaucratic elites have recognized the need for cooperation among themselves through a series of modest voluntary steps rather than premature dramatic or inflexibly binding gestures. The end result has been a highly useful and adaptable multilateral consultative mechanism to identify emergent transfrontier regional issues of mutual concern and to generate and share data relevant to the resolution of these issues.[5]

There is no question that most of us who live in Cascadia, even more so perhaps than our eastern seaboard counterparts, have certain qualities and attitudes in common. It is more than a matter of simply sharing a temperate climate. We have a love of the outdoors and a relatively high level of concern for the environment. The Native American regard for nature in Cascadia is a clearer influence than in the East. We also share an openness to Asian, as well as European, influences, perhaps as the result of lying equidistant between the two continents and having had a long history of exchange dating back to the early silk trade from China.

Indeed, immigration—particularly of Asians, who have flooded into Vancouver, and to a lesser extent, Seattle and Portland in recent years—has become a major influence in Cascadia. While somewhat controversial, the effects of immigration have been mostly positive because the vast majority of immigrants are highly motivated, hard-working, and determined to succeed. Much of this immigration is in fact by invitation. Vancouver, for example, has become "Hongcouver," as some call it, in part because British Columbia set out to attract immigrants from Hong Kong by offering tax incentives to those who were wealthy enough to start businesses and provide jobs.

Our binational regional economy is based on a combination of diverse natural resources, aerospace technology, shipping, tourism, computer software, and biotechnology. If our region were a nation, we would have a significantly positive balance of trade. Even our traditional natural resource and agricultural industries—forest products, fruit, prepared foods—are growing increasingly sophisticated, adding value by producing finished goods ready for international markets.

Partly because of this diversity, the growing regional identity that is under way in Cascadia doesn't follow any grand plan. It is a grass-roots revolution, the product of a changing world. We're not talking about a political union, but rather about a strategic alliance for competing in the new global economy.

The real revolution, it is clear, has occurred in just the past few years. As recently as the late 1980's, Gerard F. Rutan of Western Washington University in Bellingham described the relationship between Washington state and British Columbia as "mundane and dull." Yet he saw potential for progress in small steps and practical measures:

If the officials of both jurisdictions [British Columbia and Washington state] can continue their personal, problem-focused interactions and bring their efforts to bear on the mundane problems, the relationship will continue and will grow, if slowly. This is the reality of cross-border relationships in the region. It is a reality that is not exciting, nor even terribly interesting. There is little, very little, drama. But such is the stuff of microdiplomacy in the rain and fog of the Pacific Northwest.[6]

A great deal has changed in the region since Rutan wrote those words. The relationship has grown, the reality has become more exciting, and some might say there is even drama to be found.

II

To gain some perspective on Cascadia's present and future, it is helpful to reflect on the region's past. Ethnically, the early history of the settlements on both sides of the vague international line was similar, but politically, they developed apart. As Eileen V. Quigley, former editor of the *New Pacific*, wrote in the first (Fall 1989) issue of that quarterly journal:

The area was once tied together by a common, distinctive Native American culture. Washington was later ruled by the British Hudson Bay Company as part of British Columbia, and the region enjoyed dual American and British sovereignty for several decades in the 19th century. Though separate nations today, Canada and the United States are "children with a common mother," as the Peace Arch at the U.S.-Canada border proclaims. The name *British* Columbia was, in fact, necessary to distinguish one part of Columbia from the other. And the Oregon Territory once included both Washington and Oregon.[7]

Robert Saltvig, a Pacific Northwest historian at Seattle University, has emphasized the region's natural logic, quite obvious to early settlers: "The natural resources were similar, the maritime industries, the reality of mineral deposits in the mountains, the possibility of agriculture in the interior. The natural boundaries that form the region don't divide it the way the political boundaries do."[8]

Historically, the Rocky Mountains acted as a barrier to West-East communications and contributed to the development of a common culture and commercial base for Oregon, Washington, and British Columbia. One of the most often-noted shared characteristics is a strong environmental consciousness. This has always been prevalent; even in a region that exploited natural resources for their economic benefit, most people still deeply appreciated the natural beauty that surrounded them and supported the protection of large areas in parks and wilderness.

This theme was explored by Ernest Callenbach in his 1975 novel *Ecotopia*—a book that is probably cited by many more people than have actually read it. In the novel, Washington, Oregon, and northern California secede from the United States, create an independent country called Ecotopia, and seal off their borders. They reject the pollution, waste, militarism, materialism, sexism, racism, and other corrupt values of their former mother country, and form what they see as an "ecological utopia."

The name Ecotopia was borrowed by Joel Garreau in his 1981 book, *The Nine Nations of North America*, although he substantially modified its definition. Garreau's Ecotopia began in central California, just north of Los Angeles's most distant suburbs, and embraced the coastal (but not inland) portions of Oregon, Washington, British Columbia, and southeast Alaska.

Yet another environmentally based vision of Cascadia is that of David McCloskey, a Seattle University professor of sociology and human ecology. A member of an "ecocultural" movement that has argued for at least a decade that the political lines carving Cascadia into states and provinces do not reflect its ecological and cultural realities, McCloskey would have the borders of this "great green land on the northeast Pacific Rim" run from Yakutat Bay in southeast Alaska to Cape Mendocino on the California coast, inland to Yellowstone National Park in Wyoming, and along the continental divide on the crest of the U.S. and Canadian Rockies.[9]

(McCloskey, who accepts the name Cascadia, notes that the reference is not to the mountain range, but to the waterfalls along the Columbia River. When the Scottish botanist David Douglas, after whom the Douglas fir is named, stood along that river, he proclaimed Mounts Hood, Adams, and St. Helens the "mountains by the cascades.")

One successful example of environmental cooperation came in the early 1980's, when controversy arose over a proposal by Seattle City Light, a publicly owned electric utility company, to raise Ross Dam on the Skagit River, a project that would have flooded popular recreation areas north of the border in British Columbia. After months of negotiations coordinated by the U.S-Canada International Joint Commission (which had earlier produced the Great Lakes Water Quality Agreement to clean up pollution in Lake Erie and Lake Ontario), an agreement was reached between Seattle and B.C. officials. They agreed to an 80-year electricity sales pact that would send low-cost power from B.C. Hydro into the Seattle system, as long as City Light did not raise Ross Dam.

Fortunately for the citizens of Cascadia, there is a long history of regional cooperation in the management of hydroelectric resources, with British Columbia and the Bonneville Power Administration jointly running the vast power network that supplies the Northwest. Similar cooperation is growing in other domains. For example, when the central Puget Sound region was hit by a devastating windstorm in January 1993, B.C. and Oregon utility crews were among the neighbors to come to the assistance of the overworked utility companies around Seattle.

Another cooperative effort is now under way to link North Cascades

National Park in Washington with the protected Skagit Valley Recreation Area in British Columbia. Because heavy logging on the Canadian side of the border has threatened water and wildlife resources, environmentalists on both sides of the border are pushing a new park modeled after Waterton-Glacier International Peace Park in Alberta and Montana. "It's a great idea, and I would like to be remembered as a promoter and advocate of it," John Cashore, British Columbia's Environment Minister, told the *Seattle Post-Intelligencer* in 1992.[10]

On a less positive note, the environmental ties of Cascadia are currently being severely strained by an increasingly controversial issue: the city of Victoria's dumping of more than 15 million gallons a day of raw sewage into the Strait of Juan de Fuca, which divides Canada and Washington state. The practice has gone on for many years, with relatively little objection. It came under a new spotlight in November 1992, when Victoria voters, by a 57 percent vote, turned down a proposal to build a new sewage treatment plant. A primary-treatment plant would have cost individual households about $460 a year, and secondary treatment $675. Leaders of Victoria's Capital Regional District, which regulates the matter, argued that the strait's strong currents and deep waters dilute the sewage, so that it causes virtually no environmental damage. But the outcry from the United States was so great that the district's board in January 1993 announced that it would submit a plan for a secondary-treatment plant within a year—although the plant would not be built for about 25 years unless new scientific evidence from an increased monitoring program proved that it was needed.

That wasn't good enough for many U.S. officials. Slade Gorton, Washington's Republican senior senator, wrote a letter to B.C. Environment Minister John Cashore saying that a 25-year timetable was not an acceptable solution: "We must face the reality that a quarter century of pouring raw sewage and pollutants from a rapidly growing city into our shared waters is harmful."[11] And Seattle Mayor Norm Rice, speaking at a conference in Vancouver, said: "I can tell you that this is one issue that will not go away. Victoria's discharge of raw sewage into the Strait will continue to be a major irritant to regional cooperation, until steps are taken to end the dumping. It's just that simple."[12] Perhaps more effective than any politicians' statements, however, is the threat of a boycott of Victoria by convention organizers and tourists. After the November 1992 vote, the Washington Society of Association Executives canceled its 1995 convention scheduled for Victoria's Empress Hotel. Tourism Victoria estimated that the 150-member group's cancellation would cost the city about

$85,000.[13] The issue is likely to remain a sore point for some time, although it is unlikely to derail continuing efforts toward greater cooperation throughout Cascadia.

III

To tap the full potential this region holds, a regional agenda aimed at breaking down barriers, efficiently using regional resources, and promoting a regional identity is clearly in order. Similar efforts have met with success in Europe and Asia, and a comprehensive plan for regional cohesiveness is a potential model for comparable efforts elsewhere in North America. Encouragingly, much progress has been made since such an agenda was proposed by co-author Paul Schell a few years ago.[14] What follows is a recapitulation of this original agenda for Cascadia, with updates on recent developments and analysis of the current state of affairs.

Bulldoze the Checkpoints. Between 1980 and 1990 the volume of transborder traffic at Blaine, Washington, more than doubled, from 5 million crossings to 11 million a year—and the figure is predicted to reach 28 million annually by the year 2000. It is the busiest crossing point of all along the 2,500-mile border between the United States and Canada. Delays of an hour or more are not uncommon during the busy summer months, and truckers sometimes complain of delays of several hours.

A promising step toward improvement was taken in 1991, with the creation of the Peace Arch Crossing Entry (PACE) decal program. After a police background check of any criminal history, customs, or immigration violations, frequent travelers are issued PACE decals by their respective governments, allowing them to bypass regular inspection lanes during specified hours. By the fall of 1992, Canadian officials had approved 27,500 decals, and U.S. officials 19,000. This program should be more widely promoted and expanded, eventually leading to even more open borders between the United States and Canada.

Ideally, a continental North American clearance someday would make one-stop passport control available for overseas guests, and within the continent would make access between British Columbia and Washington, for example, as easy as access between Oregon and Washington today.

Planes, Trains and Automobiles—Think Intermodally. Cascadia should try to expand transportation alternatives that link the region. Our main North-South interstate freeway (Interstate 5) is jammed around all the region's urban areas. An explosion of commuter aircraft has used up much of the capacity at Seattle-Tacoma Airport. About 40 percent of the operations there are flights to Portland, Vancouver, and Spokane.

The time has come to seriously consider high-speed rail service to link our urban cores. Such a system would initially include stops at the Seattle and Vancouver airports. Seattle would gain access to Vancouver's international air routes, while Vancouver would gain access to Seattle's domestic routes. The system could be expanded to Portland and its airport. High-speed rail service would provide a convenient and practical alternative to intraregional flying.

Amtrak's service in the northeastern United States garners a larger market share than any airline. There is no reason it would not work in Cascadia as well. Indeed, there should be basic improvements to Amtrak service within Cascadia, and continuing support for the concept of "intermodalism," which can help break down the barriers between travel by car, bus, train, ferry, and airplane. The U.S. Department of Transportation has provided $150,000 to Seattle to study the possible renovation of the King Street Station, just south of downtown, as a regional intermodal transfer terminal.

The Department of Transportation in October 1992 also approved the designation of a new high-speed passenger-rail corridor from the U.S.-Canadian border to Eugene, Oregon, south of Portland. This increases the prospect of more federal funding for high-speed rail service linking Cascadia's major cities. Initially, $500,000 in federal funds was allocated to Washington and Oregon under the Intermodal Surface Transportation Efficiency Act (ISTEA). The federal government plans to spend as much as $30 million on five such corridors around the United States in the next several years.

Of course, that's only a small amount toward what could be a very expensive project. The state of Washington's High Speed Ground Transportation Steering Committee has estimated that building a 335-mile system to connect Portland and Vancouver by French- or Japanese-style "bullet" trains capable of speeds of 150 to 200 miles an hour could cost $9–$12 billion. A high-tech conventional train on existing tracks that would travel at 80–150 m.p.h. would be less expensive and perhaps more feasible.

Double Your Markets. Open borders and an improved transportation system would allow Cascadia to double its market. Seattle and Vancouver law firms, accounting firms, advertising firms, and banks are now operating or considering having offices in both cities. Vancouver viewers contribute more than 40 percent of the funds for KCTS-TV, the Seattle-based public television station.

A survey in the spring of 1992 found that 70 percent of Seattle-area residents favored the notion of sharing their baseball team, the Mariners, with Vancouver and Portland to increase its revenue base. The Mariners hired Paul Isaki, former director of Washington state's Department of Trade and Economic Development (DTED), to help build a regional advertising base for the team's cable broadcasting efforts in Vancouver, Portland, and Spokane.

Think Globally, Act Regionally. Washington and British Columbia already successfully market the "Two-Nation Vacation." Organized by the Seattle–King County Convention and Visitors Bureau, the Washington State Tourism Division, the Port of Seattle, and Canadian tourism officials, the program promotes the idea of visiting two countries in a single trip and has already been a great success with international tourists from Europe and Asia.

But we're also in an ideal spot to broker international business between Asians, North Americans, and Europeans. Cascadia is at the epicenter of the global economy, equidistant between Pacific Asia and the European Community. The relationships we develop overseas will have far more to do with our future than those we may have with Chicago, New York, and Los Angeles—or with Montreal, Toronto, and Ottawa. A joint effort might be especially effective in Europe, where it would appeal to supporters of the European Community as a smaller version of their own experiment in multinational cooperation.

One project at the Seattle-based Discovery Institute we are involved in is looking at new ways to promote tourism in the region as a whole. Some of the programs under consideration are novel, to say the least. For example, we are examining the possibility of staging trade and tourism exhibits at fairs in Europe and Asia as "Cascadia," not just as parts of our respective countries. We also are considering how provincial and state trade and promotion budgets for overseas use might be pooled in some way that would allow the whole region to operate joint offices, say, in Tokyo, or Paris—a veritable "Cascadian Embassy." (We're not serious about secession, but we don't mind pulling a few tails in Washington and Ottawa!)

Excellence in Education. A skilled, well-trained workforce is increasingly the key to global economic competitiveness. As with business and culture, the mission of higher education should be redefined in line with the region's emerging character. The world is changing quickly; the coursework and training offered by our schools must keep up.

Our approach thus far has been to throw minimal amounts of money at education without a plan. We need to decide what it is we want to teach.

We need to make sure our schools offer the latest in new technologies. We need to reassert that teaching is an honored profession, both through funding and through community support.

There are ways to cut costs and improve education. The strengths of colleges in British Columbia, Washington, Oregon, and Idaho should be coordinated to achieve centers of excellence, magnet schools of higher education that attract students from throughout Cascadia. Out-of-state tuition requirements could be eliminated for students within the region, and overlapping programs could be eliminated. A student from Victoria might study forestry at Oregon State; a student from Medford might study engineering at the University of British Columbia. The result of such a magnet school program would be less duplication, new strengths in specialized fields, and affordable quality education for the region's next generation.

As Michael Clark, a British Columbia trade official, once put it: "Suddenly, instead of two or three world-class universities you've got six or eight. Then San Francisco has nothing on us. It changes your thinking."[15]

Our children will be competing with children in Osaka, Rotterdam, and Seoul for jobs. If we are to give them the chance to be successful in the global economy, we must prepare them properly. There is no excuse for this region, one of the most progressive and internationally minded, not to have a public education system second to none.

Speak the Language. Canada is a bilingual nation. Washington is home to a substantial Spanish-speaking population, and its Asian population grew by 80 percent in the decade of the 1980's. Fluency in other languages is rapidly becoming a necessity to do business not just internationally, but also at home.

The fact that our future is tied to the global marketplace means that our best customers—and toughest competitors—may well speak another language. Studying Asian or European languages should be possible—if not required—starting in kindergarten.

Progress is being made. Washington has more high schools that teach Japanese than any other state, including California and Hawaii. This is the result not of state policy, but of local demand. Our citizens already know that a knowledge of Asian and other languages will be key to their futures.

Still, there is considerable room for improvement. While Washington ranks No. 1 in the United States in value of per capita trade, it is about average in the percentage of students who study foreign languages. Statewide, only about 40 percent of high school students study a language, and then for an average of only two years—not enough to gain fluency.

Reinforce a Regional Culture. Arts and culture are the great binders of people. Each of our urban cities is rich in symphony, ballet, jazz, theater, fine arts, and native crafts. All too often, these enterprises are heavily in debt. By sharing our cultural treasures with one another, we can enrich all our citizens and provide a strong base of support.

There have been some exchange performances by Seattle, Portland, and Vancouver symphonies, ballets, and operas, and more should be encouraged. A visual arts show that would rotate among the three cities is an excellent idea worth pursuing; a Seattle ArtFair is now in its second year, with considerable participation by Canadian artists.

The region is also fertile ground for young athletes. A disproportionate share of the National Football League's quarterbacks have prepped or attended college in Washington, Oregon, and Idaho. Regional high school championships rotating among the three states and the province of British Columbia would reinforce a regional identity and showcase the talents of Cascadia's athletes.

Cooperation, Not Competition. The economic engines within Cascadia concentrate their efforts on intraregional competition, rather than cooperation. The end result is diminished profits and increased costs for residents of the region. One notable example is our ports. The ports of Seattle and Tacoma, second only to the ports of southern California in market share in the nation, regularly find themselves in bidding wars to lure customers. They now charge shipping lines roughly half of what the ports of Los Angeles and Long Beach charge, despite projections that volumes will almost double over the next twenty years. Cooperative pricing of port facilities that sit 30 miles from each other, as allowed by federal law, would provide taxpayers the rate of return they deserve when investing in port infrastructure.

Though there will no doubt always be competition between our ports, each of which is a key gateway for U.S. exports and Asian imports, there is a growing sense that they could all benefit by a more coordinated marketing approach. The ports of Seattle, Everett, and Bellingham reached a partnership agreement to share resources and expertise and market themselves internationally. The ports of Seattle and Tacoma are helping to finance the Washington State/Ports Office in Paris. A handsome brochure markets the "Gateway Ports of Puget Sound." But broader cooperation among the major ports of Cascadia has yet to develop. As Patrick Reid, chairman of the Vancouver Port Corporation, said not long ago: "I would hope there are things we can cooperate on, but right now I'm more preoccupied with competing."[16]

Form an Effective Regional Council. Though the movement for a regional identity has risen from the ground up, much progress has been made toward formalizing the political relationship. Many of the steps needed are steadily gaining the support of the tangle of public bodies that govern the region. During Expo '86 in Vancouver, for example, Washington state government and business officials began a series of meetings with their Canadian counterparts to discuss common interests. This led to a formal agreement between the state and the province, and the creation of a fourteen-member bilateral committee. Two new agreements were signed after the U.S.-Canadian Free Trade Agreement took effect on January 1, 1989, to seal what was now officially called the Pacific Northwest Economic Partnership (PNEP). By these agreements, the state and the province committed themselves to cooperation in areas of mutual economic benefit, especially trade, investment, and tourism. Five industries—biotechnology, aquaculture, fashion, marine instruments, and aerospace—were identified for cooperative efforts. Software, information sharing, and environmental engineering technology were added later.

In contrast to the Partnership, which was primarily an executive branch initiative, the much broader-based Pacific NorthWest Economic Region (PNWER), officially established in 1991, has been led by legislative officials. It now has a 28-member delegate council and a seven-member executive committee representing Alaska, Idaho, Montana, Oregon, Washington, Alberta, and British Columbia. It too has made great progress in a very short time.

PNWER's purpose is to bring the five states and two provinces together as a single economic region to increase their competitiveness in international and domestic markets. It encourages legislators in the states and provinces to collaborate in such areas as environmental solutions, forest products, telecommunications linkages, workforce training, tourism marketing, and recycling technology.

The legislative bodies have already passed a number of identical bills that make trade and cooperation much easier. PNWER operates with staff assistance from the Northwest Policy Center at the University of Washington. Its key founder and current president is Alan Bluechel, a Washington state senator who was born in Edmonton, Alberta, and educated at the University of British Columbia. The recent (1993) appointment of Roger Bull, former Canadian consul in Seattle, as executive director of PNWER is another promising step.

There have been some other major cross-border initiatives. For example, an Environmental Cooperation Agreement between Washington and British Columbia was signed by Governor Booth Gardner and Premier Mike Harcourt in May 1992. And in September 1993, Governor Mike Lowry (Gardner's successor) convened an international conference of representatives from the Georgia Basin, Puget Sound, and Willamette Valley regions to explore ways to establish sustainable urban development across municipal, provincial, and national boundaries and jurisdictions.

The most promising recent development has been the emergence under the auspices of Discovery Institute's Cascadia Project of a Cascadia Corridor Task Force. Composed of federal, state-provincial, and local government officials under the initial chairmanship of Seattle Mayor Norm Rice, the Task Force is charged with devising a long-term strategic plan for sustainable development in the region, focusing on environmental issues and the future of "the Four T's"—transportation, trade, tourism, and technology—along the Interstate 5 corridor from Vancouver to Eugene. Though barely a year old at this writing—the Task Force emerged from legislation passed by Congress in 1992 under the cosponsorship of then Rep. John Miller (R, Wash.) and Rep. Ron Wyden (D, Ore.)—the binational group has already begun work on a plan to eliminate border crossing barriers and fees.

This group is strongly supported by the Cascadia Business Advisory Council, which represents the leading corporations in the corridor. A joint Task Force–Council dinner was held in Portland in December 1993, and others are to follow. "The Vancouver to Eugene corridor is increasingly functioning as an economic and environmental region," said Miller, who now chairs Discovery Institute's Cascadia Project; he hopes the Task Force will evolve into the formal binational Cascadia Corridor Commission originally envisioned by Congress.[17]

An encouraging development in the private sector has emerged in parallel with these government initiatives, namely, the creation, in 1990, of the Pacific Corridor Enterprise Council (PACE) by a group of regional companies eager to find ways to lower barriers to cross-border trade and commerce in the light of the FTA. PACE is a nonprofit group dedicated to helping entrepreneurs become aware of the opportunities in the regional market and learn how to be globally competitive. It works cooperatively with the region's chambers of commerce, boards of trade, universities, and government trade-support organizations. PACE hopes to accomplish its goals within a few years and, indeed, has a "sunset" clause in its charter that will end its existence on January 1, 1995, unless its members decide otherwise.

Cascadia is responding to the same forces that Martin Lubin describes for New England and Eastern Canada:

In tandem with the FTA, globalization has significantly influenced the formation and evolution of this hands-across-the-frontier strategic alliance for limited purposes. The great amount of time, resources, and commitment that cohabiting adjacent states and provinces must mobilize to adequately cope with the consequences of globalization underlines the need for loose cross-border mechanisms to enable the semisovereign member governments to dialogue and cooperate with one another for limited purposes. . . . The volume and diversity of transborder flows between the two countries as a whole continues to increase, the issues such as energy-environment trade-offs grow more complex, and the capacity of central governments to unilaterally manage these relationships shrinks.[18]

All of the groups in Western Canada and the Pacific Northwest have their strengths, but eventually they may have to combine their efforts to become a truly effective regional council for Cascadia.

IV

The vision outlined here contains few startling new concepts. It is not designed to alter the course of the region, or make it what it is not. Residents of Cascadia have no desire to emulate Los Angeles, New York, London, or Tokyo. Instead, the impetus behind the Cascadia movement is intended to make the most of the people, the culture, the natural gifts, and the geographic good fortune the region has been blessed with.

Still, the path that we are following reflects the unique character of our people. It is the people, as individuals, as businesses, and collectively as institutions, that are important: when they act, governments follow. A vision that captures the attention of a thousand people can, with energy and devotion, soon reach tens or hundreds of thousands more. At that stage, things begin to happen.

Cascadia is organizing itself around what will be the new realities of the next century—open borders, free trade, regional cooperation, and the instant transfer of information, money, and technology. The nineteenth- and twentieth-century realities of the nation-state, with guarded borders and nationalistic traditions, are giving way.

Cascadia can be differentiated from, say, Quebec, which is responding to the model of past centuries, because this region is moving toward a new, twenty-first-century model. That model will not mean a rejection of U.S. or Canadian sovereignty, laws, or traditions. But it will almost certainly mean a different role for the nation-state, one in which the State will be responsible for national defense, health care, legal systems, and other matters of broad concern, while various regions attend to their own international trade, economic development, and environmental protection.

Two countries, five states, two provinces, three metropolises, several mid-sized cities—but one region. The advantages of acting cooperatively are overcoming the past competition throughout Cascadia. It is a dynamic part of North America, ready to take its place in the new global culture and to compete in the new world economy.

The Gulf of Mexico: North America's Maritime Frontier

RICHARD KIY

For nearly 500 years the economic livelihood of the Gulf of Mexico region has been largely predicated on its strategic location as a center for foreign trade and its wealth of natural resources. Over the last five centuries, the Spanish, French, Dutch, British, and Americans have all sought to claim the riches of the Gulf, commonly referred to in this country as America's Mediterranean.

Today, nearly half of all U.S. import-export tonnage passes through Gulf waters. Four of the ten busiest U.S. ports are in the Gulf of Mexico. The United States also relies on the Gulf for much of its oil and natural gas. Additionally, the Gulf and its coastal areas are rich fishing grounds, accounting for nearly 40 percent of the total U.S. commercial landings. On top of all this, the Gulf reaps billions of tourist dollars.

With the passage of NAFTA, the Gulf region's economic importance is expected to grow, propelled by a broad expansion of trade between Mexico and the U.S. Gulf states of Texas, Louisiana, Mississippi, Alabama, and Florida. But as the most environmentally sensitive trade agreement ever negotiated, NAFTA will also impose new pressures on Gulf industries in Mexico and the United States to become more environmentally responsible. The reason is simple. Despite the Gulf of Mexico's strategic importance, its future economic sustainability has become clouded by an array of environmental problems; even now, urban and agricultural runoff, sewage and hazardous waste discharges, marine debris, and oil spills threaten its fertile wetlands and endanger a variety of species.

Because of the unique hydrographical characteristics of the Gulf's "Loop Current," no one country can effectively address these environmental problems alone—ultimately, their solution rests on joint cooperation and action on the part of the United States, Mexico, and ultimately Cuba and other Caribbean nations. Canada has an interest in the sustainability of the Gulf, too, since many of its migratory birds, including some endangered and threatened species, make their way to the Gulf of Mexico's estuaries during the winter. Moreover, Canadian waters affect the health of the Gulf, contributing via streams and tributaries to the Mississippi River's flow. Accordingly, the countries that have a stake in the future of the Gulf of Mexico can no longer afford to view questions of sustainable development in isolation. Ultimately, the future economic vitality of the Gulf depends on reconciling the region's desire for expanded trade and commerce with the need for regional cooperation in environmental protection and natural resource management. Fortunately, there are signs that national and state governments, public and private enterprises, and nongovernmental organizations are beginning to join forces in ways that will improve the Gulf's chances of evolving into a region of balanced interdependence.

The Gulf Environment

To fully grasp the complexity of the trade-environmental dilemma facing the Gulf of Mexico, an understanding of the region's unique geological, climatic, and hydrographical features is necessary.

Stretching 2,028 miles along the southern coast of the North American continent, the Gulf is surrounded almost completely by Mexico, Cuba, and the United States. There are just two gaps in what would otherwise be a solid ring of land around the Gulf—the Straits of Florida between Florida and Cuba, and the Yucatan Channel between Mexico and Cuba. Among major marine areas, only the Mediterranean Sea is more landlocked.

Measuring 600,000 square miles in total area, the Gulf of Mexico is divided into five distinctly different areas: a submerged shallow and intertidal area (about 38 percent of the total); a broad continental shelf (22 percent); steep escarpments from the shelves; three major submarine canyons (22 percent); and two large abyssal plains, the Florida Plain and the Sigsbee Plain (20 percent). At 12,425 feet below the surface, the Sigbee Deep is the deepest point.[1] Other notable features are a series of undersea salt domes (where vast deposits of petroleum, sulfur, gypsum, and, of course, salt can be found) and the Mississippi Fan, an alluvial, subsea continuation of the Mississippi River delta spreading out over the continental shelf and down the continental slope to the deeps.

The Mississippi is only the largest of nine river systems that deposit sediments and surface water into the Gulf. In addition to these—the Missouri, Ohio, Arkansas, Platte, Red, Rio Grande, Tombigbee-Alabama, and Colorado-Brazos-Trinity—it is fed by a series of smaller rivers that drain the plains and mountains of the Mexican interior.[2] All together, the Gulf receives the surface waters and runoff of 30 U.S. states and four other countries: Canada, Mexico, Cuba, and Guatemala.

One of the most dominant features of the Gulf of Mexico is the Loop Current. The parent of the Gulf Stream, the oceanic current that brings warm Gulf water up along the eastern seaboard of the United States and Canada and across the Atlantic to the British Isles, the Loop Current enters the Gulf through the Yucatan Channel, traces an arc that wanders as far north as the continental shelf off of Mississippi and Alabama, and exits through the Straits of Florida. It is roughly 20 miles wide and is exceedingly swift, carrying as much as a billion cubic feet of water a second.[3]

The Loop Current's circular nature binds the over 50 million people of the greater Gulf region in a unique way: this powerful current has been known to funnel marine debris and land-based sources of pollution from as far away as Central America and the Caribbean to their shores. In September 1993 alone over 198 tons of marine debris was removed from South Padre Island's 183-mile stretch of beach, including tagged radioactive material, medical waste, a refrigerator, a sofa bed, and a five-pound bag of cocaine. As the state's land commissioner, Gary Mauro, remarked, "Just about anything dumped in the Gulf of Mexico, from Florida to the Yucatan, can wind up on Texas beaches. The peculiar nature of the currents brings all kinds of garbage here."[4]

The Loop Current is as good an illustration as any of the need to view the Gulf of Mexico as a single ecosystem transcending political boundaries. Yet the region's rich natural resources have been a source of rivalry and conflict between nations for much of the last five centuries, creating one of the most complex and still-disputed borders on the North American continent.

The Spanish, first on the scene in the early sixteenth century, were soon challenged by their French and English mercantile rivals. In 1682 the French explorer Robert Cavelier, descending the Mississippi River and discovering the Gulf, claimed all the land drained by the river and its tributaries for France. With that claim, France effectively at once connected Canada to the Caribbean, providing a buffer against East Coast British imperialism, and split Spanish Florida from Spanish Mexico.[5] Later, through the Louisiana Purchase, Thomas Jefferson was able to secure this budding trade route for the United States. But the matter was far from settled. In fact, in one way or another, regional conflicts over the Gulf's resources are with us still.

Such conflicts have, in part, been minimized by international conventions and treaties. The most important is the United Nations Conference on the Law of the Sea (UNCLOS), which provides for a twelve-mile coastal sovereignty zone, a 200-mile offshore economic zone, encouragement to limit offshore pollution, regulation of deep-sea mining, and the right of marine vessels to free and unimpeded passage through straits under the control of individual countries. The UNCLOS, when finally concluded in 1982, after years of negotiation, was passed by an overwhelming vote of 130-4 (with 17 nations abstaining).[6] Among the Gulf Coast nations, only Mexico and Cuba endorsed the treaty. Their neighbor, the United States, worried about losing access to deep-sea mineral excavation rights, was one of the four nations to vote against it.

Subsequently, on March 10, 1983, President Ronald Reagan moved to protect U.S. mineral rights by establishing a 200-mile Exclusive Economic Zone (EEZ) around the continental United States.[7] The United States earlier, in 1976, under the Magnuson Fisheries Conservation and Management Act, had claimed jurisdiction over fisheries to 200 miles offshore, the limit sanctioned by the UNCLOS.[8]

The Gulf has a maximum width of approximately 1,000 miles east-west and an average width of just over 500 miles north-south. The UNCLOS and the U.S. EEZ establish direct jurisdictional claims by the United States, Mexico, and Cuba to 95 percent of the Gulf's harvestable living resources, 98 percent of its petroleum resources, and large amounts of its mineral wealth. But within this defined 200-mile economic zone—most of which is directly controlled by the United States by virtue of its 1,630-mile coastline stretching from south Texas to the tip of Florida—conflicts still arise. One of the latest occurred in July 1993, when a Mexican Navy patrol boat stopped and detained three American shrimp vessels off the south Texas coast until the U.S. Coast Guard informed the Mexicans that their boat had strayed ten miles into U.S. territory.[9]

A yet unresolved question involves mineral and petroleum rights in the international waters of the Sigsbee Plain. Under the UNCLOS, such resources are the common heritage of mankind and may be exploited only in accordance with the convention. Specifically, articles 136 and 137 indicate that "no state may claim, exercise sovereign rights over or appropriate any part of the deep seabed or its resources," and Annex III, which sets forth basic conditions for exploring and exploiting the deep seabed, provides that "only those applicants who are controlled by states parties to the UNCLOS or by their citizens may apply for a license to explore and exploit the deep seabeds."[10] In the case of the Gulf, the only qualifying parties are Mexico and Cuba. But the United States is at this point the only country, besides Japan, with the technological capability to exploit these resources. So far the matter has not come to issue because oil and mineral exploration in those waters remains cost-prohibitive. But development could become economically viable over time as the oil and mineral resources of the outer continental shelf are depleted.

NAFTA *and Beyond*

Cleavages linked to interest group politics drove the fight over NAFTA in the Gulf. Though trade between the U.S. Gulf states and Mexico has clearly grown since 1988, American fears of the accord's economic effects prompted the majority of Gulf state legislators to initially oppose NAFTA or remain undecided. Notable exceptions were Reps. Sam Gibbons (D, Fla.), Solomon Ortiz (D, Tex.), Mike Parker (D, Miss.), and Mike Andrews (D, Tex.), all of whom endorsed NAFTA early on.

The primary concern was the price advantage Mexican-grown winter fruits, vegetables, and sugar would have over U.S. produce. But there were a host of other fears. Some Miami import-export firms worried that NAFTA would put Mexico at a competitive advantage vis-à-vis the Caribbean Basin, while diminishing the attractiveness of U.S. foreign investment under the Caribbean Basin Initiative (CBI). Growth in U.S.-Mexico trade, it was argued, would come at the expense of the Caribbean Basin and ultimately divert port activity away from Florida to the land borders of Texas and California.[11] Since much of south Florida's new trade-related growth, especially in the textile sector, has been tied to the success of the CBI program, some Florida lawmakers conditioned their support of NAFTA on obtaining "NAFTA parity" for the Caribbean nations.[12]

Oil producers in Texas and Louisiana argued that NAFTA did not go far enough in opening up the Mexican market to the U.S. oil industry. The terms of the accord allow the Mexican government to retain its monopoly not only on all aspects of the production of crude oil, natural and artificial gas, and basic petrochemicals, but also on their export, transportation, storage, and distribution.[13] Though NAFTA does provide a market opening for U.S. suppliers of energy-related equipment and technology, and permits Mexico's state-owned oil company, PEMEX, to subcontract the services of U.S. drilling companies (see below), the oil and gas sector was not shy in saying it wanted more access to Mexico than it got under the basic NAFTA treaty.

South Florida's Cuban-American community had still another concern—that NAFTA would undermine the U.S. embargo against socialist Cuba, given Mexico's long-standing political and economic relations with neighboring Cuba. These sentiments hardened when Mexico refused to accept a boatload of Cuban refugees that had reached its shores in the summer of 1993.

Gulf coast environmentalists and shrimp fishermen joined the chorus of opposition to NAFTA with charges that Mexico's failure to require its shrimping trawlers to use turtle excluder devices (TEDs) was putting U.S. shrimpers at a competitive disadvantage and ultimately threatening two endangered species, the Kemp's ridley and loggerhead sea turtles. Interestingly, though the use of TEDs remains an issue of great dispute between U.S. shrimpers and environmental activists to this day, the NAFTA debate united these two divergent groups against a new perceived threat: Mexico's shrimp fleet.

The TED controversy was far from the only environmental concern. A much louder outcry was raised by those who insisted that NAFTA was certain to make Mexico, with its lower environmental standards and lack of enforcement, a "pollution haven" for American and Canadian industries looking to skirt regulations in their own countries. Others saw in the lax laws a clear advantage for Mexican producers. During initial industry briefings at the U.S. Trade Representative Office (USTR) in the summer of 1991, for example, this was a recurring theme among some in the U.S. oil industry. As one oil lobbyist told me, "You can do all you want on the border [to address U.S.-Mexico environmental problems], but PEMEX will continue to pollute the Bay of Campeche, sell its oil into the U.S. market at a lower overall price than us, and there is not a damn thing you are doing about it."

With 53 of the possible 218 votes required to secure passage of NAFTA, the Gulf region became a primary focus of attention for the Clinton administration and NAFTA backers in the House. Not surprisingly, on the day after the September 15, 1993, signing of the NAFTA Supplemental Agreements on Labor and the Environment, which called for greater protections and ultimately trade sanctions against signatory countries that did not comply with their own environmental and labor laws, President Clinton traveled to New Orleans for a pro-NAFTA rally with Gulf Coast shipyard workers. Though well attended, his rally was almost rained out by a tropical storm—sign of the turbulent political climate facing the pact.

TABLE I

Gulf State Congressional Votes on NAFTA, *1993*

State	Yes	No	Total
Texas	6	5	11ᵃ
Louisiana	5	2	7
Mississippi	3	2	5
Alabama	2	5	7
Florida	13	10	23
TOTAL	29	24	53

SOURCE: *Congressional Record*, roll call 575 (H.R. 3450), 103d Cong., 1st sess., Nov. 17, 1993, vol. 139, no. 160-p. II, p. H10048.

ᵃThese are the votes of the members from the coastal and southeastern areas only. With over $20 billion in exports from their state to Mexico in 1993, the 31-member Texas delegation voted overwhelmingly in favor of NAFTA (25-6). Nevertheless, Texas's Gulf coast representatives from communities such as Houston, Beaumont, and Port Arthur tended to share the same general uncertainty over NAFTA as others across the Gulf region, and many representatives shared the deep concerns of their Gulf colleagues.

Ultimately, passage of NAFTA hinged on a series of side deals nego-tiated between the United States and Mexico adding more protections for U.S. agriculture. Among the concessions secured were limits on the amount of Mexican sugar that could be imported into the United States, an arrangement that would see U.S. tariffs automatically imposed on fro-zen concentrated orange juice imported from Mexico if the price fell below a specified level for several days running, and some breaks for tomato growers.[14] Yet six days before the House vote, only three members of the 23-member Florida delegation (Reps. Jim Bacchus, Harry Johnston, and Sam Gibbons) had been locked up.[15]

In the end NAFTA passed by a vote of 234 to 200 in November 1993. Twenty-nine of the yes votes came from Gulf Coast representatives, or just over half of that group's votes (see Table 1 for a breakdown by state). Though the agreement passed by a comfortable margin, the consensus among key vote counters was that without the critical votes from Florida and Louisiana, secured through the citrus, tomato, and sugar deals, the positive momentum that NAFTA picked up in the final week following the televised debate between Ross Perot and Vice President Al Gore would have been lost, and the tide could have turned the other way.[16]

Though the treaty ultimately garnered the support it had to have from the Gulf states, the divisive NAFTA debate, which at times took on a vicious anti-Mexican tenor, sent a mixed message to Mexico. Furthermore, the array of side deals and special conditions demanded by Gulf state represen-tatives took some in the Mexican government by surprise. As one official said to me in the week preceding the vote, "What should have been a

TABLE 2

Gulf Region Exports to Mexico, 1992

(Millions of dollars)

State	Sector				
	Agriculture, forestry, and fishing	Mining	Manufacturing	Other	Total
Texas	$ 832.1	$332.3	$ 17,499.0	$175.6	$18,839.0
Louisiana	397.6	3.6	347.2	4.8	753.2
Mississippi	2.2	0.9	99.2	0.6	102.9
Alabama	2.2	2.4	257.5	1.7	263.8
Florida	10.5	0.5	636.7	16.1	663.8
TOTAL	$1,244.6	$339.7	$18,839.6	$198.8	$20,622.7

SOURCE: U.S. Department of Commerce, Office of Trade and Economic Analysis.

natural alliance based on mutual cooperation, respect, and shared economic prosperity, in the end, amounted to no more than a prenuptial agreement signed by two parties after a very stormy two-year engagement." In the circumstances, all one could do, he thought, was "wait and see how the marriage works."

For all the concerns, the region's economic prospects appear to be bright under NAFTA, which brings expanded opportunities for trade and exports with not only Mexico but the rest of Latin America, as well as for steady growth in the region's four principal sectors—shipping, oil and gas, tourism, and fisheries. Though the U.S. Gulf states have already benefited significantly from Mexico's efforts to liberalize its economy (see Table 2 for the 1992 export figures), a number of critical industries in the region will almost certainly flourish under the pact, namely, lumber and wood products, furniture, refined petroleum products, electronic equipment and scientific instruments, transportation equipment, primary metal industries, and some agriculture sectors.

Similarly, the Mexican states of Tamaulipas, Veracruz, Tabasco, Quintana Roo, Campeche, and Yucatan are expected to get an economic boost from NAFTA. As with the U.S. Gulf states, the majority of the growth will be tied to shipping, oil and gas, tourism, and fisheries. Let me take up the problems and prospects in each of these sectors by turn.

Shipping

By any standard, the Gulf of Mexico is the most important single marine waterway in North America, accounting for between 7 and 8 percent of global ship traffic. Of the ten busiest ports in the United States, four are located in the Gulf region: New Orleans, Houston, Corpus Christi, and Sabine (Texas). The two biggest Mexican ports are Tampico and Veracruz. Both countries have several other ports of significance, notably, Tampa, Gulfport, Mobile, Pascagoula, Lake Charles, Beaumont–Port Arthur, Galveston–Texas City, Freemont, Tuxpan, Coatzacoalcos, and Cieba.[17] Though located some 150 miles up the Mississippi River, Baton Rouge is also an important Gulf port.

Sea trade between U.S. Gulf ports and Mexico is concentrated in several flow patterns. New Orleans is the principal port through which U.S. agricultural products, the largest single seaborne export to Mexico, pass. By and large, other U.S. non-petroleum exports (such as grains, coal, iron, steel, fertilizers, chemicals, and industrial products) move from Houston to the nearby Tamaulipas and Veracruz coasts, and from Mobile to the Yucatan Peninsula. New Orleans and the Florida ports serve both Mexican Gulf ports and the Yucatan ports.[18] Because of the growing demand for unleaded gasoline in Mexico, U.S. petroleum exports are an ever-greater component of the Gulf shipping industry. (One estimate puts the growth rate of tonnage in the sector at over 3 percent a year.[19]) The bulk of this traffic flows from Texas and Louisiana ports to Tuxpan, the closest port in terms of transit time to the population centers of Mexico.

Unsurprisingly, given the U.S. appetite for imported oil, petroleum and petroleum products accounted for over 80.8 percent of Mexico's total waterborne exports to the United States in 1991.[20] These products flow from the oil fields of southern Veracruz and the Campeche region to U.S. refinery centers located between Houston and Mobile, Alabama. Its other exports tend to flow to U.S. population or transshipment centers on the Gulf of Mexico and to Atlantic Coast ports.

To accommodate the increased traffic expected under NAFTA, President Carlos Salinas de Gortari moved to privatize all Mexican port facilities in the early 1990's, transferring control from the state-owned firm Puertos Mexicanos to oversight by the Finance Ministry. That decision promises to eliminate decades of corruption, inefficiency, and union monopoly control at ports throughout the country.[21]

Prior to the shake-up, shipping anything through Veracruz was a nightmare, so much so that many exporters preferred to truck their goods 500 miles north to the border rather than run the risk of looting and other forms of corruption that prevailed. With the government's grant of concessions to three private companies to operate various port facilities there, productivity went up by more than 100 percent, and by 1991, the volume of traffic had climbed 8.6 percent.[22] The success of Veracruz is likely to be repeated at other ports along Mexico's Gulf Coast as well as on the Pacific.

Farther up the Gulf coast, an international task force is pushing ahead with studies to see how the U.S. Intercoastal Waterway can be extended past Brownsville to the port of Tampico. Championing the cause for the waterway extension is the Lafayette (Louisiana)-based Gulf Intercoastal Canal Association, which hopes the project will expand market opportunities for U.S. barge operators.[23]

According to the U.S. Department of Transportation, two factors could contribute to an increase in the share of waterborne commerce between U.S. Gulf states and Mexico, namely, the development of intermodal facilities in the Gulf region and the establishment of expanded rail-barge service. The Burlington Northern Railroad has already begun regular service from Galveston to Coatzacoalcos, where the rail cars are transferred to FNM, the Mexican National Railroad Company. Before such service can be expanded, however, Mexico's ports and rail system need to be modernized.

Yet as important as the U.S.-Mexico maritime trade is to the region, it accounts for no more than 10 percent of the Gulf ports' total activity. Land transportation (road and rail) is and will continue to be the predominant means of shipping goods between the two countries. Land transport accounted for fully $36.7 billion of the total $40.6 billion in U.S. exports to Mexico in 1991, or 90 percent, compared with $2.1 billion for air and only $1.8 billion for the sea.[24]

The Gulf shipping industry's future thus lies on the global trade front, and here it faces serious problems. Ports along the Gulf are confronting growing competition as railroad deregulation and the growth of intermodalism cut ever more deeply into the traditional links between the Gulf and Europe. Intermodalism is also hurting Gulf trade with Asia because steamship lines are finding it more economical to bypass the region and move their cargoes to West Coast ports by truck and rail.[25]

Additional pressure on the Gulf shipping industry is also coming from ship mutuals, known as protection and indemnity clubs, which have refused to issue certificates of financial responsibility to shipowners in accordance with the Oil Pollution Act of 1990. The reluctance of bulk and general cargo vessels to incur the additional cost associated with certification could lead to a diversion of traffic away from U.S. ports, including those in the Gulf, to Mexico.[26]

In the circumstances, NAFTA could not have come at a better time for the region, for no other ports in North America can rival the Gulf's for

North-South trade between the United States and Latin America. With prospects good for expanded hemispheric trade, the Gulf can look forward to continued growth in maritime commerce well into the future.

Oil and Gas

The presence of vast quantities of oil and gas is one of the most powerful common interests binding the Gulf region together. The United States alone, by far the largest consumer of oil and gas resources in the world, used over 16 million barrels (bbl) of oil a day in 1981. At that time, more than 60 percent of the nation's own oil production and more than 65 percent of its natural gas resources came from the Gulf region.[27] The figures have since fallen off sharply, to just 12 percent and 25 percent, respectively, causing some in the energy industry to call the Gulf of Mexico the "dead sea."[28] It is far from that, for in terms of future supplies, the Gulf contains more than 90 percent of all Mexican reserves, with more than 700 billion barrels of recuperable oil in the Bay of Campeche alone. As U.S. recoverable reserves of both oil and gas continue to fall, the result can only be an increased dependency on Mexican oil.

This vast energy wealth has created countless jobs in the region and especially on the North side of the border, where oil platforms, refineries, seaports, and pipelines are all part of an integrated system. Exploration, production, transportation, processing, derivatives, packaging, servicing, equipping, marketing, and financing combine to make the petroleum industry the leading single component of the Gulf's economic engine. The specialized skills required by the industry have drawn the region closer together, and Houston has become a common meeting ground for "players" and deal makers of both countries.

Yet this industrial overlap has not come without conflict. As is well known, Mexico and the United States have chosen different directions in the development of their energy resources. The United States relies on private capital, with government regulation only to conserve resources, protect the environment, maintain a stable price when possible, and prevent market collaboration in the form of antitrust legislation. In Mexico, oil is political and national. Some see President Lázaro Cárdenas's expropriation of foreign oil companies on March 18, 1938, as the last major act of the Mexican Revolution. In fact, Mexico was the first country to nationalize its oil industry.[29]

For the last 50 years or so, Mexico's psyche has associated oil with power, greed, exploitation, and foreigners. To protect its oil (and respond to labor grievances), Mexico established PEMEX, an arm of the government noted more for its featherbedding labor practices and undermarket pricing than for its efficient production of oil. To date, PEMEX has largely withstood the privatization tide in Mexico, treated as a special case as long as oil is seen as a sovereignty issue. Foreigners are still constitutionally prohibited from direct equity investment in Mexican oil fields.

All the same, the Salinas administration set out to reorganize PEMEX in an attempt to make this state enterprise more competitive. As the Mexicans clearly saw, the company was drowning in its own bureaucracy and debt. In 1992, for example, Atlantic Richfield, a major U.S. energy company with revenues approximately the same as those of PEMEX, had 27,000 workers; PEMEX had 170,700. In addition, PEMEX, with its vast reserves at a per-barrel cost of only $5 in the Bay of Campeche, was $15 billion in debt and had an after-tax profit of only $7 million on $15 billion in revenue. By contrast, the state-run PDV of Venezuela made $201 million profit on $10 billion in sales.[30]

Undoubtedly, Mexico's oil industry, still badly undercapitalized, would benefit from an infusion of technology and investment. The privatization of Argentina's YPF, Latin America's oldest state oil company, in 1993 could be a straw in the wind. Given the political realities and the symbolism oil still commands in Mexico, however, President Salinas kept the ownership and refining of petroleum off the table in the NAFTA negotiations. Recent changes in Mexico's foreign investment laws do permit foreign entry into such downstream areas as petrochemicals and the service sector.

PEMEX has also faced added environmental pressures at home and abroad. Partly to stem criticism in the U.S. Congress, President Salinas ordered the shutdown of the obsolete 18 de Marzo refinery, its oldest and biggest facility, located at Azcopotzalco in northern Mexico City, in April 1991. That, together with the concurrent closing of the Poza Rica refinery in Veracruz, which dried up a supply of more than 100,000 barrels of gasoline a day, or 6.25 percent of PEMEX's capacity, brought a productivity gap that continues to haunt the state-owned oil company today.[31]

The pressures have been no less severe on the home front. With rising environmental standards in the capital city and other major Mexican metropolitan areas, PEMEX has been compelled to provide its public with cleaner fuels. As a result, in 1992, the company had to import 75,000 barrels a day of unleaded gasoline, more than double what it imported in 1990.[32]

In August 1992, as a stop-gap measure, PEMEX entered into a $1 billion 50-50 joint venture with the Shell Oil company. The deal involves Shell's upgrading its 225,000 bbl/day Deer Park (Texas) refinery to process Mexico's Maya crude, which has a high sulfur content and is difficult to refine. The facility will also produce MBTE, a critical additive for unleaded gasoline. Additionally, PEMEX, hard pressed to meet domestic demand, can buy as much as 45,000 barrels of unleaded gasoline a day from Shell.[33] This investment is an example of how PEMEX has sought to circumvent Mexico's constitutional ban on foreign ownership of hydrocarbons to bring private-sector financing, as well as badly needed technology and know-how, to its operations.

The PEMEX/Shell joint venture exemplifies the type of bilateral cooperation that will not only help Mexico but lead to greater regional integration in the Gulf region. Sooner or later, the logic of fierce global competition will probably convince Mexico that it must emulate Canada's example—the debt-laden National Energy Policy was abandoned by Prime Minister Brian Mulroney in 1984, and energy is included in the 1989 Free Trade Agreement between the United States and Canada.

For U.S. energy interests, the need for expanded regional cooperation in the oil and gas industries is clear and compelling, since the Gulf states' currently available sources are beginning to reach their limits. According to the U.S. Minerals Management Service, remaining U.S. recoverable reserves in the Gulf in 1992 were 2.33 billion barrels of oil (concentrated in 143 fields) and 32 trillion cubic feet of gas (in 676 fields). While these stores are still adequate to attract the interest of small operators, at current rates of production they will soon be tapped out; in 1992, the oil fields were estimated to have a productive life of only eight years, and the gas fields only 6.8 years.[34]

If U.S. Gulf oil producers want to stay in the game, they must be prepared to substantially increase their investment in exploratory drilling and production farther offshore. One company, Shell, has already demonstrated its commitment to playing a larger role in the development of the Gulf with its planned $1.2 billion MARS project, which will see the operation of the deepest production platform yet, pumping from a depth of 2,933 feet in the Mississippi Canyon about 130 miles out from New Orleans.[35]

Alternatively, or concurrently, the United States can turn to its neighbor in the South to help meet its long-term energy needs. During the oil crisis of the 1970's, Mexico supplied billions of barrels of oil to the U.S. strategic oil reserve. In turn, the United States accelerated its purchases for the reserve in 1982, thereby helping Mexico to contain its financial crisis. Though Mexico has sought to diversify its oil market, with NAFTA and future joint ventures like Deer Park, it will continue to be a major supplier to the United States, receiving in return petroleum derivatives, oil services, and, increasingly, natural gas.

Yet another scenario would pertain if the United States, a profligate user of energy, were to reduce demand through a combination of energy efficiency and conservation. Additional savings could be obtained either by implementing a regime of full-cost pricing of energy or by imposing a carbon tax to further reduce overall energy demand in the United States. Even a modest program of energy efficiency and conservation would ease the pressure on Mexico. In the interest of greater efficiency and better environmental practices, the Mexican government might choose to open its petroleum industry still further to foreign investment. Whatever happens, the timing is ripe for a coordinated North American policy toward energy and the environment.

Tourism

From the Yucatan Peninsula to the Florida Keys, tourism is the region's second-most-important industry after oil, accounting for up to $50 billion annually in the U.S. Gulf states alone.[36] Tourists from all around the globe flock in to savor the color of cities like New Orleans and Cozumel, to soak up the sun on the beaches of seaside resorts like South Padre Island, Pensacola, and Cancun, and to scuba dive and fish in the warm Gulf waters. Most of the major cruise ship lines call in at Gulf Coast communities in Texas, Louisiana, Florida, and the Yucatan as well.

Lately more and more tourists have been drawn to the national parks, wilderness areas, wetlands, and nature preserves located on both sides of the border and birdwatchers from all parts come regularly to the Gulf's bird sanctuaries, located primarily in south Texas and home to hundreds of species that migrate from Canada for the winter. In fact, three of every four migrating water birds in North America visit the Gulf's winter wetlands. A fairly new phenomenon are the millions of Monarch butterflies that have been stopping each year on their way down from Canada to their Mexican breeding grounds, attracted to the bright yellow frames of the thousands of oil platforms that dot the Gulf coast.[37]

Unfortunately, the natural beauty that has long drawn visitors to the region is being threatened by a host of environmental problems. Each year hundreds of tons of marine debris wash up on Gulf Coast beaches. As noted earlier, Texas bears the brunt of the burden, with the highest levels of marine debris in both the Gulf and the Caribbean. Between this and sewage and industrial runoff from Matamoros, tourists visiting south Texas beaches confront serious health risks. Likewise, oil globules still mar South Padre Island's shores, a harsh reminder of the June 1989 IXTOC-I platform blowout in the Bay of Campeche.[38]

Tourist-related industries have themselves contributed to many of the environmental problems (such as beach erosion, the destruction of wetlands, and sewage runoff) that now threaten their very livelihood. Tourists are also to blame. In the Yucatan, many of the coral reefs are dying off, contaminated by slicks of suntan lotion that coat the coastal waters of many popular skin-diving destinations.

Fisheries

Benefiting from one of the most productive fishing grounds in North America, the commercial fishing industry is an economic mainstay for communities encircling the Gulf from the Yucatan Peninsula to the Florida Straits. Nearly 50 species of fish or shellfish are harvested in its waters, including oysters, shrimp, crabs, snapper, flounder, mackerel, tuna, and swordfish.

The U.S. side of the industry is among the most profitable in the country, with Gulf commercial landings accounting for close to 40 percent of the national total by weight and often exceeding $600 million a year, or 26 percent, by value. The industry is especially important in Louisiana, Texas, and Florida, which in 1990 ranked third, fourth, and fifth in value of U.S. landings (at $263.5 million, $184 million, and $170 million, respectively), outpaced only by Alaska ($1.51 billion) and Massachusetts ($263.6 million).[39] By comparison, in 1987 Mexican fisheries produced 2.3 billion pounds, with an export value exceeding $150 million.[40]

Despite the diversity of the Gulf fishery, one species, the menhaden, a kind of herring used primarily for the production of fish meal and oil, accounts for the majority of landings. In a total catch of close to 2 billion pounds in 1990, Gulf fishers landed 1.15 billion pounds of menhaden, worth $54 million. But most of the economic value of the Gulf fisheries comes from shrimp, the second-most-valuable catch (after salmon) in the United States. Of the 346 million pounds of shrimp landed in the United States in 1990, over 70 percent was caught in the Gulf.[41]

For several years now, however, shrimping, so important to regional prosperity, has been under attack for the extractive methods that are used to maximize yields. Because trawl mesh has to be fine to trap shrimp, a host of other organisms of similar or larger size are caught up along with them. An average of ten pounds of by-catch is caught for every pound of shrimp, including sharks, finfishes, and endangered or threatened sea turtles.[42] In some areas the ratio is much higher—as much as twenty to one. Since most of this by-catch is dumped overboard dead, trawling has been deemed by some environmentalists as the marine equivalent of strip-mining and clear-cutting.[43]

The most visible casualty of this practice is the sea turtle, particularly the endangered loggerhead and Kemp's ridley. It was the drowning of these creatures in great numbers that prompted the U.S. government in 1988 to require the use of TEDs in Gulf waters. Researchers are now working on an improvement, the By-catch Reduction Device (BRD), which, like the TED, attaches to the shrimp trawls and allows other organisms to escape the nets.[44] With 15–20 percent of shrimp lost through the use of TEDs, their introduction remains controversial within the industry. Some argue that it is a ploy by the environmental community to put the American shrimper out of business.

Yet as divided as Gulf shrimpers and the environmental community are on the TED issue, these groups stand united in their efforts to protect one of the most vulnerable ecosystems in the Gulf region—the coastal wetlands. Between the Mississippi border and Port Arthur, Texas, lie some six million acres of the richest, most productive lands in North America, and they are disappearing beneath the Gulf at a rate of over 50 miles a year.

What makes the loss of these coastal wetlands significant is that they are the nursery grounds for oysters, shrimp, and crabs, as well as many fishes. In Louisiana alone, wetlands produce a fifth of the nation's fish products, a third of its seafood, and half of its fur harvest. A third of all species of North American birds are either resident here or seasonal visitors.[45]

Salt water intrusion from the Gulf of Mexico, the result of dredging for ship channels, mining activity, and groundwater depletion, is only one of the threats to the marine environment. Land-based sources of pollution, including industrial sewage discharges, are wreaking their own havoc on the Gulf's wetlands, rivers, and lagoons. Over 51 percent of Galveston Bay, for example, has been permanently closed to shellfish harvesting because of contamination by coliform bacteria.[46]

Urban and agricultural runoff is still another problem. Nutrient loading from what is commonly referred to as non–point source pollution results in algal blooms that deplete the oxygen supply and cause fish and marine invertebrates to suffocate. In fact, along the Louisiana coast, from May to September, there lies a huge biological "dead zone" devoid of any form of marine life.[47] This condition, known as hypoxia, is common elsewhere in the Gulf, particularly in the very estuaries that commercial fishermen rely upon so much for the long-term sustainability of their industry.

Regional Cooperation

The plight of the Gulf fishers show that there are limits to growth within this region. It also provides a vivid reminder that the environmental carelessness of one industry can have grave consequences on the economic livelihood of another. We have seen examples of this kind of interaction throughout the Gulf region; tourism negatively impacted by oil spills, marine debris from the shipping lines, and runoff from the petrochemical, mining, and agricultural sectors is perhaps the one the public at large fastens on. The new eco-tourism industry finds itself having to confront shrimpers in order to protect the Gulf's sea turtles and to confront various other industries to ensure the preservation of the region's wetlands and wildlife habitats.

As the economic stakes increase, threatened U.S. industries are increasingly turning to the government for help or in some cases going straight to the courts. These environmental battles are inevitable, given the complex and competing interests that are at stake, and one of their consequences has been to push the federal government into a more proactive role in protecting the fragile environment. An important first step toward this end was taken in 1988, when the Environmental Protection Agency (EPA) established the Gulf of Mexico Program (GMP), with the charge to "protect, restore, and enhance the coastal and marine waters of the Gulf of Mexico and its coastal natural habitats, to sustain living resources, to protect human health and the food supply, and to ensure the recreational use of Gulf shores, beaches and waters in ways consistent with the economic well being of the region."[48] Headquartered at Stennis Space Center, Mississippi, GMP combines the efforts of four U.S. federal agencies with active state and local government participation.

Through this program, EPA, with the cooperation of state governments, has dramatically stepped up efforts to enforce U.S. environmental laws and promote greater environmental awareness in the Gulf region. Key initiatives have already been undertaken: to promote shellfish restoration in Alabama and Florida coastal communities; to reduce nutrient loading in the Mississippi River through environmental education in affected communities; and to relocate wastewater treatment facilities, sources of fecal coliform, away from commercially viable oyster harvesting areas.

Clearly, the environmental problems of the Gulf cannot be solved by one country alone. Increasingly, binational and multilateral cooperation is necessary. To this end, a number of significant conventions and protocols have been agreed to by the United States and Mexico in recent years.

In 1973 the Wider Caribbean Region (including the Gulf of Mexico) was designated as a special area of attention under Annex V of the International Convention for the Prevention of Pollution from Ships. A protocol to the Convention for the Protection and Development of the Marine Environment of the Wider Caribbean Region (Cartagena Convention) is also being developed under the auspices of the U.N. Environmental Programme to control land-based sources of marine pollution in the region. In parallel with this, EPA and Sedesol, Mexico's environmental secretariat, initiated discussions in 1992 to establish a pilot program specifically focused on land-based sources of pollution in the Gulf of Mexico.[49]

Additionally, by an agreement signed in 1980, the United States and Mexico are committed to establishing joint contingency plans for oil spills and other marine emergencies in shared waters. In 1990 the two countries also reached agreement on a protocol to the Cartagena Convention (the Special Protected Areas and Wildlife Protocol) binding them to cooperate in identifying and protecting endangered or threatened species and fragile ecosystems such as coral reefs, sea grasses, and mangroves in the Gulf region.[50] Moreover, in April 1993, heeding outcries from the U.S. environmental community during the NAFTA debate, Mexico made the use of TEDs mandatory for all its shrimp vessels in the Gulf and the Caribbean.[51]

Beyond all this, NAFTA itself will increase intergovernmental cooperation on the environment. The NAFTA text contains a number of "green" provisions never before seen in any bilateral or multilateral trade agreement. Specifically, the preamble sets out as three of its primary purposes "[to] contribute to the harmonious development and expansion of world trade in a manner consistent with environmental protection and conservation; . . . promote sustainable development; . . . and strengthen the development and enforcement of environmental laws and regulations."[52]

Among NAFTA's key environmental provisions are the recognition of a country's right to uphold existing health, safety, and environmental standards; a commitment to work jointly to improve those standards through upward harmonization; and an agreement to adhere specifically to three international environmental accords—the Montreal Protocol on Substances That Deplete the Ozone Layer, the Convention on International Trade in Endangered Species of Wild Fauna and Flora, and the Basel Convention on the Control of Transboundary Movement of Hazardous

Wastes and Their Disposal. In response to the pollution haven question, stringent provisions were added enjoining party countries from lowering their environmental laws or relaxing enforcement to attract or retain investment.

NAFTA's green provisions were later complemented by the signing of the North American Agreement on Environmental Cooperation, which established a commission for settling environmental disputes between the party countries. Charged also with fostering increased trilateral environmental cooperation, this body, the Council on Environmental Cooperation (CEC), has the potential to play an important role in promoting new initiatives between Canada, Mexico, and the United States to protect and preserve the wildlife habitats of the Gulf region, attracting as they do many migratory species from all three countries.

The CEC has a good base of cooperation at the state level to build on. For example, the first U.S.-Mexico Gulf States Governors Conference may be held in November 1994 in cooperation with business interests on both sides of the border, and the Western Governors Association of the United States, Canada's Western Provinces, and Mexico have already taken steps to promote the preservation of common bird species along the Mississippi Flyway. Other state-led initiatives include a pilot program under the Texas General Land Office (GLO) and the EPA for monitoring land-based pollution in the Wider Caribbean. GLO and EPA are also working closely to monitor the impact of Rio Grande watershed pollution on the marine life in the Gulf and Laguna Madre.

As important as bilateral and trilateral cooperation has been or will be at the governmental level, some of the most innovative work on environmental problems in the Gulf region is being done by the private sector and grass-roots organizations of the United States and Mexico. Most of these efforts to promote expanded regional cooperation have come recently.

Thanks to grass-roots lobbying on the part of various Gulf communities, President Bush declared 1992 the "Year of the Gulf of Mexico." The designation led to several important environmental education and public outreach efforts in each of the U.S. Gulf states, emphasizing the interdependence of the region. Heightened awareness of the environmental challenges facing the Gulf region also led to the establishment in that year of the Business Council for the Sustainable Development of the Gulf of Mexico (BCSDGM), an organization that aims to encourage market-based mechanisms to promote environmentally responsible commerce and industry in the region. Taking its name from the parent body formed through the efforts of Dr. Stephen Schmidheiny, a Swiss industrialist who enlisted 48 chief executive officers from around the world in his cause, BCSDGM represents 30 of the leading U.S. and Mexican companies in the Gulf region, including firms as diverse as the Conoco oil company, the pharmaceutical giant Ciba-Geigy, Florida Power & Light, and the Monterrey-based firm Grupo IMSA.[53]

BCSDGM has already undertaken some innovative binational projects. One of the more notable is an environmental cost-accounting program targeted at the region's petrochemical and refining industries, through which BCSDGM hopes to demonstrate to firms that environmentally sensitive production methods make sound economic sense. According to the Council's Executive Director, Andrew Mangan, "Conoco recognizes that the oil industry in its present form is totally unsustainable. . . . If the industry is to survive over time it must pursue a business strategy founded on the principles of sustainable development." Mangan believes that "the presence of the BCSDGM will provide a doorway through which industry and business operating in the Gulf region can join political, governmental, and environmental leaders in developing policy and projects to make sustainable development a reality."

Apart from BCSGM, much of the vision for a broader regional agenda in the Gulf of Mexico has come from Texas. Among the most important of the Texas Gulf backers are Sen. Phil Gramm, Land Commissioner Gary Mauro, and Reps. Kika de la Garza and Greg Laughlin.

Texas's leadership in these matters is not surprising, for the state has a long history of working with its many counterparts along the U.S.-Mexico land border (California, Arizona, New Mexico, Baja California, Sonora, Chihuahua, Coahuila, Nuevo León, and Tamaulipas). Thanks largely to the cooperative efforts of all these states, the U.S.-Mexico border has finally begun to receive a measure of attention and financial assistance from Mexico City and especially from Washington, D.C., as indicated by the Bush administration's commitment to fund and implement the first stage of the Integrated Environmental Plan for the U.S.-Mexico Border (1992–94) and the Clinton administration's pledge to establish two new institutions—the North American Development Bank and the Border Environmental Cooperation Commission—to help border communities finance environmental infrastructure. What Texas Gulf backers hope for is that their experience on the land border will pay off as they begin the political process of putting the Gulf of Mexico on the "radar screens" of Washington policy makers.

A key player in advancing that cause will be Land Commissioner Gary

Mauro, who served as candidate Clinton's campaign manager in Texas. As one Capitol Hill insider confided to me, "Mauro has got the ear of the President and others in the White House on issues relating to the Gulf." Through Mauro's leadership and the earlier efforts of then-Sen. Lloyd Bentsen, Congress has included in the 1994 bill to reauthorize the Clean Water Act a federally sponsored Gulf of Mexico Commission. With the eventual participation of Mexican Gulf states, the Commission would bear a striking similarity to the Cascadia Corridor Commission of the Pacific Northwest. (As of August 1994, the water bill itself was in trouble.)

Though momentum is beginning to pick up in the Gulf region for a broader regional agenda, much work remains to be done. After all, the differences that divided U.S. Gulf communities during the NAFTA debate have by no means been resolved. According to Mangan, "The key is to get Texas and Florida working together. Once this is done, he is convinced, the other U.S. states will come along.

These efforts clearly cannot and should not be limited to the United States. The Mexican and U.S. Gulf states need to formalize their relationship, to unite around a common agenda much as the provinces and states of the Great Lakes and Pacific Northwest regions have done. The first Hemispheric Summit of the Americas (scheduled at this writing to be held in Miami in December 1994) could have a spillover effect in causing greater regional cooperation in the Gulf. But for this to happen, the big states must lead.

Still, as my cocontributors Paul Schell and John Hamer make clear in their paper on Cascadia, as important as political initiatives are toward the establishment of a common regional agenda, much of the initial groundwork must be laid by the private sector. According to Mangan, "Industries in the Gulf are now beginning to realize that if they do not work together to promote an agenda based on sustainable regional development, their future long-term profitability will be greatly diminished. It is their profit motive more than anything that is bringing them to the table."

In fact, as we have seen, the Gulf business community is already a key driving force behind expanded regional cooperation within the wider Caribbean Basin. The linkage is natural, based on geography, the hydrographical connections through the Loop Current, and the growing market opportunities that will arise from expanded hemispheric free trade. Already many Florida companies and political leaders are pressing for the speedy extension of NAFTA benefits to other countries in the Caribbean region, as well as the rest of Latin America.

One critical player in both the Gulf and the wider Caribbean Basin remains off their list—Cuba, still under embargo and isolated diplomatically by the United States. Any effort to promote a regional agenda for the greater Gulf region, especially in the domain of the environment, will have to include Cuba. Here Canada, with its diplomatic ties to the Castro government, its economic stake in that country,[54] and its Commonwealth links in the Caribbean Basin, is well positioned to play a lead role. Indeed, Canadian Foreign Minister Andre Ouellet signaled his country's willingness to work together with Mexico to craft a regional agenda that would eventually include Cuba at a March 1994 meeting with his Mexican counterpart at Mexico City. Declaring that "the time has come to close the book on sour relations with the island nation," Ouellet stated: "We do not pretend that we could dramatically change American policy [on Cuba], but we believe that modestly we could have some influence and we could start a process that would be fruitful in the future . . . leading to a surprising but inevitable change in policy by the Americans."[55]

In the near term, however, Fidel Castro's refusal to introduce economic and political reforms makes a normalizing of relations with the United States unlikely. In the meantime, Cuba is seeking to exploit its oil and other natural resources through non-U.S. (and non-Russian) foreign investment, particularly from Europe.[56] As in the case of Vietnam, U.S. business interests could prove very instrumental in opening up Cuba, not just as a market, but also as a partner in developing the Gulf into a unified region.

Conclusion

As important as the Gulf's key industries are, the lessons of the past two decades, from the IXTOC oil spill to the destruction of the region's fragile wetlands, has taught Gulf coast communities just how interdependent they are. Without question, initiatives such as the "1992 Year of the Gulf" have helped to promote a greater regional consciousness among its residents. However, the intense media scrutiny of environmental issues on the U.S.-Mexico land border during the NAFTA debate did not spill over to the Gulf. And many of the same issues that divided the Gulf communities then, such as the Cuba question, Mexican competition, and environmental differences, complicate the efforts of groups like BCSDGN to promote and advance a regional identity for the Gulf.

Given the important market and hydrographical forces that bind the communities of the Gulf together, regional cooperation is inevitable and must be embraced to overcome the growing economic and environmental challenges the region will face in the twenty-first century. El Paso and Ciudad Juarez, on the U.S.-Mexico border, have learned this lesson; beset by chronic air pollution problems, the two cities have banded together to form the first binational air-management control district. It is a lesson the border communities of British Columbia, Washington, and Oregon learned even earlier, bringing them together in support of the Cascadia Corridor Commission. For the Gulf communities of the United States and Mexico (and eventually Cuba), establishment of the Gulf of Mexico Commission would open a precious window of opportunity to make North America's maritime frontier all that it ought to be.

The Mexico-U.S. Border:
A Line of Paradox

JORGE A. BUSTAMANTE

More than 200 million human crossings of the U.S.-Mexico border in 1992 suggest a unique phenomenon of interaction between two nations.[1] When one looks at the contrasts between these two bordering countries, the phenomenon appears more than a little contradictory. For the imbalance demarcated by the border cuts two ways. Economically, Mexico's output amounts to less than a twentieth of the U.S. Gross National Product. But culturally, the divide is not just between the two countries, but between one country and the whole of Latin America.

As persuasively argued in Kai Erikson's *Wayward Puritans*,[2] the United States is, culturally speaking, an Anglo-Saxon nation, notwithstanding the empirical support one might find for the melting-pot argument. To the extent that Erikson is correct, the cultural contrast across the U.S.-Mexico border, involving people of a different language, religion, and history, makes its world's record for international border crossings even more intriguing. Contrasts at this border are so many and so acute that perhaps it makes more sense to study it in terms of paradoxes rather than contradictions. But first, let's try to develop a working definition of the U.S.-Mexico borderlands, as vast in scope as they are in complexity.

I begin with the premise that the border region, however one defines it, has two sides—a Mexican side and a U.S. side. A border phenomenon, therefore, is one that has something to do with the processes of interaction between the two sides. How far do those sides extend to the North and to the South? That depends. No single spatial denominator serves all analytical purposes. The operational extension of the borderlands to the South and to the North varies in accord with the nature of the border phenomenon under study. Border economic transactions, border environmental problems, and border population dynamics all have a different geographical "reach" and project a different conceptual space upon the maps of "the Border" we carry in our minds.

Nonetheless, I have argued elsewhere that it remains valid to speak of a "border region" if for no other reason than geographical proximity.[3] This international fact is what gives support to the notion of region as applied to such a vast territory, approximately 2,000 miles long. Yet if we possess a relatively straightforward East-to-West definition, a North-to-South axis is harder to come by.[4] My suggestion is that the U.S.-Mexico border region is determined by the space empirically covered by patterns of interaction between entities located on both sides. People, institutions, and environmental factors located on the border interact either "internally" with their respective counterparts in the rest of the country or "externally" with counterparts located on the other side of the border.

For the purposes of a spatial definition of the border region, the relevant interaction obviously is the external one, the one that occurs across the border. This notion involves an epistemological assumption, namely, that the border is a man-made artifact invented to make a difference in terms of institutional ascriptions of nationality. This is not to suggest that people interacting across the border will necessarily care more about nationality than they normally do. It is simply to suggest that the border always represents an option—open to those engaged in a pattern of "external" interaction—to resort to ascriptions of national differentiation if they so choose.

Regardless of the success or failure one might achieve through exercising such an option, and regardless of the frequency with which this might happen, the border always exists, it is ever present, and it *can* make a difference in the outcome of people's interactions. On the positive side, there is a tendency to liberalize legal interactions across the border, particularly with regard to trade. But the increasingly problematic areas of drug traffic and undocumented immigration also have led U.S. politicians from border districts to promote restrictive measures as well. One example is the construction of a steel fence more than twenty miles long between San Diego and Tijuana.[5] A similar measure has been used for the border between the twin cities of Nogales (in Sonora and Arizona). These measures, viewed as unfriendly by the Salinas de Gortari administration, are hardly in keeping with the notion of "MexAmerica," as first put forward by Joel Garreau in his best-seller, *The Nine Nations of North America.*[6]

Putting a complex subject in a nutshell, the difference that the border makes for each side has to do with the nature of the citizens' relations to their respective States and the nature of the claim that each State can make about its "own" nationals. Of course, the individual's relations to the State and the claim that the State can make on its own nationals are different in Mexico and in the United States. The border implies the locus of such differences.

But there is another important difference as well, one that pervades all levels of interaction, from the most macro to the most micro. I refer to the asymmetry of power between Mexico and the United States.[7] This asymmetry of power may or may not be exercised in an "external" process of interaction, but it is always present as a possibility. As with everything else in the realm of human interaction, there is no rule to which there are no exceptions.

Returning to the problem of a conceptual definition of the North-South axis of the border region, I would posit that such a space is determined by the combination of the empirical "intensity" and "extension" of people's interaction across the border.[8] Here intensity means the actual frequency of external interactions.

These interactions could range from an American tourist buying a curio in Tijuana to a Mexican dentist in Ciudad Juárez caring for a U.S. national who resides permanently in El Paso. When such practices produce a pattern, they can be used as indicators for empirically defining the extension of one dimension of the border region. In the latter example, this could be mapped as the space covered by the process of interaction between the Mexican dentist and his or her El Paso–based patient, coupled with the actual frequency of their dealings.

The combination of these two dimensions—extension and intensity—is what makes a border region geographically distinguishable from what is not a border region. The nonborder region is likely to be characterized by a lower intensity in the frequency of its interactions in comparison to the same kinds of interactions taking place among actors whose permanent residence is physically closer to the border. Such a higher intensity of interaction across the border is the key to the suggested definition of border region. However, this definition would be incomplete if we did not combine it with the variable of extension as measured in terms of the space on both sides of the border occupied by the myriad actors involved in international transactions.

To the extent that the combination of intensity and extension of interaction is likely to be higher between people on the two sides of the border—for example, dentists and patients from Ciudad Juárez and El Paso, respectively—than the same kind of an interaction between the same type of actors farther away from the border—say, between Mexico City and Chicago—it is possible to speak of a spatially definable border region. This applies as well to processes of interaction between people, institutions, and environmental factors.

With the above stock of conceptual tools available to us, we can now focus on the notion of MexAmerica, which is the subject I was invited to write on for this book. The editors did say, "What about it?," and they then accepted my reply. As a concept, the utility of MexAmerica derives from the number of people who agree to use it in the hope of seeing it transformed into a reality. I cannot be counted among them. If Mex-America signifies a regional space that has reached a greater level of integration within itself than the integration of its two parts within their national wholes, I think it contradicts the notion of border presented above.

Of course, one easy way to dismiss my argument out of hand is to label it "nationalist" and say that it disregards the reality (border reality) that is out "there" anyway, tied to nations or not. But I maintain that borders (and certainly the U.S.-Mexican border) have abiding and distinguishable binary qualities that often are strengthened rather than weakened by interactions.

This separateness within a dynamic of apparent wholeness can be good for both sides of the border, although it may generate tensions, disequilibria, and misperceptions with regard to and on the part of the national interior. The following sections of this essay will elaborate on what I mean by border reality. This elaboration will consist of three parts. The first deals with the notion of "ethnicity" and "otherness." The second is concerned with "border integration." And the third will reflect my views on the future of the U.S.-Mexico region.

I

If one agrees that stereotypes are basically expressions of ignorance preserved and protected by the power of their users, the people on the Mexican side of the border have to deal with stereotypes originating both from the South and from the North. From the South, the stereotype most resented by *fronterizos* (those who live on the border) is one of "agringado" or "pocho." These terms allude to one who has culturally defected from his "Mexicanness" in favor of a foreign (American) cultural identity.

Northward, from the United States, fronterizos are commonly stereo-typed by the black legend that hangs over some Mexican border towns. Let's call it the "Tijuana syndrome." It's important to pause and examine these stereotypes as applied to fronterizos on the Mexican side, from both the South and the North.

The concept of ethnicity is crucial, and I would present it as a di-chotomy: "ethnicity-in-itself" and "ethnicity-for-itself." This paraphrase of Marx's concept of "class-in-itself" and "class-for-itself" should not sug-gest a Marxist approach. Rather, a closer approximation could be found in the concept of "consciousness," which has more to do with Weber's theory of social action than with historical materialism.

Ethnicity-in-itself is understood here as the actual membership of an individual in a cultural community bonded to and externally identified by its traditions. Ethnicity-for-itself is used to mean a state of mind or a desire to openly identify oneself with a cultural community bonded by its tradi-tions. What makes the difference between the two is "ethnic conscious-ness," which is absent in ethnicity-in-itself and present in ethnicity-for-itself. For example, a child more than a fully socialized adult might have ethnicity-in-itself without having ethnicity-for-itself just by virtue of be-longing to a cultural community bonded by traditions.

Ethnicity of course is an elastic concept. It might refer to macro or micro dimensions of social existence. The most macro extends to cul-tural regions comprising several countries, such as Latin America or the Arab nations. The most micro is confined to what one might identify as minority communities, such as the Papago Indian community that lives on both sides of the U.S.-Mexican border. Pleonastic or not, it is use-ful to emphasize that the cultural element is essential to the notion of ethnicity.

Having said that, I shall focus now on the stereotypes emanating from the Mexican side to the South. From the Aztecs to the present, Mexico has been a centralized nation. The most eloquent expression of this cen-tralism is the macrocephalic development of Mexico City. Efforts to decen-tralize the nation have been legion. In fact, the existence of the Colegio de la Frontera Norte, where I work, represents a successful effort on the part of Mexico City's El Colegio de México to decentralize higher education. Our institution, with its string of border offices, is a scaled-down carbon copy of the parent institution in Mexico City. Other successful efforts to-ward decentralization are growing in number, yet the fact remains that, compared with the United States and Canada, Mexico is hardly decentral-ized at all.

This historic tendency toward centralization has spawned an ethno-centric view of Mexicanness—whatever that means—among the people of the center, specifically, Mexico City. They assume that Mexicanness can be viewed as a sort of large tent, with the apex located in Mexico City and the skirts along the borders, and particularly along the northern border, where levels of Mexicanness are thought to be the lowest of all. Exacerbating this conception is a notion that might be summarized as follows: "the closer a Mexican resides to the United States, the more Americanized that Mexican is likely to be."

This stereotypical view is "confirmed" when a person from Mexico City visits a border city such as Tijuana and hears somebody saying what sounds like "te wacho a dos blokes de la marketa, ese . . ." This strange language is interpreted as evidence of cultural denationalization or loss of Mexicanness (as well as an affront to the purity of the mother tongue).

Fronterizos (at least this fronterizo) have a different interpretation when they hear this argot. It is a local nationalization of English; call it a verbal appropriation, if you will, but basically the phenomenon represents the same social process by which all languages have been created. It certainly does not defer to English speakers from the United States, who tend to be mystified by what should be like, but isn't, what used to be "their" language. In fact, this linguistic process can easily be construed as having nothing at all to do with a loss of ethnic identity, particularly when contrasted to the "ethnicity-of-the-other-side-of-the-border." For Mexican fronterizos, borrowing words from the language of the other side is in fact a process of ethnic reaffirmation. To *not* say, "I'll see you two blocks from the market" (as many fronterizos could do in perfectly correct English), is a way to reinforce the us/them distinctions of ethnicity and identity. The fact that "te wacho a dos blokes de la marketa" is addressed to another member of the same ethnic group, far from indicating a loss of Mexicanness, is a strong indication of "ethnic consciousness" and a step toward "ethnicity-for-itself."

This is the finding of a research project conducted by the Colegio de la Frontera Norte in 1982 and duplicated in a repeat project two years later. The study was based on a comparison of systematically drawn, probabilistic random samples from cities of the Mexican interior—Zacatecas, Uruapan, San Luis de Potosí, Acapulco, and Mexico City—and cities along the border—Tijuana, Mexicali, Ciudad Juárez, Nuevo Laredo, and Matamoros.[9] For our comparison, we used the scores of previously validated tests for the "use of anglicisms in casual discourse," combined with scores of test of "cultural identity," adapted from the Mexican social psychologist

Rogelio Díaz Guerrero's tests measuring traditional values of Mexican-ness, based on a scale of agreement-disagreement about what he called "sociocultural premises." [10]

What we found was so surprising that we decided to repeat our research before making public our initial findings. The second project confirmed previous findings about higher scores of Mexicanness in the border city sample than in some of the cities of the interior, with Mexico City at the bottom of the rankings! Our studies also revealed instances ranging from no correlation to weak positive correlation between the use of anglicisms in casual discourse and Mexicanness.

The first test had us stumped. We could not figure out why, among the sampled border cities, the higher the use of anglicisms, the higher the degree of Mexicanness. The initial hypothesis we wanted to test was a negative correlation, where the border cities were expected not to be higher than the nonborder ones. The explanation we came up with was along the lines of what I argued above: the use of anglicisms by border people is more a sign of ethnicity-for-itself than of ethnic rejection. This is particularly the case when anglicisms are defined as locally understood transformations (hispanicizations) of English words.

Other kinds of anglicisms were considered, such as the actual use of English words or English-language sentence construction in routine day-to-day discourse about topics held constant in taped interviews, where the respondent was asked to narrate his or her experiences during the previous week. A team of linguists was asked to systematically review the tapes in order to identify, classify, and count anglicisms found in each interview. The same respondents then took the other test, which measured distance or proximity to traditional values and perceptions previously identified as characteristic of Mexican cultural identity.

The second time around, we did something different with this research. Sample design was based on the population of each city divided into sectors, as determined by objective indicators of living standards by neighborhoods. (Our sample indicators were access to and quality of public services and quality of housing construction.) Three sectors were drawn in each city according to these criteria. We called them sector 1 (most affluent), sector 3 (poorest), and sector 2 (in-between). Here is a summary of our findings: [11]

1. The higher the standard of living, the higher the use of proper anglicisms and the lower the Mexicanness.

2. Sectors 1 of the interior cities were lower in Mexicanness than sectors 1 of the border cities.

3. The closer a border city lay to the Gulf, the higher the Mexicanness among all sectors.

4. The closer a border city lay to the Pacific Ocean, the higher the use of processed anglicisms (what in the interior are called "pochismos") in sectors 2.

5. The lower the standard of living, the higher the Mexicanness in all cities, with the border cities scoring significantly higher.

6. Generally speaking, there was no statistically significant correlation between the use of anglicisms and Mexicanness.

7. Sectors 2 showed up closer to scores of sectors 1 in the border cities but closer to sectors 3 in the interior cities.

8. Lower levels of Mexicanness were more closely associated with higher standards of living among all sectors than with geographical proximity of residence to the United States.

In our effort to explain such intriguing research findings—totally contrary to widespread stereotypes held in central Mexico about fronterizos—I suggested the factor of "otherness."[12] By "otherness," I was referring to the paradoxical effect of the intensity of face-to-face contacts at the border with the "others," namely, Americans, whatever "Americans" entails. In essence, I was arguing that, for border peoples, the notion of otherness is particularly important to one's own ethnic identity. The paradox is that otherness seems to help fronterizos reaffirm their ethnic identity as Mexicans, by helping them know what they are not. If a young Mexican from the interior is asked to define Mexicanness, he or she might have problems in selecting the proper denominators out of an array of regional ethnicities. On the border, such a question is easier to answer because otherness tells you that Mexicanness is what the gringo is not.

Otherness is less of a factor of ethnic identity as one gets farther away from the border. Along the border region itself, otherness is part of a socialization process that drives the dynamics of ethnicity-in-itself toward ethnicity-for-itself.

Mexicans from the interior tend to have a view of Americans coming from the mass media (generally positive) or from leftist ideologies (always negative). Mexicans from the border, however, tend to have a view of Americans arising from face-to-face interactions. If one conceptualizes a continuum from extremely positive to extremely negative opinions about Americans in Mexico, one would find the views of people from the interior tending more toward the extremes, and those of the border people more toward the center. It seems that the intensity of personal or face-to-face transactions experienced by border dwellers on the Mexican side results in a more pragmatic, less ideological view of Americans.

This is not to say that a more pragmatic and perhaps moderate view of Americans by Mexican fronterizos is one-sided. For Mexican border people, Americans represent both a problem and an opportunity. They learn through experience to view Americans as symbols of inequality and of asymmetrical power relationships. Americans tend to be the ones who give the orders because they are the boss, the employer, the patron, the client, or, simply, the one with more money. There's the nub of the problem. Mexican fronterizos don't like this asymmetry, and they fight against it through the conventional channels of competition. At the same time, fronterizos see the United States as an opportunity. They sell more products, services, and labor to Americans per capita than to interior Mexicans.

Furthermore, the border has suddenly become a major issue in American public life, and this is bound to affect the quality and intensity of interactions. The givens of geography dictate a joint problem-solving approach to such thorny issues as aquifer management, clean air, and sewage treatment. The six Mexican and four American border governors have been meeting annually for more than a decade to discuss a range of issues. The schools are heavily impacted: in a small elementary school like the one in Columbus, New Mexico, children from both nations mingle freely (though a current lawsuit seeks to end that). And in higher education, joint-degree programs and informatic sharing link major state universities in broad areas of teaching and research.

A firm sense of ethnicity and national identity removes the substantial insecurity that might otherwise temper, if not thwart, such vigorous exchanges. As a result, these opportunities—increasingly perceived just as clearly by Americans through the optic of global interdependence—allow fronterizos to maintain a higher-than-average standard of living. Yet this notion of opportunity is not the same as desiring to be American, as is often feared in the interior of both Mexico and the United States. I say this despite the fact, or perhaps because of it, that the United States has more to do with the life histories of Mexicans throughout Mexico than is true of Mexico with respect to Americans.

Again, the asymmetry of power works its stern stuff on history and can be seen in the massive relocations of populations, but the suspicion lingers that a deeper force is at play in border life. If, for instance, political parties in opposition to the dominant Partido Revolucionario Institucional (PRI) are more electorally successful along the border, people from the interior automatically think it is because of the democratic culture and values emanating from the nearby United States. But this isn't necessarily what is happening, and to elaborate, I turn next to the subject of "integration."

II

Critics of NAFTA in the Mexican interior have argued that it will result in a loss of Mexican cultural identity or a thoroughgoing Americanization. This fear assumes a fatalistic spiral from economic integration to cultural integration. Fronterizos are skeptical, however.

Looking at the history of the Zonas y Perimetros Libres system (a type of duty-free zone), one finds that the most nationalist president of Mexico in this century, Lázaro Cárdenas, promoted it vigorously. His public policy goal was to attract Mexicans to the border in order to create a buffer against U.S. expansionism.[13] The paradox is that this nationalistic objective was sought and achieved by offering duty-free access to American goods to citizens who would move to the newborn border settlements, particularly toward the Pacific Ocean end. Obviously, the policy of creating such duty-free commerce meant integrating the economies of the Mexican border cities and the United States. But Cárdenas was not contradicting his nationalist views. He just did not believe that cultural integration would necessarily follow from economic integration. If the research findings cited above are correct, history has confirmed his judgment.

The key to understanding Cárdenas's insight is fairly simple. Human beings' ethnic identities are not the result of a zero-sum game, where a new element from a foreign culture automatically expels an old element from the indigenous culture. Cosmopolitanism sees to that. The use of other languages or the enjoyment of foreign cultures is not necessarily at the cost of one's ethnic identity. But this is not to deny that an original ethnic identity can be lost, as indeed happens. As noted under point 8 of the study cited above, it is what we could see with regard to living standards in the most affluent sectors. Yet even as we have seen Mexican border cities maintain their cultural identity, a paradoxical parallel phenomenon has occurred on the economic side. Yes, the economies of the border cities have integrated with the U.S. economy, but at the same time, there has been an increasing Mexicanization of business in these cities.[14]

Those Mexicans who fear that NAFTA will cause a loss of national identity simply do not know the history of their own border. If cultural integration necessarily followed economic integration, Mexican fronterizos long since would have begun singing *The Star-Spangled Banner* in the morning.

What actually happens is that ethnic identities change; they are not static but evolve and often spread into ethnic subidentities. A Yucatan version of a Mexican ethnic identity is just as authentic as a Veracruz version or a fronterizo version. They are all different subidentities, and one is no more Mexican than the other, particularly when they are viewed from within Mexico. From outside Mexico—that is, in contrast to other national ethnic identities—all of them together and each one of them separately stands out even more distinctively as "Mexican." Let's say the border identity is more cosmopolitan than interior identities, but let's not go so far as to say that because I enjoy jazz and speak English, I have lost my identity as a Mexican.

Within the context of the relative independence that exists between economic integration and cultural or ethnic integration, important cultural phenomena *do* take place on the border. Electoral victories, especially by the opposition Partido Acción Nacional, or PAN, derive in part from the increasing "middle-classification" of border populations.

Tijuana epitomizes this phenomenon. In contrast to most medium-to-large Mexican cities, Tijuana never had an agriculturally based economy; rather, early on it was based on catering to the whims of Americans, especially during Prohibition. Regardless of the peculiar type of "services" that characterized the beginnings of this economy, the fact remains that a service economy produces a value structure more clearly middle class in nature than that of an agriculturally oriented economy. In addition to the formative history of Tijuana's economy, it bears noting that Tijuana's social makeup draws on migrants from all over the country. This tends to produce another important deviation from what is typical throughout Mexico. Tijuana's family structures tend to be nuclear rather than extended, as in the rest of Mexico. The economic effect of this difference is that family income tends to be distributed among relatively few members, and this in turn pushes upward the social mobility of the Tijuana families. Their counterparts elsewhere, with their financial resources distributed among a larger number of individuals, display less upward social mobility.

The middle-class values I am referring to are common to all middle classes in the Western world, from Boston and London to Madrid and Buenos Aires. These values are associated with individualism, a preoccupation with upward social mobility, and an abiding concern for those things that both thrust a person upward and preserve his or her well-being: education, health, the work environment. Given their relative financial success, middle classes are also deeply concerned with the return value of the taxes they must pay. They demand accountability of public officials and monitor public expenditures closely. In short, they demand democracy. In this respect, Tijuana's middle class is no different from any other middle class. Its vote for the PAN is not so much a direct reflection of

American values as the result of a fast-growing middle-classification of its society at large.

Using income distribution to define social classes, one finds that Tijuana's is very atypical of the rest of Mexico. In the nation as a whole (as well as in the majority of Mexican cities), income distribution resembles a triangle, with the poorest (the majority) at the bottom. In Tijuana, by contrast, income distribution resembles an irregular pentagon, with the majority above the bottom and the poorest making a shorter line at the bottom than the more affluent at the top. This atypical shape of income distribution represents the rising importance of middle-class values in Tijuana, values that link Tijuanenses with their middle-class cohorts in Mexico City, Guadalajara, and Monterrey, to be sure, but with the difference being that in those cities, the middle class is not the majority of the population. And in some important measure, this factor lies behind the alternating electoral successes of the competing political parties in border cities like Tijuana.

Even though Tijuana represents the middle class's high point along the border and probably around the country, it is a border phenomenon set in the context of a very heterogeneous region. In terms of conventional indicators of socioeconomic levels, a comparison between the cities of the northern border places Tijuana at the top, Matamoros at the bottom, and Ciudad Juárez somewhere in the middle. Nevertheless, as a region the border's standard of living is higher than the national average. Paradoxically, the opposite is true of the U.S. side of the border. With the exception of southern California, U.S. border areas have a lower standard of living than the national average, with the per-capita income of counties in southeast Texas among the poorest anywhere in the country. This creates a real difference in perception: for Americans, the indicators suggest a host of social problems in a stressed physical environment; for Mexicans, the border is a region that is pulling ahead.

Having introduced yet one more paradox about the U.S.-Mexican border, the final question, the question about the future, remains. If not toward MexAmerica, where is the border heading?

III

Now that NAFTA has been ratified by the U.S. Congress and has been signed into law by all three countries, it can be argued that the agreement will only accelerate a process of economic integration already well under way between Mexico and the United States: this process is irreversible.

Furthermore, economic integration will be more strongly and swiftly felt along the border than in Mexico's interior. This is not to suggest that NAFTA is an irrelevancy, for the fact remains that by accelerating the process of economic integration, NAFTA will bring about opportunities for all three countries that might not emerge in its absence.

More than for the interior of Mexico, this would be particularly the case for the Mexican side of the border. Here, trade liberalization is as old hat as the duty-free system launched under Cárdenas. In this sense, the Mexican side of the border, especially Baja California, has lived under NAFTA-like conditions for decades. Fronterizos have been socialized within a world-class consumer culture; they expect good quality at a good price. But the interior of Mexico is only beginning to harbor the same expectations, having spent long decades playing under the very different rules of import-substitution economics. That strategy, once common among underdeveloped countries and especially strong in Latin America, probably made sense in its early stages to the extent that it attracted foreign investment and industry that might not otherwise have come to Mexico. But it evolved into a captive consumer market, where competition was absent, prices were high, and quality was low. Thus NAFTA will have a much greater impact on the interior than on the border regions of Mexico.

When one turns from consumption to production, one finds the *maquiladora* in-bond assemblage and manufacturing industry operating along the border in tune with industrial standards common to world competition everywhere. "Total quality" and "just-in-time" are everyday watchwords. Maquiladoras have brought to the border a lot of good in terms of job creation and some bad in terms of environmental degradation and the overburdening of public services: strong evidence indicates that the balance is positive. Partly because of the maquiladoras, the workforce knows the meaning of punctuality and error-free production. Without losing its national identity, this workforce has pushed standards upward and kept pace with the cross-border institutional cooperation in other sectors I mentioned above—in education and local and state government. Further, it has become the focus of international cooperation on environmental matters. While the maquiladora's environmental record is mixed, its overall track record of competitiveness and efficiency augurs well for a long-term improvement, especially when backed and prodded by federal governments that have come to understand something of the border's rapidly emerging centrality in bilateral relations. Given the pragmatic ethic of border residents' experience in exploiting fresh opportunities, it is not too much to expect a potentially strong and positive response to the environmental challenge of fast growth in fragile deserts. However distantly, the border population feeds on Cárdenas's confidence in its ability to preserve and protect Mexico; but this in no way limits interest in new forms of cooperation with U.S. counterparts. The fact that border employment levels and wages are among the highest in Mexico underscores the relentless push toward those middle-class values and aspirations we have noted. Thus, the Mexican side is apt to bring fresh intensity and perhaps an extension of aspirations to the border region as a whole.

All this does not add up to a marbled MexAmerica, a supposedly distinct region of interchangeable cultures, ethnicities, and languages, with its own personality and values, and above all distinctive from both "interiors." But it is difficult for me to lament that fact, since I (and others) question why anyone would hold up such an unlikely entity as a criterion of "success." We can do quite well as the two separate peoples and nations that we are.

No, the more ominous scenario for me is one in which NAFTA and related processes lead not to MexAmerica, but to three Mexicos: a prospering Northern Mexico, a Plateau Mexico, with its ponderous administrative core, and an impoverished Central American Mexico. The dynamics of this scenario are based on the increasing socioeconomic gap between the populations of the northern and southern states, with Mexico City's giant metropolitan area in the middle. Is Mexico developing its version of the classic North-South problem within nations?

The gap even now has widened to the point that we already see early signs of resistance from sectors of the northern states to "sharing the burden" of aiding the southern states. Some northerners resent any thought of achieving national equalization by compensatory income transfers to the underdeveloped South. As ridiculous as it might sound in a country of Mestizos, there are certain elements of racism in the North's attitude toward helping the South, where the Indian population is, proportionately, much higher.

I would argue that this gap in levels of socioeconomic development between the North and the South could be bridged under NAFTA but might well have widened without it. Free to move across the border, tropical agriculture in the South should have a unique opportunity to compete advantageously in the market niches of fruits and vegetables in the United States and Canada. If it does not grasp that opportunity, southern Mexico is apt to slide toward Central America, in figurative economic terms, and to experience a still-greater gap between its living standards and those of the prospering northern border.

My impression is that the metropolitan area of Mexico City would not join either the North or the South. Rather, it would follow a middle path, caught in the midst of unhappy national tensions—and highly sensitive to those tensions, too, since Mexico City is, after all, made up of immigrants from all over the nation. Having achieved its own species of macrocephalic ethnicity would not immunize it from vast contradictions on both sides.

Presented in this way, I think we can see that North America as a whole can have considerable effects on its constituent national and regional parts. Further, NAFTA can play a big part in this. If economic integration does not deeply affect "who" we are, it may be said to condition "how" we are, by influencing the material resources and opportunities we all have at our disposal to realize our identities. At any rate, my fear about the future of Mexico, as I have said, is not the scenario of "MexAmerica," but the scenario of three Mexicos. Comparative data on the socioeconomic levels of the Mexican State support such a hypothetical scenario. I have suggested it here not as a fatalistic prediction but rather as a way of analytically signaling a challenge to be faced by all Mexicans. As we manage our affairs in relation to the weighty Other of economic interdependence with neighboring nations, certain asymmetries persist and may spawn new ones in their wake.

Conclusion: The Search for Community

ROBERT L. EARLE AND JOHN D. WIRTH

As international trade in North America burgeons toward $300 billion a year, and workers, consumers, and investors enter ever more deeply into a broad range of commercial and environmental relations, the question of some form of continental community inescapably arises. The givens of geography, coupled with changes in the world economy, are creating a new regionalism. This convergence of utilitarian interests sets the stage for other kinds of association, but how will these associations develop and mature? How can Mexicans, Canadians, and Americans, so decidedly different in culture, history, and outlook, find the common ground of shared pride and understanding that lifts discrete groups into functional, if not formal, communities?

As those who have tried working with this trinational tableau know, these are awkward questions: awkward because North America has been a land of conventional, and often distorting and dysfunctional, perspectives. A place where Canadians revel in, yet also resent, their invisibleness to American eyes. A place where the United States sees only itself. A place where Mexico has one eye fixed on the legacy of Spanish authoritarianism and the other on the nation as victim, often at the hands of the United States. Given North America's disparities in power, population, and wealth, how, indeed, could it ever come together in some broad social consensus on a set of values?

Such different countries, one is tempted to suggest, ought to deal only in carefully measured arrangements of candid self-interest. Let there be courtesy, respect, proper form, good manners, yes, but with low expectations for community; these are the limits that, because of history and current conditions, ought to be accepted when it comes to the spirit of North

American cooperation. On the face of it, there are no deep lessons commonly available from centuries of North American culture; few points of intersection that could possibly join the deeply indebted remaining superpower, the culturally schizoid natural-resource palace, the poor giant of Spanish America.

Readers of Richard Morse's influential *El espejo de Próspero* will find confirmation of the deep cultural gap between *America anglosaxónica*, which is the majority of Canada and the United States, and *America latina*, in this case Mexico. Probe deeper into the essential characteristics of *México profundo*, Guillermo Bonfil Batalla tells us, and the authentic worldview of Indian collectivism conflicts with the superficial cosmopolitanism of westernized elites, all within one nation. The two nations of the North, both overwhelmingly immigrant societies, will find scant resonance in Federico Ortiz Quesada's take-home message that "the key to understanding Mexico lies encoded in three millennia of history."[1]

What to do? If there must be rituals of friendship in the three universes of North America, relegate them to the surface of things? For leadership defer to the technocrats and money engineers in government and business who coolly calculate the economic rewards of proximity? Clear the decks of history, culture, and worldview, and especially of fuzzy and intangible notions like "identity"? The whole point of competitiveness, after all, is to shape our peoples to the global challenge. In the calculus of conventional wisdom among realists, economic interdependence provides enough consensus to keep things going for a while. In sum, it is regionalism that is bringing us together, and we should, of course, make the best of it. However plausible, such limited views misrepresent the possibilities for North American association on at least two counts. For one thing, the North American peoples already are creating the conditions for community through a myriad of individual and group choices, and their institutions are straining to respond. For another, there is a historical openness of thought, institutions, and practices in North America. This distinctive *amplitude of vision* offers the basis for a shared sense of continental community. Liberal in the broadest sense, this tradition is a restless faith in our ongoing search for better definitions of ourselves and our societies— definitions built on broad public participation, cultural diversity, and the practical value of experience in individual as well as institutional settings. In short, many of us have not been listening to what people do and what they want; and we have focused overlong on the wrong past.

Consider the movement of peoples. With 15 million Mexican Americans in various degrees of concourse with Mexico, and with one out of every seven Québécois wintering in Florida at a given time, profound and deep-running exchanges link North America's far-flung regions. Many small-town businesses in rural California could not survive without revolving credit accounts based on the deposits of Mexican farmworkers. The Vancouver Community Foundation runs a program to advise Canadians who want to make bequests to the Mexican and American towns and places where they have lived.[2] Consider also that the mass media, popular culture, and the astonishing growth of nongovernmental organizations (NGOs) and such manifestations of the "information revolution" as Internet are enabling us to learn much more about one another than before.

The complexity of North American society still needs explaining, something that the new lessons of market economics cannot fully address. Since we are all tumbled together as never before, we need a road map for this diverse, churning North American reality that is finding expression in an emerging community—the rich interplay of peoples, ideas, cuisines, architectures, and extended sense of "home" that defines our interdependent identities.

Let us be clear at the outset. Given the distinct histories and trajectories of three very large federal states, and their disparities in economic power, the model of a federated, European-style community with a capital "C" is unlikely to apply to North America. Yet as we sort out the distorting perspectives of history and unexamined stereotypes, it is plausible to envision a loosely structured and largely informal community with a small "c."

The fact is that Mexicans, Canadians, and Americans have reached a watershed. They have realized that the Soviets are no more, Mother England is far away, and Latin America is not the main event, and that for all three, the Pacific Basin looms larger all the time. They are realizing that they must work out a new sense of international Other explicitly in the North American context. For them, North America is where the action is, and it is more than just geography. North America has become a partnership, a multidimensional flow, that is rapidly dispensing with the attitudes that once raised our psychological borders so much higher than our political ones.

Precisely *because* of North America's diversity and internal contradictions, humanity at large has a stake in this experiment. Global affairs matter, but at the outset this is a site-specific undertaking. Government matters, but in a broader sense North American culture, thought, and institutions will have to do the job. Are they up to creating a regional community of such mass and scope?

"A community," as Robert Bellah and his associates inform us in *Habits of the Heart*, their influential study of American values, "is a group of people who are socially interdependent, who participate together in discussion and decision making, and who share certain *practices* [that] both define the community and are nurtured by it."[3] In their useful definition, "community attempts to be an inclusive whole, celebrating the interdependence of public and private life and of the different callings of all."[4] The achievement of wholeness is the subject of *The Good Society*, their next book, which looks at the role of "institutions [that are] not only constraining but also enabling. They are the substantial forms through which we understand our own identity and the identity of others as we seek cooperatively to achieve a decent society."[5] Institutions, thus, are essential building-blocks of community.

Bellah and his colleagues have been criticized for their focus on the majority culture of America, for neglecting the diverse strands that, woven together, produce the true cultural fabric of a nation of immigrants. They are said to neglect the fact that "wholeness" in community is inseparable from diversity. Specifying the *we* in community becomes a key operating question. We agree with this critique, all the more so when the diversity that draws our attention includes the contributions of peoples from all three nations to form a *continental* community. But we think the definition of community Bellah and his colleagues have constructed can be refashioned to accommodate this larger social vision, and we believe they are right in emphasizing the key role of institutions and practices in building community.

It is our thesis that fundamental social institutions and practices are on a convergent path in North America, and that they are the necessary instrumentalities for fleshing out a common intellectual heritage that we call liberal for its breadth and experimentalism and lessening of state constraints on individuals. However, we would note that the content of this liberalism and the institutions it nourishes is more and more defined by a tension between individual and group rights, a tension that affects the role and identity of the State as well. Although this phenomenon is similar in all three countries, their national histories matter a great deal here; they are approaching a new equilibrium—and each other—from different directions.

In this respect, Mexico and Canada share a greater emphasis on group rights and the State's role in promoting group rights, as Keith Spicer notes in his lead essay. In the United States, procedural liberalism is based fundamentally on choices made by individuals, as Marc Pachter tells us. We address this point at greater length below, while noting that taking pleasure in *shared differences* (a Ruy-Sánchez concept) will help in the resolution.

To understand this liberal tradition in North America, we begin with a search for the openness and novelty of North American experience in a triad of writers, starting with Mexico's Sor Juana Inés de la Cruz and proceeding on, in turn, to William Carlos Williams and Margaret Atwood. Each offers us a sense of North America's originality, breadth of possibilities, local particularities, and dependence upon the creativity of individuals.

Moving next to political philosophy, we touch upon the social thought of Octavio Paz, John Dewey, and Charles Taylor. These philosophers develop the common themes of individual responsibility and the demands of true community on modern society (although each leaves the means of achieving more authentic and discriminating relationships between the individual, the group, and society imperfectly defined).

Then, we identify the institutions that in our opinion best exemplify the core values and the finest achievements of each nation: Mexico's civic action program, Solidaridad; Canada's universal health care scheme; and the American university system. Here we encounter means for grounding liberal beliefs in institutions and practices ample enough to accommodate an individual's skills and goals in the framework of social needs.

Finally, having triangulated our continental map among the reference points of values, political philosophy, and institutions, we conclude by linking identities to the emerging possibilities of North American regionalism.

I

Culture doesn't count for much in international affairs because it gets in the way, or so say the realists. If culture is what you believe, it's nonnegotiable, a real impediment to business and diplomacy. If culture is what you *say* you believe, there may be some room for a deal, but even then the hypocrisy of stale forms and customs creates uncertainty and irritating delays. Besides, in international affairs, real culture isn't culture as commonly understood, which is to say, costumes and cuisine at the lower end and the arts at the higher end. No, for realists, culture is simply the cloth of power and control, their adornment and concealment. The thoroughly discredited totalitarian regimes of our century understood this well. Nationalists in the post–Cold War world are equally cynical in their manipulation of cultural forms. Besides, to emphasize culture in the radically diverse context of North America is to counterpose conflicting values to the highly legitimate utilitarian linkages so essential to relations between nations. When all is said and done, isn't the United States the real agglutinating factor in the trinational relationship?

In Mexico, after all, the underlying cultural reality, as history seems to shows us, is illiberalism. Counter-Reformation Mexico long has drawn on its inheritance from the other side of an earlier continental (in this case, European) divide. And that's glossing over three millennia of indigenous state theocracies that came before the Spaniards. How can an illiberal culture like Mexico's enter into community with its partners in twenty-first–century North America?

Even an exception to this interpretation of Mexico does much to reinforce its weight. But the moment has come to push into Mexican culture and examine its counterintuitive and often contradictory strengths. Is the Mexico the rest of North America thinks it knows—the Mexico of the poor and the powerful, the Mexico of authoritarianism, hierarchical control, and closed-mindedness—the only real or *essential* Mexico? Embedded in its past is a broadly cosmopolitan, even universal, spirit of inquiry and individual enterprise. In the *Labyrinth of Solitude*, the Nobel laureate Octavio Paz calls this universal spirit Mexico's positive and sunny inheritance from Spain, an open and engaging gift for exploration and experimentation (as contrasted with Spain's dark and rigid medieval militarism, so much better known in the Anglo-Saxon world).[6] He links this aspect of Mexican culture to the seventeenth-century poet Sor Juana Inés de la Cruz, an illegitimate child who took religious orders and yet became the advocate of science and inquiry as the foundation of belief—only to fall into the trap of being a woman unable to free herself of the illiberal men and doctrines that silenced her genius without real debate.[7]

The idea that such a brilliant woman could have emerged as the New World's First Poet (although Anne Bradstreet also is a candidate) and First Feminist says something to us about Mexico and the New World in general. It says that Mexico has long been intimately engaged in the West's great rationalist debate centered in Europe. Even in the times of the Inquisition, a Sor Juana could emerge: dependent but independent, dominated but free. Did she think she enjoyed real liberty or simply impunity as she made bold with the languages of love, science, and mystery in her verse? At times, yes, she benefited from the protection of viceroys and archbishops, but could she have "happened" in Madrid even with the same kind of patronage?[8] A certain distance from Spain enabled her to use Spain's own "universal" spirit to access the rest of the West.

This amplitude of vision is a central aspect of New World thought. In the case of Sor Juana, it seems to us that her genius used this detachment from Old World constraints to help define a tragically premature moment in the life of free inquiry and expression here—in the end, a self-destructive moment, since she failed to cast off the lot of what might be called "the least estate," simply being female. Yet when read today, Sor Juana's defense of her rights as a female human being strikes at the core issues of sexism in contemporary society. Mexico is *that* deeply vested in both gender-rights and counterdoctrinal thinking; its critical spirit isn't exclusively a function of either Revolutionary ideologues or U.S.-trained cabinet members.

Paz sums up Sor Juana's continuing relevance by citing her "Reply to Sor Filotea," a defense of individual and women's rights:

The fact that she wrote this defense and dared to proclaim her fondness for disinterested thought makes her a modern figure. If it is accurate to see her affirmation of the value of experience as an instinctive reaction against traditional Spanish thought, then there is an implicit defense of the intellectual conscience and consciousness in her conception of knowledge. . . . This gives her thought an originality that deserved something more than the eulogies of her contemporaries or the reproaches of her confessor, and in our own day demands a deeper judgment and a more daring examination.[9]

Some two centuries after Sor Juana's death, the great American poet William Carlos Williams understood that the history of Mexico (and Canada as well) had important and little-studied messages for the United States. To him all three countries were "America," a community of individuals whose natural and best bond was the shared willingness to see the New World as truly new, open, and uncorrupted, not a fresh stage set for rehashing Europe's old ways of dogma, greed, power, and manipulation. In his continental tableau, Williams found the reality of the American Other as much in such quotidian events as a woman dressing herself in a second-story window as in the grand image of Champlain founding Quebec.

Heir to the literature of Edgar Allan Poe, Ralph Waldo Emerson, Emily Dickinson, and Walt Whitman (a literature that wrenched itself free of Old World forms and motives), Williams forged a poetry that fits within what the Canadian philosopher Charles Taylor would call the "authenticity of recognition." In his poetry and his autobiography, and especially in his singular work of imaginative history, *In the American Grain*, Williams insists upon the moral and aesthetic virtue of the encounter experience in which America was born and still, however much diminished, struggles to survive.[10] Like Sor Juana before him, he asserts a distinctively New World liberal right to confront history, knowledge, and desire in his own personal consciousness. Thus he shares in and authenticates the life of what he would recognize.

Williams argues that the threat to this American community lies in succumbing, individually and collectively, to the propaganda of interests and ideologies, whether it flows from that arch-instrumentalist Alexander Hamilton (whom Williams loathed) or from the Puritans. His eclectic response is to use antiheroes and heroes alike to chip away at the received wisdom of Indian-haters like the American historian Francis Parkman. He despises Eurocentric prejudices and small-minded jealousies that whittle away at the grandeurs of America's native genius, and he fights back by turning instead to the themes of space, place, action, and character to make us remember that America from Tenochtitlan to Paterson (his New Jersey home) and the Georges Bank is a fresh chance for the human spirit.

As Octavio Paz described Williams's approach, "America is not a given reality but something we all make together with our hands, our eyes, our brains, and our lips. . . . American man speaks a language different from the European original."[11] This is the essence of Williams's generosity and adventuresomeness. He looked aghast (and with contempt) at T. S. Eliot's "The Wasteland" because it cowered before the vitalizing wilderness of the American spirit and celebrated bondage to the European tradition. Rather than looking to Europe for communal space, Williams would have Americans stare at Canadian ice and Mexican fire.

To this day, Williams remains an intellectually cantankerous but vital figure in American literature. His insistence upon the "value of experience" is as disruptive as Eliot's insistence upon "the value of tradition" is stabilizing. It is grass roots and democratic, Whitman-like. And it is unmistakably contrarian, defying the rigid paradigms of three resolutely separate countries in North America, married in geography, divorced in spirit. We got North America all wrong, Williams writes in *In the American Grain*. For Williams, our destiny was always part of a larger, continental New World of shared encounter. Whatever some might think of his selective and idiosyncratic methods, his relevance today lies in his dogged pursuit of social and cultural possibilities far greater than those offered by the United States alone.[12]

A Canadian poet, novelist, and critic who studied the Puritans, Margaret Atwood no doubt would agree with Williams about the limits of U.S. culture. In her novelistic nightmare *The Handmaid's Tale*, a futuristic and totalitarian version of the United States straps Sor Juana down for state-sponsored sex in search of the unradiated egg.[13] Puritan order, Puritan purpose, and Puritan hypocrisy inform this vision of humanity sacrificed on the altar of ideas. Strange how well this book and most of Atwood's work over the last two decades has sold in the United States, her largest market. Here is a Canadian who severely criticizes U.S. culture—who conflates anyone prone to solving problems by violence and aggression as "American"—and yet who holds the stature of the home-grown giants of contemporary American letters: the Updikes, the Morrisons, the Percys, the Oateses. And doubly strange because Atwood is the Canadian writer who has perhaps most gone out of the way to take on the problem of Canadian, not American, literature, despite her early studies at the Harvard of the Puritans.

Her message is at least twofold. First, the very liberalism (shared by William Carlos Williams) that makes Atwood critical of the United States is exactly what makes her appealing to the nation's own self-questioning irreverence and iconoclasm. It is a satirical, ironic liberalism that Americans understand (not unlike the liberalism of the Mexican novelist Carlos Fuentes, who also is widely read in the United States), a liberalism that doesn't accept exclusions when, for any reason, one's interest is engaged. Second, Atwood's importance in Canada, the United States, and elsewhere derives at least in some measure from the fact that she is a shaper and symbol of Canadian culture.

Unlike Williams's vision in *In the American Grain*, Atwood's literary interpretation of Canada in her seminal book *Survival* (a concept that both Keith Spicer and Daniel Latouche nicely define for their own purposes in this volume) doesn't cross borders.[14] In the early 1970's, Atwood concluded that Canadian literature as such had never been defined, and this is the job she set for herself, emphasizing the crucial, if not wholly deterministic, influence Canada's harsh and demanding natural environment has had on its social outlook. In *Survival* and succeeding works, Atwood (like Williams) has granted physical reality a leading role in terms of both the human body, especially the woman's body, and Canada's body, that vast, harsh, life-threatening, and yet inspiring presence in the national psyche. In Atwood's interpretation, "the sense of northernness and space" that Canada's Group of Seven painters captured on canvas after the First World War haunts its literature as well.[15] The north questions the individual and collective will to become either victim or survivor; it demands responses, crushes alibis, and works on timetables indifferent to human history. We would take special note of this view as a literal grounding of social thought in the limits and mysteries of organic and inorganic ecologies. Unlike

Europe, Atwood seems to be implicitly saying, Canada (and all of North America) is not exclusively a social endeavor. Though her treatment of the broad themes in Canadian literature is still debated as vigorously as when she first proffered it, the rise of environmentalism in the ensuing twenty years has given her indirect support from a separate field. The earth to which she attaches so much importance hasn't finished speaking yet; its voice can be heard even in the corridors and avenues of the cities. Further, the *fact* of Atwood's having consolidated a view of one aspect of Canada's cultural production gave her (and Canada) a stance to take inside and outside the country—in dialogue with the United States, Britain, or any other country. Absent such self-knowledge and self-criticism, what is the worth of an interlocutor? But given such self-knowledge and self-criticism, the interlocutor gains in interest and value, even as she turns her powers of critique on you.

This trio of literary figures—the nun, the doctor, and the critic—may appear grouped more by convenience than reason. It can be said that they "have nothing to do with one another," and in some literal sense, that is arguable, but in cultural terms, each embodies a stance of free and restless inquiry that is more North American than European. In the Mexican case, it is precisely the difficulty of understanding Sor Juana in the context of a bright, as opposed to a dark, Spanish heritage that makes her so intriguing and relevant. She is wittier than her American contemporary, Mistress Anne Bradstreet; she is Atwood-like and Williams-like in her nonconforming qualities. But in the end all three of them, each in her or his own way, are insistently original because their context is original: named or unnamed, it is the New World, and it is North America.

II

The case for reservoirs of continental understanding and relevance may emerge more directly from political thinkers and philosophers than poets, whose chosen role, after all, is to tear down paradigms of conventional thought, not build them up. But if the United States and Canada are self-styled liberal democracies, where does Mexico fit in, with its 70-plus years of one-party rule and its Indo-Hispanic tendency to govern by group interest rather than individual rights? And where does the United States fit in, with the massive imperatives of its internal dynamics; its one federal representative per 400,000-plus people and dozen lobbyists per giant corporation; its juggernaut debt; its magnetic pull with respect to the Mexican poor and to Canadians of all kinds? Or Canada, perpetually cleaved within itself: English against French, West against East, the whole relentlessly pulled South?

The unifying trendline we see in North American political thought is a persistent, hence recuperable, liberal tradition, plagued with interruptions and contradictions though it may be. By liberal, we mean respectful of individual rights through democratic political values and processes that are nurtured by an openness to the consequences of free inquiry. Liberalism's way of economic life is essentially capitalist in orientation, but in all three national traditions, we find a willingness to have the State act as a counterbalancing tool against large, vested interests and address common problems that the market, left alone, cannot. We see political liberalism and capitalist economics as motive forces in North American thought as far back as Mexican Independence right through the rise of the U.S. military-industrial complex and down to the debate about diversity and multiculturalism in Canada today.

For Mexico, one might argue that the current regime of privatization, free trade, and control of state governments by opposition parties is exclusively a response to contemporary international circumstances and recent internal difficulties—a dysfunctional economy as well as dysfunctional State governance. Lodging the case for Mexico's recent changes within the last ten years of debt crisis and recovery creates the satisfying illusion that national experience is policy-sensitive. Yet these changes are such radical turnabouts as to finally belittle policy analysis and raise the question of whether Mexico has suddenly given up on its own national identity. After all, it has undone post-Revolutionary agricultural reform, reestablished relations with the Vatican, and dared to enter into a free trade agreement with the United States and Canada. Few Mexicanists prior to 1988 would have predicted much if any of this.

We would argue that nations and their leaders do not enter into such changes without a sense of rootedness and ballast lodged in the national past (or if they do, it is at their considerable peril). We look back, then, at Mexican history and search for antecedents to contemporary liberalism grounded in the rule of law, the rights of the individual against vested interests, and the ability of the nation to spawn socioeconomic progress through *less-centralized* institutions.

That such a Mexico once asserted itself may seem jarring to Canadians and Americans accustomed to another view of Mexico. Yet former President Miguel de la Madrid made this point when he said that the will for a liberal order had existed early on; it was simply that, without the socioeconomic conditions to sustain it, the State was able to resume its strong centralizing role.[16] The historian Charles Hale, who argues the case at length in *Mexican Liberalism in the Age of Mora*,[17] sees Independence-era Mexico as deeply attuned to the liberal philosophical principles that motivated the French and American revolutions. He is exactly right. Mexico was indeed a country that was intellectually cosmopolitan, even more heavily influenced by France than by Spain, and an enemy of ancient tyrannies—the Church, the military, the nobility. Mexicans *wanted*, in many ways, to achieve a liberal democracy analogous to the democracy of Madison and Jefferson. That they failed to avoid civil wars, foreign interventions, dictatorships, and the traps of one-party rule does not discount the enlightened impulses of earnest, learned constitutionalism in the first half of the nineteenth century. Fundamentally, those who would question Mexico's ability to relate politically to the other two North American democracies either do not understand or miss entirely this intellectual and historical grounding available to contemporary Mexican reformers.

Still, Octavio Paz emphasizes two cautionary points about this period. First, there was its discontinuity with colonial thought and governance, as well as indigenous models: "The democratic ideas adopted by the liberals were the negation of everything that New Spain had been."[18] Second, liberalism was all the more unstable because it lacked a middle class to sustain it against the powerful and entrenched institutions of the Church and the army.[19]

On top of these uncertain internal conditions, Mexican liberals were thunderstruck by the actions of the United States in the war of 1846. For them, the United States, till then a virtuous paragon of representative democracy, showed another, horrendous face, as an insatiable monster that consumed half of Mexico's territory. Worse, U.S.-style imperialism gained force in the hemisphere: "The fragmentation of our countries [i.e., of Latin America], the civil wars, their militarism and dictatorships, were, naturally, not invented by the United States. Yet that nation bears a primordial responsibility, since it seized upon this state of affairs in order to turn a profit, to further its own interests, and to dominate."[20]

As Paz and others retell the tale, Mexico gradually—through the liberal Reform of 1857, the Revolution of 1910, and subsequent modifications—limited the roles of the Church and army in national life while banishing the aristocracy completely. Mexico also incorporated aspects of pre-Columbian cultural forms into its governance. Revolutionary Zapatismo, a radical program of return to small-scale agricultural communitarianism, found expression in Mexico's (recently reformed) *ejido* system of communal lands. And post-Revolutionary Mexican presidents have, ac-

cording to Paz, represented not so much the Hispano-arabist and person-
alist political boss (*caudillo*) found in other Latin American countries as
the institutionalized and impersonal Aztec leader-priest (*tlatoani*). "Hence
the abstract figure of the president corresponds to a bureaucratic and hi-
erarchic corporation like the Institutional Revolutionary Party, which has
ruled Mexico since 1935."[21]

Although Paz confesses that Mexico has had "many a tlatoani and
many a caudillo in [its] history," his case for the "secret supremacy of the
Aztec model" is impressively substantiated by Mexico's remarkable stability for the better part of this century, while so many other Latin American
regimes have tottered and fallen under caudillo-style leadership or unstable
military regimes.

Yet Paz does not offer this critique of the Mexican experience as self-
satisfied praise. Rather, he suggests that cultural legitimacy is a necessary
but insufficient condition for meeting Mexico's problems and aspirations.
Here, for Paz, is where liberal democracy enters in. In fact, liberal democracy—rooted or unrooted—he insists, is an idea that will not let Latin
America, or Mexico, alone. Writing in an essay entitled "Latin America
and Democracy," he comments: "Our nations were democratic by birth,
and, despite crimes and tyrannies, democracy was a sort of historic act of
baptism for our peoples."[22] And with regard to Mexico specifically, "the
central and most urgent question in Mexico is to achieve a political reform
that assures, once and for all, the rotation in power of the different parties
through free elections."[23]

Again, cultural legitimacy alone will not do. Else why has it failed to
help Mexico or any other Latin American country "modernize" itself? Setting aside his misgivings about "progress," Paz notes that every Latin
American revolution since the days of Independence has been implicitly
founded on the promise of improving the material welfare of its impoverished citizens. With regard to the institutions necessary to achieve social
and material well-being, Paz is not an unremitting critic of the United
States, and it would be a serious mistake to read him that way. Indeed, he
can be as generous in his praise as he is severe in his criticism:

One of the great achievements of the American people has been to preserve democracy in the face of the two great threats of our day: the powerful capitalist
oligarchies and the bureaucratic State of the twentieth century. Another positive
sign: Americans have made great advances in the art of human cohabitation, not
only in terms of different ethnic groups that live peacefully together but also in
domains heretofore ruled by the taboos of traditional morality, such as sexu-
ality. . . . Finally, the development of the sciences and technology is a direct con-

sequence of the freedom of investigation and criticism predominant in the universities and cultural institutions of the United States.[24]

What Paz seeks from the United States is a wise use of its critical vision in understanding and accepting Mexico's historical and cultural reality. He argues that this is in our best interests as well as Mexico's: "Not only do we 'others' make up the majority of the human race, but also each marginal society, poor though it may be, represents a unique and precious version of mankind. If the United States is to recover fortitude and lucidity, it must recover itself, and to recover itself it must recover the 'others'— the outcasts of the Western World."[25]

At the same time, Paz asks a great deal of Mexico, and has been asking it for many decades. The elements of his critique, coupled with his call for the rotation in power of different Mexican parties through free elections, appear to add up to a truly indigenous version of liberal democracy.

The staying power and enduring imperatives of Mexico's indigenous cultural forms should be clear to all by now, but has the time in fact come when the dream of Mora and his fellow nineteenth-century liberals can be realized and wedded to them? Only time can resolve this complex question, but we would note that two significant factors that detracted from liberal democracy in Mexico in the nineteenth century appear to support it at the end of the twentieth.

First, it has been clear since the late 1960's, if not before, that what Mora and his cohorts lacked by way of general support—an educated and concerned middle class and an articulated national market and financial system—now exists. As a consequence, some political change has been occurring in Mexico (governorships, city offices, and other positions coming into the hands of various "opposition" parties all over the country), and more pluralism is likely. And second, the United States's increasing ease with the multiple "Others" within its borders, and its growing appreciation of economic interdependence across borders, have opened it to Mexico in new, positive ways. Canada, too, has the same interest in constructive cooperation with Mexico, providing fresh room for growth.

That said, we must note again that Paz's perspective on the United States, the West, and modernity in general is cautionary. He warns of the "suicide cult of progress,"[26] and believes that modernity, which is, after all, the product of liberal democracies, is showing its age in the degraded environment, the surge in drug use, the decay of the cities, and the alienation of workers from their work. His jeremiad on these points ultimately leads him to call for the deepest kinds of communal intimacy within the individual soul and between members of society. Confessing that this is an impossible dream, a problem of existence, he accordingly shifts from the poetic plane to that of political criticism, where (as we will shortly see) he offers an agenda that is deeply compatible with the thought of John Dewey. In his essay "The Other Mexico," Paz writes: "We must break up the existing monopolies—whether of the state, of parties, or of private capitalism—and discover forms, new and truly effective forms, of democratic and popular control over political and economic power and over the information media and education. A plural society, without majorities or minorities: not all of us are happy in my political utopia, *but at least all of us are responsible.*" [27]

Turning now to the United States, we preface our discussion by acknowledging that the first act in the post–Cold War era could indeed be the worldwide assertion of a new Manifest Destiny of American culture, technology, and power. We don't rule that out. As the sole standing superpower, the United States casts its gaze globally beyond North America deep into Europe, Africa, the Middle East, and the Pacific. There certainly was such a strain in American thought evident in the last twelve years of Republican administration, but despite the tremendous attractions and imperatives of American globalism, the Democrats won the 1992 presidential election by emphasizing the domestic, not a foreign, agenda.

So, as foreign commentators often lament, America lurches this way and that. It is impulsive and inconstant. But any thoughts that it can ignore the world are illusory, especially when its destiny is now coupled so tightly with that of its two continental neighbors. In fact, its largest export markets, principal immigration concerns, and most pressing international environmental agenda all are lodged in North America.

In our view, a stabilizing principle of philosophical thought is seeking to reassert itself in the American scheme of things—a principle of thought, founded on individual self-fulfillment in a context of community, that is well suited to a more meaningful conception of North American relations. We refer to that strain of American liberalism called "pragmatism" in the works of John Dewey. Much more than simple "utilitarianism," pragmatism is an anti-zealous, anti-absolute, sober exercise in the search not just for *what works,* but for *what benefits, what fulfills, what untroubles and untangles,* and *what clarifies.*

Using all the tools of the philosophical tradition and borrowing from the method of scientific empiricism, Dewey based his philosophy on the belief that the individual and society can and must form an interrelationship guided by human intelligence in pursuit of the ultimate goal of community. His thesis was that the two were distinct but inseparable realities.

As in the case of the mind and the body, one could not possibly exist without the other. "In fact, both words, individual and social, are hopelessly ambiguous, and the ambiguity will never cease as long as we think in terms of antithesis."[28]

Compounding the challenge of resolving individual and collective interests is the fact that any individual is likely to hold multiple allegiances and be a complex society in his or her own right:

An individual as a member of different groups may be divided within himself, and in a true sense have conflicting selves, or be a relatively disintegrated individual. A man may be one thing as a church member and another thing as a member of the business community. The difference may be carried as if in water-tight compartments, or it may become a division as to entail conflict. In these facts we have the ground of the common antithesis set up between society and the individual. Then "society" becomes an unreal abstraction and "*the* individual" becomes an equally unreal one.[29]

Yet Dewey believed human beings are capable of assessing their interests and doing so in terms that are remarkably similar to those posed by Paz. What Dewey called "effective democracy" would counter the alienating effects of industrial modernity. In accord with Paz's call for "new and truly effective forms of democratic and popular control,"[30] Dewey proposed: "All those who are affected by social institutions must have a share in producing and managing them. The two facts that each one is influenced in what he does and enjoys and in what he becomes by the institutions under which he lives, and that there he shall have, in a democracy, a voice in shaping them, are the passive and active sides of the same fact."[31]

As Robert Westbrook observes in his impressive biography, Dewey did not construe democracy as limited to political democracy.[32] His concept of democracy was broader and led beyond political institutions to the larger goal of community. Again, like Paz he was aware (as we are aware) that such thinking would be tarred as "utopian." Walter Lippmann took great trouble to chop down the notion of the "omnicompetent citizen" capable of informing himself on all the arcana of modern public policy.[33]

Yet Dewey stiffly resisted any concept of democratic elitism that overlooked the value and meaning of community: "The clear consciousness of a communal life, in all its implications, constitutes the idea of democracy. Only when we start from a community as a fact, grasp the fact in thought so as to clarify and enhance its constituent elements, can we reach an idea of democracy which is not utopian. . . . Fraternity, liberty and equality isolated from communal life are hopeless abstractions."[34]

To be sure, Dewey's central conception of community was that of "local communities," full of "abundant meanings" and "smaller intimate unions of human beings living in immediate contact with one another,"[35] but he, like Paz and Williams, was more than willing to trade grand false starts for small home truths. However challenging "the reconstruction of face-to-face communities" might be, Dewey insisted on a pragmatic engagement with the situation at hand as the final epistemological verdict. "The local is the ultimate universal, and as near an absolute as exists."[36]

Dewey, the quintessential twentieth-century voice for the philosophy of democracy as a relationship between the individual and society, rose and fell away in the United States, as Mora and his cohorts had done in nineteenth-century Mexico. As Westbrook relates, there was a time when he was necessary to complete all public debates—Dewey on God, Dewey on schools, Dewey on art, Dewey on war—but the gigantism of America's response to the Second World War gradually ground him down and pushed him away. The precise, site-specific ethical procedures of pragmatic liberalism advanced by Dewey were too fine, too doubting, to guide a nation confronting the armies of fascism. More complete and sweeping judgments were needed than he would admit. Or so it was said by critics like Reinhold Niebuhr and Lewis Mumford, who feasted on misreadings of his work.

Yet Dewey has not been long forgotten, being highly relevant as a political thinker today. The military-industrial complex that concerned Eisenhower was something Dewey foresaw; "small is beautiful" and "think globally, act locally" are mottoes consistent with his thought. A few scholars and activists in the 1960's, then more in the following decades, saw fit to revisit Deweyism from biographical, political, educational, and philosophical perspectives. Quality circles in manufacturing are consistent with Deweyism; respect for cultural diversity is consistent with Deweyism; the use of the media in narrow-casted "electronic townhalls" is consistent with Deweyism; and certainly the clear-eyed engagement of Americans, Mexicans, and Canadians on the basis of an interdependent and continental context is consistent with Deweyism.

Were he alive today, John Dewey would start the march toward a new agenda of global concerns right here in North America, placing community building higher on his list of priorities than productivity, the environment higher than profits, the goals and aspirations of people higher than their effective use as atomized factors in the international division of labor. In unblinking fashion, John Dewey would move along the networks of interdependence in North America and rethink them all from the perspective of human interests and values.

The Canadian philosopher Charles Taylor draws on the Dewey tradition in his cogent analysis of the ways liberalism is being redefined in our postmodern age. The tension between the search for authenticity in the form of being true to oneself and the new imperatives of group recognition as manifest in multiculturalism is one of Taylor's central themes. In a series of influential books and essays, Taylor has established himself as perhaps the most lucid and sophisticated North American thinker on individual and group identities in the liberal state.[37]

But unlike Dewey, who wrote generations ago from what was then the great melting pot of the United States, Taylor has contemporary Canada, a different immigrant society, as his point of reference. While writing broadly about Western values, he cares deeply about Canada, and it is here that the creative tension between two different and competing concepts of rights liberalism is being played out on a national scale.

On the one hand, there is the concept of individual-based procedural liberalism, codified in Canada's 1982 Charter of Rights, which reflects the U.S. Bill of Rights. The bedrock principle here is equal treatment. But on the other hand, there is the equally strong claim of group liberalism to safeguard certain historically grounded group values. Quebec is of course the foremost champion of this principle, whose watchword is *la survivance*, or cultural survival, though native rights are also being pressed. But a liberal society like Quebec based on group rights unquestionably challenges the model of a liberal society like Canada as a whole based on individual rights. Such incompatible aims, it would seem, are a prescription for national breakup, something Canada is putting to the test. And this is happening despite broad, shared agreement on basic individual and political rights, such as the security of the person and of the vote. So how can liberalism accommodate certain collective goals, granting differential treatment to diverse groups, while remaining true to the rights of the individual? This is the question Taylor explores in his seminal essay on multiculturalism.[38]

The answer, Taylor says, lies in allowing ourselves to differ while preserving a larger social connectedness by achieving the wider sense of community any society needs to survive.[39] If accommodating difference is what Canada is all about, then what happens in this northernmost nation of North America is centrally important to us all.

This is because the civic values of *all* modern societies increasingly are subject to what Taylor calls the rising demands of "recognition." And it doesn't take a Quebec to force the issue. At its most elemental, Taylor defines "recognition" as the call for the equal dignity of genders, ethnicities, and cultures,[40] all in the name of permitting members of those genders, ethnicities, and cultures to enjoy their own authenticity, being true to themselves. Yet what Taylor calls "the politics of equal dignity" has two conflicting requirements that are symptomatic of the tensions between group and individual rights. One would have us treat people "in a difference blind fashion." The other would have us "recognize and even foster particularity." Don't these divergent requirements place us in a classic dilemma? If we are not blind to difference, we run the risk of violating the principle of nondiscrimination. But if we *are* blind to difference, we run the risk of negating "identity by forcing people into a homogeneous mold that is untrue to them."[41] This can be construed as a form of morally unjust oppression. What we are faced with, fundamentally, is the requirement for universal recognition of authentic difference, a deep and demanding ethical vision that honors the characteristics of identity emanating either from the individual-as-individual or from the individual-as-member-of-group, as the case may be and as the perceived individual may desire.[42]

In the social and political tableau of North America, this difficult playing out of individual and group identities is likely to be less pressing in Mexico, with its more culturally based identity, than in the two immigrant societies to the North, where nationality is essentially defined by political compact. Nonetheless, a commingling of perspectives is inevitable. As Taylor notes: "All societies are becoming more multicultural and more porous."[43] We have to live together more and more—in our cities, throughout our countries, and across the continent of North America. This requires the acceptance of difference, originality, and diversity. Building community requires an appreciation of, even pleasure in, if not love for, the differences of others.

Americans, with their strong commitment to procedural liberalism, have more difficulty with group and corporate rights. After all, Canada has within it "the Quebec fact," which establishes a condition of deep diversity as an a priori feature of the national self-image.[44] Yet deep diversity is just the challenge that Native Americans in the United States (as well as in Canada and Mexico) have posed for generations. And it is within the concept of deep diversity—a diversity that turns on the characteristics of past and future generations, as well as of the current generation—that Taylor looks for a justice that honors both group and individual rights, a justice that also would amplify North America's capabilities for self-understanding and acceptance.

For Taylor, like Dewey, the individual derives the mass of his identity from his relationship with society. But Taylor goes beyond Dewey by adding "groups" as a form of mediation between the individual and society. In effect, Taylor is calling for a *relativistic* liberalism, amplifying Dewey's *pragmatic* liberalism by allowing space for the rights of such distinct groups as Francophones and First Nations. In their claim to recognition and authenticity, these groups project distinctive gender, ethnic, or cultural identities through time; not unlike national identities on a larger scale, groups are history in human motion, attaching their ongoing collective meanings and identities to individual subjects. And if not recognized, they are effectively denied, an aggressive act.

The operational logic of Taylor's search for dignity and justice is that as long as what group X needs by way of recognition does not detract from the vital interests of anyone else's individual rights, it merits that recognition. The key to this concept, we would emphasize, is the question of need, always a debatable but at least a specific issue. The fear procedural liberals have of this construct is that the assertion of group rights might go on and on, eventually blotting out the concept of individual rights altogether. This "give an inch, take a mile" argument has a strict, lawyerly logic to it, no doubt. However, the groups in question are a historical and present fact whose requirements for identity are neither discretionary nor arbitrary. Is there room for them in Canada or in the makeup of all of North America, with its vast storehouse of ethnicities and nationalities? As we and Taylor suggest, in a truly liberal community, diversity can find its voice because community is a harmonizing force, *especially if, in true Deweyian fashion, the cost/benefit analysis of the allocation of rights is performed on the spot and not in some abstract field of general principle.*

The American law professor George P. Fletcher, in his 1993 essay on the ethics of loyalty, calls for a "melding of [these] two systems, the universal and the relational, the impartial and the partial."[45] One needs both: an overemphasis on historically grounded rights and personal loyalties leads to rigid particularism; an overarching universalism violates those things we hold near and dear. The upshot is that "the ethics of loyalty doom us to a mixed system of independent but compelling systems of thought," not unlike the mixed economy, with its awkward but workable mix of market signals and the State's guiding hand.[46] For example, the historically grounded exclusive right of Pueblo Indians to market their jewelry under the portal of the Palace of the Governors in Santa Fe was recently affirmed. Rejecting the claim of an Anglo merchant that to deny him a place was a violation of his individual rights, the court considered Indian sales as a legitimate Palace "program."

The pragmatic resolution of this local drama is a good example of Taylor's relativistic liberalism. To see differences not as obstacles, but as building-blocks to community is the challenge in Taylor's thought.

III

If these are the cultural and intellectual perspectives contributing to North America's outlook on itself, what are the instrumental outcomes? Specifically, what institutions have each people generated that have value in both the national and the subregional context? And what are the potential borrowings and gains that might accrue in North America from a sense of community that goes beyond capital investment, products of exchange, and other profit-seeking ventures?

Fortunately for North America, the locus of change related to the issues of rights, values, and identity are working themselves out in small subnational units, where efficacy and community combine in functional practices and institutions. As we have seen elsewhere in this book, transborder regions are reworking the socioeconomic landscape of North America. The dynamics of federalism are very active in Canada and the United States, and are gaining force in Mexico in an attempt to overcome or bypass the limitations of its centralized state system. Thus it is in subnational units that the play of individual and group rights will be most clearly revealed within the context of three national citizenships.

Our short list of national institutions is emblematic of a North America that is open to diverse conditions, yet coherent. These institutions function between the global and the local, perhaps countering by their effectiveness the forces of integration/disintegration unleashed by the global economy. We place on this list Mexico's civic action program, called the National Solidarity Program (PRONASOL) or Solidaridad; the U.S. system of higher education; and the Canadian health care plan.

The liberalism practiced by the Salinas administration is a conditioned liberalism, according to Salinas himself, who calls it "liberalismo social," or "social liberalism." It is a liberalism of individual rights and competition in the marketplace up to the point where market forces and economics do not reach or meet the needs of society. A highway can be privatized, and so it should be. A bank can be privatized, and so it should be. But where the private sector has little incentive to do anything—in providing electrical power to a distant mountain village, say—the government seeks to provide a partnership with the members of society themselves. Under

Solidaridad, a $2–3 billion per annum program of civic works and start-up capital for small, service-oriented businesses, the Mexican government deals directly with the community: it will provide something if the community provides something in response. Let the community dig the cable ditches, and Solidaridad will provide the cable. Let the community provide a health clinic building, and Solidaridad will provide the medical equipment.

Throughout Mexican history (and throughout Latin America), such programs traditionally have been maladministered exercises in pork and paternalism. There have been charges that Solidaridad falls into the same category, at least in part,[47] but it undeniably does have the focus of activism and genuine cooperation. In the main, it is limited to specific community-oriented plans, not national goals. It is Dewey-like in this regard, a wholly fresh way of linking the State with civil society so effective that it promises to outlast Salinas's personal vision and endure as a major Mexican institution. As one Solidaridad official suggested to us: "Our way of sponsoring local enterprises works. Why don't you try it in Los Angeles?"[48]

The acceptance of "co-responsibility" between government and citizens in responding to society's needs gets results. Both the United States and Canada can learn from Solidaridad's success in linking the State with grass-roots civil society.

Has history now overtaken this judgment? The severest test and criticism of the Solidaridad program and Mexico's progress toward a fuller experience of democratic liberalism came with the insurrection of the Zapatista National Liberation Army in January 1994. The question of whether this movement indicts the value of the entire Solidaridad program remains open as of this writing. It would appear that the good works and community spirit Solidaridad has generated remain valid in and of themselves but are, at least in Chiapas, insufficient. Donaldo Colosio, the PRI presidential candidate, was raising the theme of unmet demands for social and economic recognition when he was assassinated in March 1994.

We see a positive relationship between NAFTA-inspired optimism about Mexico, the promise of social liberalism, and the Zapatistas' expression of grievance. As Bustamante foresaw in his essay (written in mid-1993), economic developments focused on the north of Mexico highlighted underdevelopment in the south. The Zapatista movement appears to claim a different kind of economic justice than that witnessed in the north, however, and this justice is linked to new expressions of democracy, indigenously conceived expressions of democratic self-rule, and entitlement.

Dramatic change is occurring throughout Mexico, and free trade has opened up the concept of free politics. Liberalization works this way: whether one begins with political opening or economic liberalization is more a question of timing than substance. In the end, at least in the West, civil society acquires and expresses both kinds of power. The passing of an old order, especially a strained, relatively poor order, brings with it varieties of nationalistic utopianism and withdrawal as the old ways of doing things give way. It also mandates adjustments and concessions to realities on the ground—hence the galvanized responses to the Chiapas rising—which may vary in a large, complex country like Mexico.

It seems reasonable to expect that Mexico will continue to move in the direction of democratic self-expression, open channels of internal debate and communication, and liberalized economic activity. This trend may not advance as swiftly as the modernizers once imagined. Nonetheless, the concepts of community, group rights, and individual contributions to the greater whole, of democracy and market capitalism, have come more seriously into play in Mexican national experience. The expectation is for greater commitments to Solidaridad and the like, not simply to buy off disgruntlement and alienation or to extend entitlements, but to reach hitherto vulnerable and marginal groups demanding recognition in the sense that Charles Taylor defined it.

In the United States, one institutional achievement stands out as quintessentially American. We refer to the U.S. university system—including the old-line private schools as well as the land grant and state colleges. Open to all socioeconomic sectors, providing massive grants-in-aid, and dedicated to the impartial development of socially useful knowledge, U.S. colleges and universities, with their 13 million students, are where U.S. resources and values come together better than anywhere else. Though they could not attain the diverse excellence for which they are noted without billions of federal research dollars each year and the support of private donors, financial strength alone is not the secret to U.S. schools. The secret has more to do with the proposition that they are wedded to the needs of society in general—that knowledge cannot be indifferent to the fate of the nation but rather is, in the benefits (and risks) of free inquiry, its lifeblood. This is a distinctively U.S. approach, one good enough to share in and emulate. (And Canada has done so, while going a step further to erase the fee differences between public and private universities.) As Dewey suggested, it is an emblem of the inextricable link between individual and society. Every student and faculty member on every campus must understand (or should be reminded) that they are bound to a community at large that supports their work with many millions and, in fact, billions of dollars' worth of critical infrastructure.

In essence, the U.S. philosophy of education is that individual excellence blends with team efforts to produce knowledge, much of it targeted explicitly to the public good and readily transferable, as in the Silicon Valley phenomenon. Put another way, knowledge is not disconnected from society or simply linked to the perpetuation of certain class entitlements or privileges. This approach to knowledge is a highly flexible engine for competitiveness, as well as a training resource for humankind.[49]

Similarly, the Canadian health care system has raised a positive example for its neighbors to the south. Isn't a guarantee of medical attention to any and all a brilliant keystone for a polity that prides itself on service to people? The motto is simple but profound, "Canada Cares," and the message is one that speaks to the deepest and most vulnerable recesses of every Canadian's identity: a person's right to physical well-being and welfare in time of critical need, and the responsibility of a community-oriented government to secure this right. The development of the Canadian health care system in the 1960's marked a turn toward shared responsibility and unity in Canada, even as the forces of French Canadian separatism and Western independence were rising in national life.[50]

Universal health care is something Americans have not known. The obverse of the Canadian motto is that the United States Does Not Care, although the Clinton administration has made such coverage a priority.[51] Unlike the United States, Mexico now achieves almost universal vaccination against common childhood diseases. With its tradition of collective services, Mexico can also aspire to comprehensive health care, increased national wealth permitting.

IV

The purpose of this essay is to identify available ideas that support the dynamics of common interests in North America. Its thesis is that through self-knowledge, North America can reap the benefits of self-actualization. The Germans use a word—*schadenfreude*—to signify joy at the misfortune of one's enemy. It is for North Americans to invent a word to signify the opposite: joy at the good fortune of one's friend.

Aptly enough, Charles Taylor cites the German philosopher Hans-Georg Gadamer's concept of a "fusion of horizons" in his long essay on multiculturalism cited above: "What has to happen is that we learn to move in a broader horizon, within which what we have formerly taken for granted as background to valuation can be situated as one possibility alongside the different background of the formerly unfamiliar culture. The 'fusion of horizons' operates through our developing new vocabularies of comparison, by means of which we can articulate these contrasts."[52]

Needed for a fusion of horizons to occur is a willingness to accept why and how we—all of us—act from different national perspectives, without having to abandon our own beliefs. Our respective national civic cultures are deepened thereby: what is our own, what is most near and dear, is broadened and enriched by convergence, proximity, and understanding, to the point of taking pleasure in the civic culture of our neighbors. The result is to develop multiple allegiances, without necessarily giving up our original one. In this era of continental partnership and increased flows of all kinds, the mind-set to go with them is at once broader, but also deeper.

To reap the benefits of a larger whole, liberalism itself must be married with community in order to overcome or at least counterbalance its historic tendency to undervalue the collective dimension of human existence. As Ken Jowett points out, those hostile to "liberal capitalist democracy [scorn it] for an inordinate emphasis on individualism, materialism, technical achievement, and rationality."[53] To us, the amplitude of vision based on liberal thought, institutions, and New World experiences offers a framework and a foundation. In all three countries, the State compensates for some of the "collective" shortfalls of neoliberal economics. Yet at this moment of regionalization and convergence, it is exactly at the point of community building that liberalism needs a sharper focus.

Thus our argument is not State-centered; rather, it seeks the wellsprings of community in an era when sovereign states, though still important, no longer dominate the realm of collective action. The argument seeks first to bring individuals into more direct contact with the common interests and perspectives they share with their neighbors, while appreciating, even valuing, the differences, and then to prompt them to act upon those interests and perspectives in communities forged through social institutions, practices, and associations.

The interests of the individual and society are inextricably linked, as Dewey said. To search for community is thus to pose a direct challenge to those American social critics who, through a failure of nerve or vision, bear agonizing witness to a society they see being polarized by division and the rise of barriers among groups. To search for community is also to suggest a new agenda for those in Canada and Mexico who fear that market integration is the inevitable prelude to a loss of identity and distinctiveness.[54]

Conceptually well armed, we are now prepared to link the larger North American community with the question of identities. What follows by way of conclusion are some examples of community building in the emerging institutions and practices going on around us.

Border cities, especially twin communities like "Ambos Nogales" on the Sonora/Arizona border, with their myriad physical crossings, shared facilities, and interlocked economies, are an obvious place to start, and the literature is abundant. These cities (and those of the Great Lakes) are commingled by more than geography. Transborder regionalism will intensify. The Mexican schoolchildren being bused over the border to New Mexican schools (paid for by localities on the American side) are tomorrow's bilingual citizens and consumers. As this example and Dewey suggest, the local community is the truest of communities; and such communities already form the most fluid and functional links in North America. Along our borders, citizens of all three countries live in a constant state of cultural adaptation and adjustment, fine-tuning their social frequencies in accord with which side of the border they are on.

Less well documented as yet are "functionally" connected areas far from the border, such as the giant metropolises of Mexico City and Los Angeles, united by the need to cope with a shared problem—in this case, two of the world's most polluted air basins. The search for meliorating anti-pollution techniques and policies has led to regular and sustained contacts between officials of the South Coast Air Quality Management District and their Mexican counterparts in the Federal District. These officials have a compelling interest in sharing information and cooperating. In 1992, an organization called North American Cities International was formed to establish partnerships between Canadian and American cities. Toronto, Detroit, and Cleveland are forming the nexus of a Great Lakes superregion to foster economic cooperation.[55]

The transborder regions are seedbeds for nurturing community, even as they address a range of regional problems that are either ignored at the federal level or best handled by local authorities. Recently, George F. Kennan has lamented the onset of a "bigness" in American government and institutions that seems to him to threaten to obliterate traditional and cultural differences among regions. Perhaps, he muses, a different sort of framework based on something like twelve loosely federated republics could rescue, and even nurture, "the interaction between different values, different outlooks, and different goals, which here as elsewhere has served in the past as one of the greatest sources of intellectual and aesthetic fertility."[56] The élan of a Cascadia and the inventiveness of the Gulf of Mexico region, with its maritime frontier, may be the harbingers or functional equivalents of Kennan's republics, but operating on a continental tableau.

Dewey himself was deeply concerned with what he called the Great Society's ability to invade face-to-face communities and strip them of control over their own destiny. "Only in local, face-to-face associations could members of a public participate in dialogues with their fellows, and such dialogues were critical to the formation and organization of the public."[57] Yet, as his biographer relates, Dewey was vague on the ways the local community might be reconstructed in the midst of the Great Society.[58] Latter-day theorists might equally lament how the forces of an increasingly globalized world economy are eroding the loyalties to, and the purview and functions of, the nation-state, opening space to a series of increasingly disarticulated regions. Other than the market, what is the glue that will hold North America together? This focuses our attention on what Bellah and his colleagues have called the key role of institutions and practices in building community.

All three nations are federally organized, however different their practices: Canada's decentralized system granting substantial powers to the provinces; the United States's generally benign recognition of state experiments that may later become national; Mexico's current effort to decentralize its top-heavy national structure and in doing so create the underpinnings of a more liberal society. Dynamic federalism accommodating transborder regionalism is surely a major transforming force for our times, something Dewey missed and Kennan sensed but did not develop because of his preoccupation with the American, rather than a North American, system. Subnational and transfrontier changes will open space to the communitarianism that so engaged Dewey, while providing the innovations, necessities, and identities that will spur the development of functional interconnections between locations in North America.

We are entering a community with a small "c," different from the regulatory thrust of European federalism to date, but nonetheless open to institution building at the trinational level. In fact, certain problems like environmental protection can only be handled at this level and the environmental side agreement to NAFTA is a case in point.

The cabinet-level Council on Environmental Cooperation will have monitoring, fact-finding, and investigative powers, seeking enforcement primarily through transparency and through citizen access, employing fines and trade sanctions only as instruments of last resort. The Council is not a supranational regulatory body in the European sense. Porosity, co-operation, and timely reporting on freely exchanged information among three governments with equal standing and using their own courts are the practices on which the Commission will be built.[59] This is a model for what may become a series of institutions. Canada will host the Environ-mental Council in Montreal, Mexico will house the NAFTA Secretariat in Mexico City, and the heretofore much weaker Labor Commission is slated for the United States, in Dallas.

Judging from current U.S.-Canada practice, much government busi-ness in the future will be handled far below the treaty level. A great deal of signaling is already going on. A continental forum for ministers, key leg-islators, and private sector leaders to exchange ideas and set an agenda was recently suggested by the diplomat and foundation officer Clint Smith.[60] Bilateral meetings of parliamentarians already take place, but these are often marred by either indifference or the assertion of excessive proprie-torship by U.S. participants. The real test and benefit will be to get U.S. legislators to commit some of their time to developing substantial exper-tise in North American issues.

Other examples of possible trinational institution building readily come to mind. Community service is the mission of the recently estab-lished Border Volunteer Corps for the U.S.-Mexican border. This grants-driven program could readily be extended to the Canada-U.S. border. The experience will foster understanding of the social and ecological "whole-ness" of the North American continent. Links between North American universities are accelerating. Europeans and Asians make better current use of U.S. university exchanges than either Canadians or Mexicans; be-cause of funding difficulties, Mexicans in fact have only recently gotten back to the high-water marks they set in the early 1980's. For their part, U.S. universities clearly understand the need to develop more continental educational exchanges. During the years 1989–92, for example, we wit-nessed a veritable flood of university presidents and senior administrators visiting Mexico. As the then president of Stanford University, Donald Kennedy, said of his visit to Mexico: "The connectedness of our cultures, languages and economies is extensive—and believe me, it is sensed and understood far better in California than it is in Washington."[61]

Efforts to coordinate degree standards and the recognition of diplo-mas are now under way, notably in Cascadia, where a plan to rationalize graduate training among the region's universities is under consideration. But much better language studies are required, especially in the United

States. With only 15 percent of U.S. high school students studying a foreign language, Americans have a pressing need to ensure that future generations can speak French and Spanish. Joint research projects will open opportunities for young scientists at the postdoctoral level. The curriculum will benefit from trinational perspectives, which will affect the training of K–12 students as well.

Taken together, these measures can be a counterpart to the "Eurokids" phenomenon, the result of two decades of educational exchanges and planning by the EEC, and to Project Erasmus, which guides European research, graduate training, and degrees. In all advanced societies, leaders principally emerge from university systems; ours, like Europe's, can and should have the faculty of familiarity, as well as the broadened cultural perspectives enabling them to respond to diversity more intelligently and creatively at home. The passage of NAFTA will accelerate these flows and promote creative regional solutions based on our own traditions.

As Tony Judt, Remarque Professor of European Studies at New York University, noted in a lecture at Stanford in 1993, such efforts in Europe are needed now more than ever. With a rising trend toward particularism and fragmentation undermining European intellectuals' faith in a united Europe, they are beginning to probe the bases of Anglo-American liberal thought. Judt argues that these analysts see liberalism's openness as a *condition* tied to the universal values that make modern public life possible, whereas its economic manifestation, the free market, is no more than a limited *project*, not a political philosophy in the broadest sense of the word.[62]

By force of example, Canada already has made a signal contribution with its health care program. While not immune to the galloping costs of medical technology and the financial crisis of health care in general, Canada leads in the social concept of community through universal care. However, as the costs of medical research soar, coordinated programs of research make increasing sense. The United States may have the largest share of financial and scientific resources, but informal professional mobility in the medical field has been great in North America for decades, and there are specialties in which Canadian and Mexican researchers are at the forefront. Public health is another area in which there is already substantial cooperation.

In this information age, the expanding role of what David Ronfeldt calls "multi-organizational networks" of change agents of all sorts is a North American phenomenon with immense implications for building community:

Some exist between big traditional institutions, but the main growth is occurring among organizations that seem too small to be called institutions. They are mostly non-governmental organizations (NGOs) that are linking together and setting in motion new dynamics to build local, national, regional, and what some people call *global* civil societies. I refer mainly to a range of advocacy and activist organizations in all three North American countries and to political action committees in the United States as examples of this trend. NAMI is also a kind of organizational network, for it has offices in all three countries and no centralized hierarchy.[63]

As hierarchies decline and knowledge proliferates faster than governments or large organized groups can react, *networking* among voluntary groups will increasingly take a place among the dynamic forces intersecting our continental social space. Foundations are actively promoting networks among these change agents. What is so impressive is the union of new communications technology with the need for groups of all kinds to seek out and make common cause with counterparts throughout North America. Community building by networking is a powerful new connecting force. The institutions and processes are still too much in ferment for us to go beyond speculation,[64] but it is certain that the underlying forces creating this ferment will continue to assert themselves.

The movement of peoples looms large on the North American policy agenda: interdependence means more, not less, migration in the future. Powerful push-pull factors have gone beyond the economic realm to the social dimension as well. Whole families, that most powerful network of all, stand ready to welcome "home" people who have never before even visited the country in which they are arriving—by the tens and hundreds of thousands and perhaps by the millions each year.

As Richard Estrada makes clear, this population movement from nearby sending countries will continue confronting North America with hard choices, given the real and disturbing pressures already being felt; this is true not just for Americans on the receiving end, but also for Mexicans and Canadians on the sending ends, who are losing precious talent and human capital to the large market in the middle. Yet there are also regional variations in the direction of travel. Vancouver is a magnet for creative newcomers, and NAFTA is promoting a flow of senior Canadian and American managers to Mexico. The situation is dynamic and complex.

Rattled by migration, California is discussing ways to intensify police actions and policy incentives to keep people, many of them Mexicans, in their native lands. To do so would conform to some of the traditional models of North America we alluded to in the opening passages of this essay, but such approaches have not worked in the past and offer little hope for the future. To resist the massive forces now deeply embedded in North America's socioeconomic dynamics runs the risk of transforming a free and open continent into a tense, claustrophobic, and xenophobic one. To regulate and channel the migratory flow with dignity and under full legal protections is a challenge as yet unmet by government. When all is said and done, the more enlightened and promising path for North America is the path of inclusiveness, a path that understands that migration, however shaped by the coordinated labor policies that must come soon, is a central feature of the continent's essential wholeness.

What then of identity and its link with community? Learning to live with more than one identity, to be comfortable with several "others," is almost certainly a condition of our times. Historically given identities are commingled with market-driven identities, overlapping media markets, and great spatial mobility. We are different, Canadians, Americans, Mexicans. Our artists and philosophers make this clear, but they, like our institutions and practices, also make clear that we all are New World peoples learning to live in a shared regional space. To paraphrase Paz and Taylor, we are recognizing the complex boundaries of the Other as a means both of accepting and of transcending them in the search for understanding, respect, and cooperation. This fusion of social and cultural horizons is the main motive force in redefining our emerging sense of who we North Americans really are.

Reference Matter

Notes

Introduction

1. David J. Weber, *The Spanish Frontier in North America* (New Haven, Conn.: Yale University Press, 1992).

2. Bernard Bailyn, *The Peopling of British North America: An Introduction* (New York: Knopf, 1986).

3. Patricia Nelson Limerick, *The Legacy of Conquest: The Unbroken Past of the American West* (New York: Norton, 1987).

4. Seymour Martin Lipset, *Continental Divide* (New York: Routledge, 1990).

5. Comments of Daniel Latouche at authors' meeting, Sol y Sombra Center, Santa Fe, N.Mex., Jan. 30, 1993.

6. Comment of Robert Earle at authors' meeting, Jan. 30, 1993.

7. Mordecai Richler, *Oh Canada! Oh Quebec! Requiem for a Divided Country* (New York: Knopf, 1992), p. 107.

8. Robert Suro, "Poll Finds Desire by Hispanic Americans to Assimilate," *New York Times*, Dec. 15, 1992, pp. 1, 18.

9. Comments of Marc Pachter and Alberto Ruy-Sánchez at authors' meeting, Jan. 30, 1993.

10. Joel Garreau, *The Nine Nations of North America* (New York: Avon Books, 1981), pp. 207–44. In this book, brilliantly prescient for its time, Garreau defined his evolving regions in cultural and economic terms; government was irrelevant. Between the global and the local, we would say today, government plays a role, but this is changing rapidly. Also, Garreau hewed to an earlier definition of North America, leaving out Mexico, which Louis B. Casagrande then addressed in his article "The Five Nations of Mexico," in the American Geographical Society's *Focus* (Spring 1987), pp. 2–9.

11. This question may have a great deal to do with North America's economic prospects as well. The editors concur with Samuel Huntington that culture has a major impact on economic and other aspects of international relations. "The success of the North American Free Trade Area depends on the convergence now

underway of Mexican, Canadian, and American cultures. Huntington, "The Clash of Civilizations," *Foreign Affairs*, 73.3 (July/Aug. 1993), p. 27. The Moynihan quote is from an article by David Bender, *New York Times*, Feb. 7, 1993, pp. 1, 14.

Canada: Values in Search of a Vision

AUTHOR'S NOTE: This paper reflects only my personal views and in no way expresses official positions of the Canadian Radio-Television and Telecommunications Commission.

1. Other actors include Michael J. Fox, Leslie Nielsen, Martin Short, Rick Moranis, Eugene Levy, Margot Kidder, Lola Davidovich, and the late John Candy. Among hit TV programs, *Saturday Night Live*, with longtime founding producer Lorne Michaels, stands out. In the print media, I would cite *SCTV* and *Mad* magazines. Graydon Carter, founding editor of the popular *Spy* magazine, which ceased publication in 1994, is a Canadian.

2. Keith Spicer et al., *Citizens' Forum on Canada's Future: Report to the People and Government of Canada* (Ottawa: Canadian Government Publishing Center, 1991).

3. Herschel Hardin, *A Nation Unaware: The Canadian Economic Culture* (Vancouver: J. J. Douglas, 1974).

4. Ernest Renan, *Qu'est-ce qu'une nation?* Reprint. (Paris: Pierre Bordas et fils, 1991.)

American Identity: A Political Compact

1. Richard Reeves, "You'll Never Drive Alone," *Travel and Leisure*, 23.1 (Jan. 1993), p. 39. Baskin-Robbins is a U.S. ice cream company that built its reputation on its menu of 31 flavors.

2. Charles Sealsfield, *The Americans As They Are* (1828), reprinted in Sealsfield, *Samtliche Werke*, ed. Karl J. R. Arndt, vol. 2 (New York: Georg Olms Press, 1972), p. 186.

3. Thomas Jefferson to James Madison, Dec. 20, 1787, quoted in Michael Kammen, *The Origins of the American Constitution: A Documentary History* (New York: Penguin, 1986), p. 91.

4. Kammen, *ibid.*, p. xx.

5. Marcus Cunliffe, *The American Presidency* (Boston: Houghton Mifflin, 1987), p. 24.

6. James Madison, "Federalist No. 51," quoted in Kammen, *Origins of the American Constitution*, p. 203.

7. James C. Kirby, "The Right to Vote," in Norman Dorsen, ed., *The Rights of Americans* (New York: Pantheon, 1971), p. 203.

8. James MacGregor Burns and Stewart Burns, *A People's Charter: The Pursuit of Rights in America* (New York: Knopf, 1991), p. 60.

9. The Reverend Jackson and Dr. Guerra are quoted in Bernard A. Weisberger, *Many People, One Nation* (Boston: Houghton Mifflin, 1987), pp. 235, 286, respectively.

Approaches to the Problem of Mexican Identity

AUTHOR'S NOTE: I want to thank Phillip Hutchinson and Roberto Tejada for their help with the English text. Thanks also to Robert Earle and John Wirth for their constant patience and their warm and intelligent communications with me as we pursued this project.

1. Samuel Ramos, *El perfil del hombre y la cultura en México* (Mexico: Imprenta Mundial, 1934); Octavio Paz, *El laberinto de la soledad* (Mexico: Cuadernos Americanos, 1950). Republished in altered form in 1959.

2. Samuel Ramos, *Ensayo sobre Diego Rivera* (Mexico: Imprenta Mundial, 1953). Originally published in 1935.

3. Emilio Uranga, *Análisis del ser del mexicano* (Mexico: Editorial Porrúa y Obregón, 1954).

4. Alberto Ruy-Sánchez, "New Forms for a Century's End," in the art catalogue *Through the Path of Echoes: Contemporary Art in Mexico* (New York: Parallel Project/Turner, 1990); "New Moments in Mexican Art: Fantastic Fundamentalism," in the catalogue *New Moments in Mexican Art* (New York: Independent Curators, Inc., 1990); "El Fundamentalismo fantástico del arte joven de México," *Revista de la Universidad*, no. 508 (May 1993); "Una nueva geografía imaginaria," in *Mito y magia en América: los ochenta* (Monterrey: Museo de Arte Contemporáneo, 1991).

5. Henri Focillon, *The Life of Forms* (New York: Zone Books, 1992), p. 142. Originally published in 1934: *La Vie des formes* (Paris: Presses Universitaires de France).

6. Ramos, *El perfil*, p. 32.

7. *Ibid.*, pp. 32, 33.

8. Octavio Paz, "El laberinto de la soledad," in *México en la obra de Octavio Paz* (video; Televisa, 1990).

9. Octavio Paz, "Vuelta a El Laberinto de la Soledad, conversación con Claude Fell," in Paz, *El ogro filantrópico* (Mexico: Joaquín Moritz, 1979), pp. 20, 21.

10. This dissonance is clearly explained in Margarita De Orellana, *La Mirada circular: el cine norteamericano de la Revolución Mexicana, 1911–1917* (Mexico: Joaquín Moritz, 1992).

Pluralism and Ecology in Canadian Cities

1. Charles McC. Mathias, "Limits of Leadership: The United States," in Steven Muller and Gebhard Schweigler, eds., *From Occupation to Cooperation: The United States and United Germany in a Changing World Order* (New York: Norton, 1992), p. 74.

2. For a comparison of Canadian and American cities based on a wealth of data from the 1980 censuses, see Michael A. Goldberg and John Mercer, *The Myth of the North American City: Continentalism Challenged* (Vancouver: University of British Columbia Press, 1986).

3. Tony Hiss, "Experiencing Cities," sec. 1 in his *The Experience of Place* (New York: Knopf, 1990).

4. J. M. S. Careless, *Careless at Work* (Toronto: Duderin, 1990), p. 149.

5. J. M. S. Careless, *Frontier and Metropolis: Regions, Cities, and Identities in Canada Before 1914* (Toronto: University of Toronto Press, 1987), pp. 9, 29, 93. A recent study of Chicago takes the same city-as-leader approach. See William Cronon, *Nature's Metropolis: Chicago and the Great West* (New York: Norton, 1991).

6. In the 1990's, the violent presence of Jamaican drug gangs, with their continental and Caribbean links, began to challenge this civic code. Tensions between the Toronto police and the black community also emerged.

7. Identifying gun-related violence in the streets as a public health issue, rather than as the unfortunate by-product of a "right," is a promising new approach by the Clinton administration.

8. Goldberg and Mercer, *Myth of the North American City*, p. 40. The authors are far more interested in the differences between the nations—language cleavage is "as profound for Canada and particularly urban Quebec as race relations are a vitally important issue for urban America" (p. 43)—than they are in comparing the multiculturalist movements in both countries or, for that matter, patterns of assimilation.

9. Arthur Schlesinger, Jr., *The Disuniting of America* (New York: Norton, 1992), p. 13. He continues: "Attracted variously to Britain, France, and the United States, inclined for generous reasons to a policy of official multiculturalism, Canadians have never developed a strong sense of what it is to be a Canadian." Goldberg and Mercer give a Canadian view: "If Canada has a national culture, a collective self-portrait, it is likely to be intrinsically more fragmented than that of its self-confident, powerful neighbor." *Myth of the North American City*, p. 41.

10. Gov. Mario Cuomo, statement on multicultural education, July 15, 1991, as quoted in Schlesinger, *Disuniting of America*, p. 18.

11. Northrop Frye, *Divisions of a Ground: Essays on Canadian Culture* (Toronto: House of Anansi Press, 1982), p. 62.

12. Given the differences in political culture (see Pachter's and Estrada's chapters), one is nonetheless compelled to note that a rather murky area of some overlap might include patterns of assimilation. According to the outside reader of this manuscript, it could even be said that in practice the melting-pot process in English-speaking Canada has been indistinguishable from that in the United States. Official multiculturalism lending legitimacy to immigrant groups may actually facilitate that process, since if you are accepted by the general community, you have less reason to resist incorporation within it. It follows that, knowing the game and its intended result, Quebec nationalists refuse to play by multiculturalist rules established by the majority.

13. Careless, *Frontier and Metropolis*, p. 93.

14. Pierre Trudeau, as quoted in Reginald W. Bibby, *Mosaic Madness: The Poverty and Potential of Life in Canada* (Toronto: Stoddart, 1990), pp. 49–50.

15. Robert F. Harney, *Gathering Place: Peoples and Neighbourhoods of Toronto, 1834–1945* (Toronto: Multicultural Historical Society of Ontario, 1985), p. 13.

16. Hugh Brody, *Maps and Dreams: Indians and the British Columbia Frontier* (Vancouver: Douglas and McIntyre, 1981), p. 148.

17. Lewis Mumford, *The Culture of Cities* (New York: Harcourt, Brace, 1938). See also Jane Jacobs's famous critique of Mumford's penchant for urban renewal: *The Death and Life of Great American Cities* (New York: Random House, 1961), pp. 19–21.

18. Nuala Beck, *Shifting Gears: Thriving in the New Economy* (Toronto: Harper Collins, 1992), p. 74.

19. Jacobs, *Death and Life*, revised ed. (New York: Modern Library, 1993), Introduction, p. xvi.

20. *Regeneration: Toronto's Waterfront and the Sustainable City*. Final Report of the Royal Commission on the Future of the Toronto Waterfront (Ottawa: Queen's Printer of Ontario, 1992).

21. Jacobs, *Death and Life*, revised ed., p. xviii.

The Dynamics of Assimilation in the United States

1. On the damage to life and property, see "The Untold Story of the LA Riot," *U.S. News and World Report*, May 31, 1993, p. 36.

2. In this chapter, I use the term "assimilation" loosely to refer to both the knowledge and acceptance of the language and civic culture of the American nation, and socioeconomic mainstreaming. When one facet of assimilation is being stressed more than another, this should be clear from the context in which the term is employed.

3. Fred Harris and Roger Wilkins, "Cities Losing Race with Time," as cited in "Report Says U.S. Cities Are 'Resegregating,'" *Dallas Morning News*, Mar. 1, 1993.

4. The term "political apartheid" was used by Associate Justice Sandra Day O'Connor in writing the majority opinion in *Shaw* v. *Reno*, July 1993.

5. In stark contrast, some nations have flatly declared themselves to be "not countries of immigration," and several, including France, the United Kingdom, Switzerland, and Sweden, have set up new, more restrictive rules to prevent large influxes of foreigners. See, for example, these stories, in the *New York Times*: Henry Kamm, "Migrants Wear Out Welcome as Numbers Grow in Europe," Feb. 10, 1993; "Prague Fears Being Last Stop for Refugees Heading West," June 30, 1993.

6. Maldwyn Allen Jones, *American Immigration*, 2d ed. (Chicago: University of Chicago Press, 1992).

7. In 1986, a Ku Klux Klan leader in Idaho told over 1,000 cheering people that violent acts would curtail illegal immigration from Mexico. "Supremacists Target Mexicans at Rally," *Miami Herald*, July 14, 1986, and the former Klansman David Duke raised immigration restriction in a racial context during his candidacy for the 1992 Republican presidential nomination.

8. See, for example, Jack Miles, "Black Versus Brown," *Atlantic Monthly*, Oct. 1992, p. 54.

9. Peter Skerry, *Mexican Americans: The Ambivalent Minority* (New York: Free Press, 1993), p. 60.

10. Leon F. Bouvier and Bob Weller, *Florida in the 21st Century: The Challenge*

of Population Growth (Washington, D.C.: Center for Immigration Studies, 1992), p. 10.

11. Peter Skerry and Michael Hartman, "Latin Mass," *New Republic*, June 10, 1991, pp. 19, 20.

12. George F. Kennan, *Around the Cragged Hill: A Personal and Political Philosophy* (New York: Norton, 1993), p. 154.

13. Brilliant in its historical overview, though misguided in its highly ideological conclusions, is Chris Harman's "The Return of the National Question," *International Socialism*, 56 (Sept. 1992), pp. 3–60.

14. The rationale for learning good English is graphically portrayed in Richard Rodriguez, *Hunger of Memory* (Boston: D. R. Godine, 1981).

15. Barry R. Chiswick, ed., *Immigration, Language and Ethnicity: Canada and the United States* (Washington, D.C.: American Ethnographic Institute Press, 1992), p. 1.

16. "Spanish Station Tops L.A. Radio Market," *Wall Street Journal*, Feb. 24, 1993.

17. John Hingham, "Introduction: The Forms of Ethnic Leadership," in Hingham, ed., *Ethnic Leadership in America* (Baltimore: Johns Hopkins University Press, 1979), p. 2. Hingham here follows the ideas of the social psychologist Kurt Lewin.

18. Peter J. Duignan and Lewis H. Gann, *Hispanics in the United States: A History* (Boulder, Colo.: Westview Press, 1986).

19. Robert Suro, "Poll Finds Desire by Hispanic Americans to Assimilate," *New York Times*, Dec. 15, 1992, pp. 1, 18. Puerto Rico is a special case: in part for cultural reasons, the island voted in 1993 to maintain Commonwealth status, which is a halfway house between statehood and independence. Mainland Puerto Ricans and islanders are vested in a binational/bicultural birthright, with the option to opt out, that is, assimilate.

20. Skerry, *Mexican Americans*, pp. 337–38.

21. "The time horizon over which individual incomes can increase sufficiently to remove the economic incentive for emigration from migrant sending countries to the United States must be measured in decades or generations. The short term in this context is therefore at least ten years. It is probably longer." Report of the Commission for the Study of International Migration and Cooperative Economic Development. *Unauthorized Migration: An Economic Development Response* (Washington, D.C.: Government Printing Office, July 1990), p. 5.

22. Morris Janowitz, *The Reconstruction of Patriotism: Education for Civic Consciousness* (Chicago: University of Chicago Press, 1983), pp. 129, 137, cited in Skerry, *Mexican Americans*, p. 4.

23. According to Richard L. Nostrand, some 100,000 Mexicans, about 1 percent of Mexico's population, stayed on the U.S. side of the new border, including 75,000 in New Mexico and some 12,000 each in Alta California and Texas. See his "The Spanish Borderlands," in Robert D. Mitchell and Paul A. Groves, eds., *North America: The Historical Geography of a Changing Continent* (Savage, Md.: Rowman and Littlefield, 1990), p. 61.

24. "Citizenship Campaign Targets 10 Million Immigrants, *Dallas Morning News*, Mar. 16, 1993, p. 18.

25. George I. Sanchez, "Education," in Rudolph Gomez, ed., *The Changing Mexican-American* (New York: Meridian, 1972), p. 33.

26. Eugene Robinson, "Worldwide Migration Nears Crisis: Politics, Economics Cited," *Washington Post*, July 7, 1993.

27. See David E. Simcox, *Many Hands, Few Jobs* (Washington, D.C.: Center for Immigration Studies, 1987).

28. Rodriguez interview with TV host Bill Moyers, Public Broadcasting System, World of Ideas series, 1990.

Mexico: Culture and Identity in the Information Age

1. Manuel Montes Collantes, "La desmexicanización de México," *Excélsior*, Nov. 28, 1955, p. 6A.

2. Jonathan Weber, "Tuning in the Global Village," *Los Angeles Times*, Oct. 20, 1992, special supplement, pp. H1–H12.

3. For more information on Televisa's TV activities and other business interests, consult Raúl Trejo Delarbre, ed., *Televisa el quinto poder* (Mexico: Editorial Claves Latinoamericanas, 1985).

4. Raúl Trejo Delarbre, comp., *Las redes de Televisa* (Mexico: Editorial Claves Latinoamericanas, 1988), p. 177.

5. Emily Mitchell, "Sightings: The Russians Also Cry," *Time*, Sept. 14, 1992, p. 54.

6. IBOPE, ratings for the period Aug. 24–Sept. 24, 1992.

7. "Metrónomo," Organización Radio Centro network, hit parade list for Sept. 1992.

8. Julia Palacios, lecture, Instituto Mora, Sept. 24, 1992.

9. *La fabrica de sueños: Estudios Churubusco 1945–1985* (Mexico: IMCINE, 1985), p. 24.

10. Montes Collantes, "La desmexicanización de México."

11. Alma Guillermoprieto, "Report from Mexico: Serenading the Future," *New Yorker*, Nov. 9, 1992, p. 99.

12. Paz is quoted in the Introduction to Jacques Lafaye, *Quetzalcoatl y Guadalupe: La formación de la conciencia nacional in México* (Mexico: Fondo de Cultura Económica, 1977), pp. 18–19.

13. Ricardo J. Zevada, *Calles, el Presidente* (Mexico: Editorial Nuestro Tiempo, 1971), p. 144.

Quebec in the Emerging North American Configuration

AUTHOR'S NOTE: The comments of Alain-G. Gagnon of McGill University have been much appreciated. Many of the ideas expressed here came about in our ongoing dialogue about where precisely the Quebec experience fits in.

1. My use of "vanquished" here picks up on a term that many Native leaders, in an ironic turn-of-the-table, have come to apply to the Québécois.

2. E. J. Hobsbawm, *Nations and Nationalism Since 1780: Programme, Myth, Reality* (New York: Cambridge University Press, 1990), p. 182.

3. John Breuilly, *Nationalism and the State* (Chicago: University of Chicago Press, 1985), p. 422.

4. In the countries involved, such questions are usually answered in equally simplistic terms by both sides of the nationalist battle. The Québécois, it is said by defenders of the federal option, are too rational, too aware of their pocketbooks, and too in tune with the integration mood of the times to embark on the separatist adventure. Not so, comes the answer: the Québécois are simply prudent, somewhat alienated, and profoundly entangled within a carefully nourished and confusing situation.

5. Whether or not 1960 marked such a rupture is now a matter of open debate. For recent systematic overviews of Quebec since 1960, see Gérard Daigle, ed., *Le Québec en jeu: Comprendre les grands défis* (Montreal: Les Presses de l'Université de Montréal, 1992); Fernand Dumont, ed., *La Société québécoise après trente ans de changements* (Quebec: Institut québécois de recherche sur la culture, 1990); Simon Langlois, ed., *La Société québécoise en tendances, 1960–1990* (Montreal: Institut québécois de recherche sur la culture, 1990).

6. So dominant is this vision of a monolithic and reactionary French-Canadian nationalism that it has become accepted even by nationalist sympathizers eager to differentiate modern Quebec nationalism from its reactionary first incarnation.

7. For a general presentation of this pre-1960 nationalism with accompanying culturalist interpretations, see the articles collected by Ramsay Cook, ed., *French Canadian Nationalism* (Toronto: Macmillan, 1969).

8. The best presentation of this "generally agreed upon" vision is to be found in Louis Balthazar, *Bilan du nationalisme au Québec* (Montreal: L'Hexagone, 1990).

9. This vision has been especially popular among antinationalist English-speaking Canadian historians. See Ramsay Cook, *The Maple Leaf Forever* (Toronto: Macmillan, 1967) and *Canada, Quebec and the Uses of Nationalism* (Toronto: McClelland and Stewart, 1986); and Michael Behiels, *Prelude to Quebec's Quiet Revolution: Liberalism Versus Neo-Nationalism, 1945–1960* (Montreal: McGill–Queen's University Press, 1985). For a different vision, see Claude Couture, *Le Mythe de la modernisation au Quebec: Milieus d'affaires francophones à Montréal au tournant du siècle* (Montreal: Éditions du Méridien, 1991); Fernand Roy, *Progrès, harmonie, liberté. Le libéralisme des mileus d'affaires francophones à Montréal au tournant du siècle* (Montreal: Boréal, 1988).

10. Fernand Dumont, *The Vigil of Quebec* (Toronto: University of Toronto Press, 1971). For a fascinating controversy around the exact nature of the Quebec difference in North America, see his "Parlons Américain . . . si nous le sommes devenus," *Le Devoir*, Sept. 3, 1982. In the late 1970's, Dumont was Deputy Minister of Cultural Affairs and as such was responsible for designing the Parti Québécois's much-criticized but theoretically rich blueprint for cultural development: *A Cultural Development Policy for Quebec* (Quebec: Éditeur official du Québec, 1978).

11. Richard Handler, *Nationalism and the Politics of Culture in Quebec* (Madison: University of Wisconsin Press, 1988), pp. 50–51.

12. One of Quebec's most influential scholars and intellectuals, Léon Dion's views of nationalism can be found in his *Nationalismes et politique au Québec* (Montreal: Hurtubise-HMH, 1975), probably the most elaborate vision of the various "types" of nationalism in Quebec. His *Québec 1945–2000: A la recherche du Québec* (Quebec: Les Presses de l'Université Laval, 1987), remains the most systematic attempt to pull together all the various components of the Quebec identity. For a review of Dion's importance in Quebec intellectual life, see Raymond Hudon and Réjean Pelletier, eds., *L'Engagement intellectuel: Mélanges en l'honneur de Léon Dion* (Quebec: Les Presses de l'Université Laval, 1991).

13. See Marcel Rioux, *Quebec in Transition* (Toronto: James Lewis and Samuel, 1971), and *Les Québécois* (Paris: Le Seuil, 1974). Rioux, who died in late 1992, should also be read for one of the few Canada-Quebec intellectual "conversations" on the notions of culture and nationalism. See Susan Crean and Marcel Rioux, *Two Nations: An Essay on the Culture and Politics of Canada and Quebec in a World of American Pre-eminence* (Toronto: James Lorimer, 1983). He is also well known for his structuralist account of the Quebec case.

14. For a literary presentation of this theme, see the novels of Jacques Godbout, especially his *Les Têtes à Papineau* (Paris: Le Seuil, 1981). The schizophrenic myth has been translated electorally in the belief, also unfounded, that Québécois tend to vote for a federalist party in federal elections and for a nationalist one provincially. See Gérard Bergeron, *Notre miroir à deux faces: Trudeau-Lévesque* (Montreal: Québec/Amérique, 1985). For an interesting presentation from a Quebec political scientist strongly opposed to Quebec nationalism, see Stéphane Dion, "Explaining Quebec Nationalism," in R. Kent Weaver, ed., *The Collapse of Canada?* (Washington, D.C.: Brookings Institute, 1992), pp. 77–121.

15. The challenge has been met successfully by Kenneth McRoberts, *Quebec: Social Change and Political Crisis* (Toronto: McClelland and Stewart, 1988).

16. For a general formulation of this explanation, see Michael Hechter, "Group Formation and the Cultural Division of Labor," *American Journal of Sociology*, 84.1 (1978), pp. 6–29. Its applicability to the Quebec case has been reviewed by Kenneth McRoberts, "Internal Colonialism: The Case of Quebec," *Ethnic and Racial Studies*, 2 (1979), pp. 293–318.

17. See Hubert Guindon, *Quebec Society: Tradition, Modernity and Nationhood* (Toronto: University of Toronto Press, 1988).

18. From *Indicateurs de la situation linguistique au Québec. Édition 1992* (Quebec: Conseil de la langue française, 1992). On the volatile issue of language and revenues in Quebec, see *Langue et statut économique au Québec, 1980–1985* (Quebec: Conseil de la langue française, 1991).

19. Nevertheless, total revenues of Anglophones are still 16 percent higher than those of Francophones.

20. This thesis is well presented in Dominique Clift, *Quebec Nationalism in Crisis* (Montreal: McGill–Queen's University Press, 1982). For another "end-of-nationalism" vision, this one stressing the incapacity of nationalist thinking to integrate the intellectual rupture required by the New Age, see Pierre Valliéres, "Vers un Quebec post-nationaliste," in Serge Proulx and Pierre Valliéres, eds., *Changer*

de société (Montreal: Québec/Amérique, 1982), pp. 21–57. One of the founders and theoreticians of the Front de libération du Québec, Pierre Valliéres is the author of the influential *White Niggers of America*. Yet another diagnosis has it that post-modernity, with the death of the "grands textes," is slowly killing the nationalist discourse in Quebec and elsewhere: Marc Henry Soulet, *Le Silence des intellectuels* (Montreal: Éditions Saint-Martín, 1987).

21. The definitive statement of this hypothesis is to be found in Gilles Bourque and Nicole Laurin-Frenette, "Social Classes and Nationalist Ideologies in Quebec, 1760–1970," in Gary Teeple, ed., *Capitalism and the National Question in Canada* (Toronto: University of Toronto Press, 1972), pp. 185–211.

22. All the empirical studies point out the growing insignificance of traditional so-cioeconomic factors (revenue, education, occupation), as well as geo-demographic factors (sex, residence), in explaining support for the PQ or independence. Age remains the only exception. For a longitudinal study of Quebec public opinion since 1960, see Édouard Cloutier, Jean H. Guay, and Daniel Latouche, *Le Virage: L'évolution de l'opinion publique au Quebec depuis 1960* (Montreal: Québec-Amérique, 1992).

23. The consociational argument has been best put forward by Kenneth McRae, "Consociationalism and the Canadian Political System," in McRae, ed., *Consociational Democracy: Political Accommodation in Segmented Societies* (Toronto: McClelland and Stewart, 1974), pp. 238–61. See also his more recent "The Meech Lake Impasse in Theoretical Perspective," in Alain-G. Gagnon and A. Brian Tanguay, eds., *Democracy with Justice* (Ottawa: Carleton University Press, 1992), pp. 140–53. Although the late Donald Smiley would certainly dispute the consociationalist label, he was one of the most articulate proponents of the "elite breakdown" approach to the rise of Quebec nationalism. See his "French-English Relations and Consociational Democracy," in Milton J. Esman, ed., *Ethnic Conflict in the Western World* (Ithaca, N.Y.: Cornell University Press, 1977), pp. 179–203. Smiley's vision of executive federalism borrowed heavily from this elite compact perspective on Canada. See his *The Federal Condition in Canada* (Toronto: McGraw-Hill Ryerson, 1987).

24. For an early and still applicable critique, see Jules Savaria, "Le Québec est-il une société périphérique?," *Sociologie et société*, 7.1 (1975), pp. 115–28. For a more general presentation of these early "neocolonialist" visions, see Gérald Bernier, "Le Cas québécois et les théories de développement et la dépendance," in Edmond Orban, ed., *La Modernisation politique du Québec* (Quebec: Boréal Express, 1976), pp. 19–54.

25. Alain-G. Gagnon and Mary Beth Montcalm, *Quebec: Beyond the Quiet Revolution* (Scarborough: Nelson Canada, 1990). Many have noted that Quebec separatism played a role in the rise of Toronto, since it made Montreal less attractive to Anglo-Canadians.

26. Illustrations of this approach can be found in Gérard Bergeron and Réjean Pelletier, eds., *L'État du Québec en devenir* (Montreal: Boréal, 1980); and Gérard Bergeron, *Pratique de l'État au Québec* (Montreal: Québec/Amérique, 1984). "I use the term "managerial-pluralist" gingerly here. In fact, a typology of Quebec State

theoreticians is not easy to produce, since they tend to borrow elements from both the French tradition (Poulantzas, Boyer) and the Anglo-American one (Alford, Miliband, Skocpol).

27. This defensive vision of nationalism has been well articulated by Louis Balthazar, "La Dynamique du nationalisme," in Bergeron and Pelletier, *L'État,* pp. 37–58.

28. See Marc Renaud, "New Middle Class in Search of Social Hegemony"; Jorge Niosi, "The Rise of French Canadian Capitalism"; and Pierre Fournier, "The New Parameters of the Quebec Bourgeoisie," in Alain-G. Gagnon, ed., *Quebec: State and Society* (Toronto: Methuen, 1984), pp. 15–228. English-speakers of whatever class have generally been excluded from the government of Quebec as well.

29. For a presentation of this view, see Reg Whitaker, who stresses the lack of legitimacy of the Canadian bourgeoisie in "Images of the State," in Leo Panitch, ed., *The Canadian State, Political Economy and Political Power* (Toronto: University of Toronto Press, 1977), pp. 28–68; and Garth Stevenson, *Unfulfilled Union* (Toronto: Gage, 1989).

30. Gérard Boismenu, "The Federated State and the Heterogeneity of Space," in Garth Stevenson, ed., *Federalism in Canada: Selected Readings* (Toronto: McClelland and Stewart, 1989), p. 279. This very complex analysis is more fully developed in Gérard Boismenu and Lizette Jalbert, eds., *Espace régional et nation* (Montreal: Boréal, 1983).

31. Anne Légaré and Nicole Morf, *La Société contre l'état* (Montreal: Hurtubise-HMH, 1989), p. 42.

32. The most recent of these "bottom-line" analyses is that of François Rocher, ed., *Bilan québécois du féderalisme canadien, Montreal* (Montreal: VLB Éditeur, 1992).

33. As symbolized by a permanent list of so-called "traditional constitutional claims" that all Quebec governments have scrupulously maintained since 1976, presumably to be able to "evaluate" more systematically any set of constitutional proposals coming out of Ottawa. See *Les Positions traditionnelles du Québec en matiére constitutionelle, 1936–1990* (Quebec: Secrétariat aux Affaires intergouvernementales canadiennes, 1991).

34. The Quebec "concertation" model has been extensively studied. See, especially, Clinton Archibald, *Un Québec corporatiste* (Hull: Asticou, 1984); and A. Brian Tanguay, "Concerted Action in Quebec: Dialogue of the Deaf," in Gagnon, *Quebec: State and Society,* pp. 365–85.

35. There are few serious studies of this new business bourgeoisie. See Alain-G. Gagnon and Khayyam Zev Paltiel, "Towards Maitres chez nous: The Ascendancy of a Balzacian Bourgeoisie in Quebec," *Queen's Quarterly,* 93.4 (1986), pp. 731–49; Matthew Fraser, *Quebec, Inc.* (Toronto: Key Porter Books, 1987); and Yves Bélanger and Pierre Fournier, *L'Entreprise québécoise: Développement historique et dynamique contemporaine* (Montreal: Hurtubise-HMH, 1987). The concept of "market nationalism" is borrowed from Tom Courchene, one of Quebec's most astute observers. See his *In Praise of Renewed Federalism* (Ottawa: C. D. Howe Institute, 1991).

36. This view is best expressed by Bruce Wise, "The Changing Face of Class Politics in Quebec: The Representation and Expression of Business Interests in the Policy Process," in Gagnon and Tanguay, *Democracy with Justice*, pp. 340–51. See also Daniel Drache and Harry Glasbeek, *The Changing Workplace: Reshaping Canada's Industrial Relations System* (Toronto: James Lorimer, 1992), for an effective argument on how rapidly the Quebec labor difference has disappeared under world economic pressures.

37. On the Quebec Commission, see Alain-G. Gagnon and Daniel Latouche, *Allaire, Bélanger, et les autres* (Montreal: Québec/Amérique, 1991); and Richard Fidler, ed., *Canada, Adieu. Quebec Debates Its Future* (Halifax: Institute for Research on Public Policy, 1991).

38. Andrew Parker et al., *Nationalism and Sexualities* (New York: Routledge, 1992), p. 5.

39. Nevertheless, we should be careful, as Eve Kosofsky Sedgwick reminds us, to understand the limits of the paradigm of "otherness," which fails "to do justice to the complex activity, creativity, and engagement of those whom it figures simply as relegated object." *Ibid.*, p. 239.

40. Benedict Anderson, *Imagined Communities* (London: Unicorn Hyman, 1989), p. 5.

41. *Ibid.*, p. 17.

42. See Micheline Plasse, "La Politique d'internationalisation de Montréal: Un politique en devenir," *Politique*, 19 (1991), pp. 37–67.

43. The recent White Paper of Quebec's Department of International Affairs is a case in point: *Le Québec et l'interdépendence: Le monde pour horizon* (Quebec: Ministère des Affaires internationales, 1991).

44. One surprising result of the free trade debate was the lack of effectiveness of the Ontario government. Any similar opposition by the Quebec government would have "killed" the deal. See G. Bruce Doern and Brian W. Tomlin, *The Free Trade Story: Faith and Fear* (Toronto: Stoddart, 1991). On the role of Canadian provinces in the FTA, see Leslie Delagran, "Conflict in Trade Policy: The Role of the Congress and the Provinces in Negotiating and Implementing the Canada-U.S. Trade Agreement," *Publius*, 22.4 (1992), pp. 15–30.

45. There is a vast literature on the subject, most of which is summarized in Ivo Duchacek, Garth Stevenson, and Daniel Latouche, eds., *Perforated Sovereignties and International Relations* (New York: Greenwood Press, 1989).

46. See E. Fry, L. H. Radebaugh, and P. Soldatos, eds., *The New International Cities Era* (Provo: Brigham Young University Press, 1989).

47. Elsewhere I have argued that the rise of international "regimes" has contributed to the emergence of subnational units on the international scene and could eventually facilitate their incorporation in international society. See Daniel Latouche, *Le Bazar* (Montreal: Boréal, 1991).

48. I have examined this and other related arguments in my article "Le Québec est bien petit et le monde est bien grand," in Alain-G. Gagnon and François Rocher, eds., *Réponses au détracteurs de la souveraineté du Québec* (Montreal: VLB Editeur, 1992), pp. 345–72.

49. Parti Québécois, *Le Québec dans un monde nouveau* (Montreal: VLB Editeur, 1993).

50. This theme is treated at length in Daniel Latouche, *Canada and Quebec, Past and Future: An Essay* (Toronto: University of Toronto Press, 1981).

51. Sylvia B. Bashevkin, *True Patriot Love: The Politics of Canadian Nationalism* (Toronto: Oxford University Press, 1991), p. 157.

52. See David J. Bercuson and Barry Cooper, *Deconfederation* (Toronto: Key Porter Books, 1991); and J. L. Granatstein and Kenneth McNaught, eds., *English Canada Speaks Out* (Toronto: Doubleday, 1991).

53. Anthony D. Smith has come to recognize the crucial role played by this ethnic core in the establishment of a national identity. See his *The Ethnic Origins of Nations* (Oxford: Basil Blackwell, 1986), and *National Identity* (New York: Penguin, 1991).

54. The more "ancient" Tory streak of this English-Canadian nationalism always had an anti-Quebec and anti-French orientation. What is different this time is how widespread that orientation has become among progressive and left-wing nationalists, groups that had always professed their support for the Quebec "struggle." The already classic presentation of this view is to be found in Philip Resnick, *Letters to a Québécois Friend*, with a reply by Daniel Latouche (Montreal: McGill–Queen's University Press, 1990). For a rare Quebec vision of English-Canadian intellectuals, see Serge Denis, *Le Long Malentendu* (Montreal: Boréal, 1992).

55. The existence of a distinct set of English-Canadian values has been a much-debated issue, especially since the foremost proponent of this "cultural" thesis has been an American, Seymour Martin Lipset, whose first foray into this minefield led him to suggest that English Canadians were more elitist, ascriptive, and conservative than Americans. See his *Continental Divide* (New York: Routledge, 1990). See also Robert J. Brym, *From Culture to Power: The Sociology of English Canada* (Toronto: Oxford University Press, 1989).

56. For obvious strategic reasons, Quebec pro-sovereignty leaders prefer to ignore all signs of saber-rattling coming out of English Canada, even from such respected organizations as the Canadian Institute of Strategic Studies, whose 1991 conference on the "security" implications of the constitutional quagmire prompted ominous headlines in the *Montreal Gazette* ("Separation Could Spur Violence") and the *Globe and Mail* ("Canada Could Require US Might") and an even more ominous comment by Canada's foremost military historian, Desmond Morton, who told a *Christian Science Monitor* reporter: "Croatia is not absolutely unthinkable here." For the conference report, see Alex Morrison, ed., *Divided We Fall: The National Security Implications of Canadian Constitutional Issues* (Toronto: Canadian Institute of Strategic Studies, 1991).

57. This elevation of the continental aspect is not an entirely new phenomenon. It simply used to pass under the name "mappism." That is to say, the very cartographical representation of the country as a huge (because of the Mercator distortion) blur on the map, always colored in red, came to represent a source of pride for Canadians. The importance of spatial archetypes in both English and Quebec

thinking has been aptly illustrated by Luc Bureau. See his *Entre l'Eden et l'Utopie* (Montreal: Québec/Amérique, 1984) and *La Terre et moi* (Montreal: Boréal, 1991).

58. These concessions have given rise to a flourishing "industry," that of "Canada-without-Quebec" map making, which usually involves the entire southern segment of the province, together with parts of the Eastern Townships and the western half of Montreal Island. Such territorial speculations no longer are the by-product of a few English-Canadian fanatics, but are now openly discussed in academic journals. See Linda M. Gerber, "Referendum Results: Defining New Boundaries for an Independent Quebec," *Canadian Ethnic Studies*, 24.2 (1992).

59. See Robert Chodos and Eric Hamovitch, *Quebec and the American Dream* (Toronto: Between the Lines, 1991).

60. Quebec's North American identity has been the subject of much speculation. See, for example, Jean Morisset, *L'Identité usurpée* (Montreal: Nouvelle Optique, 1985). For a novelist's viewpoint, see Jacques Godbout, *Une Histoire américaine* (Paris: Le Seuil, 1986).

61. "When English Is Foreign Tongue: Census Finds a Sharp Rise in 80's," *New York Times*, Apr. 28, 1993, p. 1. After Spanish, French is the second-most-spoken foreign language in the United States.

Cascadia: The New Binationalism of Western Canada and the U.S. Pacific Northwest

1. All dollar amounts are in U.S. currency.

2. Douglas M. Brown and Earl H. Fry, eds., *States and Provinces in the International Economy* (Berkeley: Institute of Governmental Studies Press, University of California, 1993), p. 10.

3. *Ibid.*, p. 57.

4. Barton Reid, "The Debasement of Bio-regionalism," *City Magazine* (Vancouver, B.C.), Summer-Fall 1992, p. 17.

5. Martin Lubin, "The Routinization of Cross-Border Interactions: An Overview of NEG/ECP Structures and Activities," in Brown and Fry, *States and Provinces*, p. 150.

6. Gerard F. Rutan, "Micro-Diplomatic Relations in the Pacific Northwest: Washington State–British Columbia Interactions," in Ivo D. Duchacek, Daniel Latouche, and Garth Stevenson, eds., *Perforated Sovereignties and International Relations: Trans-Sovereign Contacts of Subnational Governments* (New York: Greenwood Press, 1988), p. 182.

7. Eileen Quigley, "Coming of Age in the New Pacific Era," *New Pacific*, Fall 1989, p. 5.

8. Saltvig, as quoted in the *Christian Science Monitor*, July 20, 1992.

9. McCloskey, as quoted in *New Pacific*, Winter/Spring 1990, p. 3.

10. Cashmore, as quoted by Joel Connelly, *Seattle Post-Intelligencer*, Dec. 3, 1992.

11. Gorton to Cashmere, printed in *Seattle Post-Intelligencer*, Feb. 5, 1993.

12. Rice, as quoted in *New Pacific*, Winter 1992–93, p. 19.

13. *Seattle Post-Intelligencer*, Dec. 10, 1992.

14. Schell, speech to the Greater Seattle Chamber of Commerce, Apr. 1990. For a succinct assessment of the dynamics underlying this and other transborder agendas from a central Canadian point of view, see Lawrence Martin, "An Explosion of Relations," chap. 16 in his anti-NAFTA book, *Pledge of Allegiance: The Americanization of Canada in the Mulroney Years* (Toronto: McClelland and Stewart, 1993), pp. 204–15. The perspective of central Canada is a tendency to view the whole west coast, including California, as the emerging region, which raises doubts about the viability of a country based on East-West ties. See also Latouche, above.

15. Clark, as quoted in the *Seattle Times*, Apr. 11, 1992.

16. Reid, as quoted in *ibid*.

17. U.S. House Res. 383, passed in 1992 (and supported by House-Senate Conference Report 102-918 adopted the same year), called for the State Department to provide one-quarter of the funding—up to $400,000—for the first two years of a binational organization called the Cascadia Corridor Commission. Matching funds were to come from the Canadian federal government, as well as American and Canadian local governments. The Task Force, now financed primarily by local governments, may prove to be permanent or an interim vehicle leading to a formal binational commission.

18. Lubin, "Routinization," pp. 162–64.

The Gulf of Mexico: North America's Maritime Frontier

1. Robert H. Gore, *The Gulf of Mexico: A Treasury of Resources in the American Mediterranean* (Sarasota, Fla.: Pineapple Press, 1992), p. 52.

2. *Ibid.*, p. 63.

3. Michael Weber, *Environmental Quality in the Gulf of Mexico: A Citizen's Guide*, 2d ed. (Washington, D.C.: Center for Marine Conservation, 1992), p. 9.

4. "Beach Cleanup Turns Up Cocaine," *Dallas Morning News*, Sept. 23, 1993, p. 30a.

5. Gore, *Gulf*, p. 24.

6. *Ibid.*, p. 240.

7. For details, see Louis B. Sohn and Kristin Gustafson, *The Law of the Sea* (St. Paul, Minn.: West Publishing, 1984), pp. 122–23.

8. By act of Congress, U.S. maritime states have jurisdiction over the waters out to three miles. But thanks to a 1960 Supreme Court ruling, Florida and Texas are exceptions. With jurisdiction extending nine nautical miles out, those two states have control of not only the outlying intertidal and submerged intertidal lands, but also the critical oil-rich continental shelf lands beyond. Everything within these territorial limits falls under their purview, from Outer Continental Shelf (OSC) oil leases to fishing rights, law enforcement, and environmental protection.

In July 1994, the Clinton administration accepted UNCLOS as amended to address technology and access issues.

9. "Mexicans Err, Halt U.S. Shrimpers as Season Starts," *Dallas Morning News*, July 8, 1993, p. 27a.

10. Sohn and Gustafson, *Law of the Sea*, p. 180.

11. Glen Segal, "Miami Jockeys for Position in Free Trade Arena," *Bobbin*, Mar. 1993, pp. 84–92. *Bobbin* is a textile trade publication.

12. And indeed, at the time of this writing, the United States had just signaled its intention to minimize the Mexican apparel industry's competitive advantage over Central American and Caribbean producers by gradually lowering tariffs on their goods and eventually allowing them the same duty-free entry that most clothing from Mexico will ultimately enjoy under NAFTA. Speech by Alexander F. Watson, Assistant Secretary of State for Inter-American Affairs, Institute of the Americas, La Jolla, Calif., Mar. 3, 1994.

13. "NAFTA: The Energy Sector," *U.S./Latin Trade*, Sept. 1993, p. 52a.

14. David Rosenbaum, "Administration Sweetens Trade Agreement Terms," *New York Times*, Nov. 4, 1993, p. 3.

15. Paul Anderson, "Floridians No Pushovers for Their NAFTA Support," *Miami Herald*, Nov. 14, 1993, p. A-1.

16. As a Legislative Fellow and vote counter for House Chief Deputy Whip Bill Richardson, the author played a key role in the NAFTA debate.

17. Weber, *Environmental Quality*, p. 47.

18. *Ibid.*, p. 80.

19. *Ibid.*, p. 51.

20. *Ibid.*, p. 48.

21. Gregory Morris, "Mexico: Port Privatization Edges Slowly Towards Reality," *Chemical Week*, June 23, 1993, p. 9.

22. U.S. Department of Commerce, International Trade Administration, Office of Mexico, Fact Sheet on Veracruz Port Privatization, 1993.

23. "A Long Way to Go in Mexico: Roads, Rails Hurting," *Chemical Week*, Feb. 17, 1993, p. 39.

24. U.S. Department of Commerce, International Trade Administration, Office of Mexico, Fact Sheet on U.S.-Mexico Trade Flows, 1991.

25. See "Not in My Backyard," *World Trade*, 4.2 (Apr. 1991), pp. 50–56.

26. "Oil Spill Liability Crisis," *Business Insurance*, Aug. 2, 1993, p. 2.

27. Jesus-Agustin Velasco-S., *Impact of Mexican Oil Policy on Economic and Policy Development* (Lexington, Mass.: Lexington Books, 1983), p. 151; Gore, *Gulf*, p. 251.

28. "Dead Sea Bubble," *Economist*, Mar. 5, 1994, p. 70.

29. C. Jonathan Brown and Alan Knight, *The Mexican Petroleum Industry in the Twentieth Century* (Austin: University of Texas Press, 1992).

30. U.S. Agency for International Development, Office of Energy and Infrastructure, *Environment, Market Conditions, and Business Opportunities in Key Latin American Countries* (Arlington, Va., Oct. 1992), pp. 122, 127.

31. Johannes Werner, "Return of the Gas Crisis Jitter," *Business Mexico*, June 1993, p. 32.

32. "Mexico: The Role of State Oil Companies," *Oil & Gas Journal*, Aug. 16, 1993, p. 60.

33. U.S. Department of Commerce, International Trade Administration, Office of Mexico, Fact Sheet on Shell-PEMEX Deer Park Joint Venture, 1992; Werner, "Return of the Gas Crisis," p. 32.

34. A. D. Koen, "Warning Flag Hoisted Over Gulf of Mexico Longevity," *Oil & Gas Journal*, Dec. 21, 1992, p. 19.

35. Steven Selzer, "Deep Rig: Light Weight, Heavy Yield," *Engineering News Record*, Oct. 18, 1993, p. 8.

36. Gore, *Gulf*, p. 258.

37. "Butterfly Bivouac," *Environment*, Mar. 1993, p. 22.

38. Weber, *Environmental Quality*, p. 285.

39. *Ibid.*, p. 38.

40. Gore, *Gulf*, p. 251.

41. Weber, *Environmental Quality*, p. 39.

42. *Ibid.*

43. Frederick Turner, *A Border of Blue: Along the Gulf of Mexico from the Keys to the Yucatan* (New York: Holt, 1993), p. 42; Weber, *Environmental Quality*, p. 43.

44. Weber, *Environmental Quality*, p. 43.

45. Turner, *Border of Blue*, p. 162.

46. Gore, *Gulf*, p. 281.

47. Turner, *Border of Blue*, p. 158.

48. U.S. Environmental Protection Agency, "Gulf of Mexico Program, Annual Report," Oct. 1, 1993, draft, p. 2.

49. U.S. Environmental Protection Agency and Secretaría de Desarrollo Urbano y Ecologia, *Integrated Environmental Plan for the U.S.-Mexico Border Area, First Stage (1992–1994)*, Feb. 25, 1992, p. III-11. SEDESOL (Secretaría de Desarrollo Social) is the successor agency.

50. *Ibid.*, p. III-37.

51. SEDESOL, "A Better Mexico, a Better Environment," Oct. 1993, Sec. VI.

52. *The North American Free Trade Agreement*, Sept. 6, 1993, draft text, p. I-1.

53. Personal communication, Andrew Mangan, executive director of the Council, Feb. 22, 1994. The following quotes come from our telephone conversation of this date.

54. In recent years, a spate of Canadian investors have seen opportunities in the development of Cuba's hotel resorts and its energy sector. Personal communication, Drew Fagan, Washington *Globe and Mail* correspondent, Mar. 12, 1994.

55. Kevin Hall, "Canada, Mexico Seek End to U.S. Embargo to Cuba," *Journal of Commerce*, Mar. 3, 1994.

56. In 1991 Cuba produced 788,000 tons of crude petroleum and nearly 8 million tons of petroleum-related products. Much of this capacity was developed through a joint venture with two French companies. Gore, *Gulf*, pp. 243, 331. Mexico may purchase a Cuban refinery. Andres Oppenheimer, "Mexico's Proposed Oil Refinery May Help End Cuba's Energy Woes," *Journal of Commerce*, Mar. 21, 1994.

The Mexico-U.S. Border: A Line of Paradox

1. As reported by the U.S. Immigration and Naturalization Service. The figure is for the fiscal year.

2. Kai T. Erickson, *Wayward Puritans: A Study in the Sociology of Deviance* (New York: Wiley, 1966).

3. Jorge A. Bustamante, "La interacción social en la Frontera México–Estados Unidos: Un marco conceptual para la investigación," in R. Gonzalez Salazar, ed., *La frontera del norte interacción y desarrollo* (Mexico: El Colegio de México, 1981). See also J. A. Bustamante, "Frontera México–Estados Unidos: Reflexiones para un marco teórico," *Frontera Norte*, 1.1 (Jan.–June 1989), pp. 7–24.

4. For a general discussion of geographic space in the border region, see Niles Hansen, *The Border Economy: Regional Development in the Southwest* (Austin: University of Texas Press, 1981), pp. 53–76. See also, on the Texas southern border, John W. House, *Frontier on the Rio Grande: A Political Geography of Development and Social Deprivation* (New York: Oxford University Press, 1982), pp. 55–69. The border economy is discussed in Jan Gilbreath Rich and David Hurlbut, *Free Trade with Mexico: What's in It for Texas?* U.S.-Mexican Policy Report no. 1 (Austin: University of Texas, 1992).

5. Rep. Duncan Hunter (R, Calif.), a ranking member of the House Armed Services Committee, continues to campaign strongly for militarizing the border. It was he who successfully promoted the construction of the steel fence that has so significantly changed the landscape of the San Diego–Tijuana border.

6. Joel Garreau, *The Nine Nations of North America* (New York: Avon Books, 1981). It is noteworthy that this book, so successful in the United States and Canada, went virtually unnoticed even by Mexican commentators who assiduously follow U.S. publications on Mexico and the bilateral relationship.

7. The concept of "asymmetry of power" applied to U.S.-Mexican relations was first advanced by Mario Ojeda in "The Structural Context of U.S.-Mexican Relations," in Tommie S. Montgomery, ed., *Mexico Today* (Philadelphia: Institute for the Study of Human Issues, 1982).

8. For a discussion of these concepts, see Bustamante, "Frontera México–Estados Unidos."

9. Research findings from this project were first reported in J. A. Bustamante, "Identidad nacional en la frontera norte: hallazgos preliminares," in A. Carona Renteria, ed., *Impactos regionales de las relaciones economicas México–Estados Unidos* (Mexico: El Colegio de México, 1984).

10. See Corona Renteria, *Impactos regionales.*

11. According to the scale drawn from the scores, the highest "Mexicanness" corresponded to the value of 3.00 and the lowest to 1.00.

12. This concept is discussed in Bustamante, "Frontera, México–Estados Unidos."

13. A classic study of the Zonas y Perimetros libres is the two-volume work by Ulises Irigoyen, *El problema economico de las fronteras mexicanas* (Mexico: n.p., 1935).

14. This process, as transpiring in Tijuana, is documented in J. A. Bustamante, *Historia de la Colonia Libertad* (Tijuana: Colegio de la Frontera Norte, 1986).

Conclusion: The Search for Community

1. Richard M. Morse, *El espejo de Próspero: Un estudio de la dialectica del Nuevo Mundo* (Mexico: Siglo Veintiuno, 1982); Guillermo Bonfil Batalla, *México profundo: Una civilización negada* (Mexico: Grijalbo, 1990); Federico Ortiz Quesada, *Yuhcatiliztli: Ser y identidad nacional* (Mexico: Editorial Némisis, 1992), p. 147.

2. Richard Mulcaster, president of the Vancouver Community Foundation, comments to John Wirth, Oct. 15, 1991.

3. Robert N. Bellah, Richard Madsen, William W. Sullivan, Ann Swidler, and Steven M. Tipton, *Habits of the Heart: Individualism and Commitment in American Life* (Berkeley: University of California Press, 1985), p. 333.

4. *Ibid.*, p. 72.

5. Robert N. Bellah, Richard Madsen, William W. Sullivan, Ann Swidler, and Steven M. Tipton, *The Good Society* (New York: Knopf, 1991), p. 12.

6. Octavio Paz, *The Labyrinth of Solitude* (New York: Grove Press, 1985).

7. For her poetry, see Alan S. Trueblood, tr., *A Sor Juana Anthology* (Cambridge, Mass.: Harvard University Press, 1988). See also Paz's extended commentary in *Sor Juana, or the Traps of Faith* (Cambridge, Mass.: Harvard University Press, 1988).

8. Paz, *Labyrinth*, p. 115.

9. *Ibid.*, pp. 114–15. The "value of experience" Paz speaks of is a concept that neatly sums up much of John Dewey's philosophy, as discussed below.

10. William Carlos Williams, *Selected Poems*, ed. Charles Tomlinson (New York: New Directions, 1985); *The Autobiography of William Carlos Williams* (New York: New Directions, 1951); William Carlos Williams, *In the American Grain* (1925). Reprint (New York: New Directions, 1956).

11. Octavio Paz, *On Poets and Others* (New York: Arcade Publishing, 1986), pp. 13–14.

12. See Bryce Conrad, *Refiguring America: A Study of William Carlos Williams' 'In the American Grain'* (Urbana: University of Illinois Press, 1990), for a discussion of Williams's use of sources and his historical method.

13. Margaret Atwood, *The Handmaid's Tale* (New York: Ballantine Books, 1985).

14. Margaret Atwood, *Survival: A Thematic Guide to Canadian Literature* (Concord, Ont.: Anansi, 1972).

15. See Peter Mellen, *The Group of Seven* (Toronto: McClelland and Stewart, 1981).

16. Miguel de la Madrid, comments at the Ninth North American Institute Forum, Santa Fe, N.Mex., Nov. 7, 1992.

17. Charles Hale, *Mexican Liberalism in the Age of Mora, 1821–1853* (New Haven, Conn.: Yale University Press, 1968).

18. Octavio Paz, *One Earth, Four or Five Worlds* (New York: Harcourt, Brace, Jovanovich 1985), p. 142.

19. "A middle class barely existed, and our bourgeoisie had scarcely gone beyond the mercantilist stage." *Ibid.*, p. 166.

20. *Ibid.*, pp. 168–69.

21. Paz, *Labyrinth*, p. 316.

22. Paz, *One Earth*, p. 173.

23. *Ibid.*, p. 172.

24. *Ibid.*, pp. 40–41.

25. Paz, "Mexico and the United States," in *ibid.*, p. 376.

26. Paz, *One Earth*, p. 153.

27. Paz, "The Other Mexico," in *Labyrinth*, pp. 282–83 (our emphasis).

28. John Dewey, *The Later Works, 1925–1953*, vol. 2 (Carbondale: Southern Illinois University Press, 1976), p. 351.

29. *Ibid.*, pp. 354–55.

30. Paz, "The Other Mexico," in *Labyrinth*, p. 282.

31. Quoted in Robert B. Westbrook, *John Dewey and American Democracy* (Ithaca, N.Y.: Cornell University Press, 1991), p. 432.

32. *Ibid.*, p. 434.

33. James Gouinlock, Introduction, in Dewey, *Later Works*, vol. 2, p. xxiii.

34. *Ibid.*, pp. 328–29.

35. *Ibid.*, pp 367–77.

36. *Ibid.*, p. 369.

37. Charles Taylor: *The Ethics of Authenticity* (Cambridge, Mass.: Harvard University Press, 1992); *Multiculturalism and "The Politics of Recognition"* (Princeton, N.J.: Princeton University Press, 1992); "Alternative Futures: Legitimacy, Identity and Alienation in Late Twentieth Century Canada," in Alan Cairns and Cynthia Williams, eds., *Constitutionalism, Citizenship and Society in Canada* (Toronto: University of Toronto Press, 1985); "Shared and Divergent Values," in Ronald L. Watts and Douglas Brown, eds., *Options for a New Canada* (Toronto: University of Toronto Press, 1991). See also his collected essays on Canada, *Reconciling the Solitudes: Essays on Canadian Federalism and Nationalism* (Montreal: McGill–Queens University Press, 1993).

38. Taylor, *Multiculturalism*, p. 52.

39. Taylor, "Shared and Divergent Values," p. 184.

40. Taylor, *Multiculturalism*, p. 27.

41. *Ibid.*, p. 43.

42. Taylor, *Ethics of Authenticity*, p. 50.

43. Taylor, *Multiculturalism*, p. 63.

44. Taylor, "Shared and Divergent Values," pp. 75–76.

45. George P. Fletcher, *Loyalty: An Essay on the Morality of Relationships* (New York: Oxford University Press, 1993), p. 165.

46. *Ibid.*, p. 172.

47. Lorenzo Meyer, "Estilo oriental de governar," *Excelsior*, Feb. 4, 1993. Denise Dresser sees Solidaridad as fundamentally a political control mechanism, antidemocratic and congruent with Salinas's neoliberal development model. See "Neopopulist Solutions to Neoliberal Problems," *Current Issue Brief* no. 3, Center for U.S. Mexican Studies, University of California, San Diego (1993).

48. Santiago Portillo, conversation with John Wirth at Solidaridad office, Mexico City, Dec. 10, 1992; Presidencia de la República, "National Solidarity Program," *Mexican Agenda*, 13th ed. (July 1992), pp. 151–59. These proven results could be carried across the border. In fact, Solidaridad Internacional will match migrant

remittances used to start new businesses in Mexico. The Fundación Progresso Fronterizo / Border Progress Foundation is sponsoring the new federally funded Border Volunteer Corps. See also Mark R. Sills, "Empowering Poor People: Lessons from Mexico," Human Services Institute *Monthly Communication*, Nov. 1993, pp. 6–7.

49. The system is not without critics, including most notably Allan Bloom, who sees the social function of U.S. universities as their demise and advocates instead the purity of vision associated with the great ideas of the West. Allan David Bloom, *The Closing of the American Mind* (New York: Simon and Schuster, 1987). For another view of the undergraduate curriculum, see W. B. Carnochan, *The Battleground of the Curriculum: Liberal Education and American Experience* (Stanford, Calif.: Stanford University Press, 1993).

50. On the Canadian health care system, see the papers from the Health Policy Conference on Canada's National Health Care System, 1985, in R. G. Evans and G. L. Stoddart, eds., *Medicine at Maturity: Achievements, Lessons, and Challenges* (Calgary: University of Calgary Press, 1986); and John K. Inglehart, "Canada's Health Care System," *New England Journal of Medicine*, 3 parts, 315 (1986), pp. 202–8, 778–84, 1623–28 (July 17, Sept. 18, Dec. 18).

51. At this writing, rising costs in the Canadian program are often cited by those who are against a single-payer system as the answer to the crisis in the delivery of services in the United States. For an informed comparison of the Canadian and U.S. systems, see Victor R. Fuchs and James S. Hahn, "How Does Canada Do It? A Comparison of Expenditures for Physicians' Services in the United States and Canada," *New England Journal of Medicine*, 323 (1990), pp. 884–90 (Sept. 27).

52. Taylor, *Multiculturalism*, p. 67.

53. Ken Jowett, "The New World Disorder," in Larry Diamond and Marc F. Plattner, eds., *The Global Resurgence of Democracy* (Baltimore: Johns Hopkins University Press, 1993), pp. 252–53.

54. See Michiko Kabutani, "Against the Tide: Making a Case for Shades of Gray," *New York Times*, June 18, 1993, pp. B1, B10; Lawrence Martin, *Pledge of Allegiance: The Americanization of Canada in the Mulroney Years* (Toronto: McClelland and Stewart, 1993); and Alberto Ruy-Sánchez's paper, above.

55. Martin, *Pledge of Allegiance*, p. 213. See also David Crane, "Forging a Great Lakes Community, *Toronto Star*, Aug. 14, 1993. Crane concludes: "The question still to be answered for Ontario and Canada—as this regionalization occurs, spurred on by free trade—is how the Canadian [national] identity will be maintained in the process."

56. George F. Kennan, *Around the Cragged Hill: A Personal and Political Philosophy* (New York: Norton, 1993), p. 151.

57. Quoted in Westbrook, *John Dewey*, p. 314.

58. *Ibid.*, pp. 315–16. See also Timothy V. Kaufman-Osborn, "John Dewey and the Liberal Science of Community," *Journal of Politics*, 46 (1984), pp. 1158–59.

59. "North American Agreement on Environmental Cooperation," in *The NAFTA Supplemental Agreements* (Washington, D.C.: Government Printing Office, Sept. 13, 1993), pp. 1–42. For a precursor document, see North American Institute, "The North American Environment: Opportunities for Trinational Co-

operation by Canada, the United States, and Mexico. Report and Recommendations (Santa Fe, N.Mex., Feb. 12–14, 1993).

60. Clint Smith, *The Disappearing Border* (Stanford, Calif.: Stanford Alumni Association, 1992), pp. 113–14.

61. Donald Kennedy, "The North and the South: Education in a Global Environment." Remarks given at Stanford University's Second International Centennial Celebration, Mexico City, Feb. 10, 1990, and cover letter, Apr. 1990.

62. See Paul Kennedy, *Preparing for the Twenty-First Century, New York* (New York: Random House, 1993), for a broader discussion of how education relates to global interdependence and competitiveness. On Euro-kids and the new cultural fusion they seem to be creating, see *New York Times*, Mar. 28, 1993, p. 3. Professor Tony Judt's ideas were presented in the Bliss Carnochan Lecture at the Stanford Humanities Center, April 16, 1993.

63. David Ronfeldt, "Institutions, Markets, and Especially Networks," in Rod Dobell and Michael Neufeld, eds., *Learning for Life: Education for an Economically Competitive and Socially Responsible North America* (Vancouver: Oulichan Books, 1992), p. 84. See also David Ronfeldt and Cathryn Thorup, "NGOs, Civil Service Networks, and the Future of North America," in Rod Dobell and Michael Neufeld, eds., *Citizens, Networks, and New Institutions in the North American Community* (Vancouver: Oulichan Books, 1994).

64. Consult Dobell and Neufeld, *Citizens*. For a list of organizations, see Ricardo Hernandez and Edith Sanchez, eds., *Cross-Border Links: A Directory of Organizations in Canada, Mexico, and the United States* (Albuquerque, N.Mex.: Inter-Hemispheric Education Resource Center; coproduced with Action Canada Network and Equipo Pueblo in Mexico, 1992).

Index

In this index an "f" after a number indicates a separate reference on the next page, and an "ff" indicates separate references on the next two pages. A continuous discussion over two or more pages is indicated by a span of page numbers, e.g., "57–59." *Passim* is used for a cluster of references in close but not consecutive sequence.